D1739169

STUDIES IN GERMAN LITERATURE,
LINGUISTICS, AND CULTURE
Vol. 57

Jean Paul Friedrich Richter

Army-Chaplain Schmelzle's
Journey to Flaetz

and

Life of Quintus Fixlein

Reprint of the first edition of Carlyle's *German Romance*,
Vol. III (1827).

For ease of reading, this edition was reproduced at
approximately 120% of the original. The original copy used comes
from the Camden House Collection of German Literature in
Translation

Jean Paul Friedrich Richter

Army-Chaplain Schmelzle's Journey to Flaetz

and

Life of Quintus Fixlein

Translated by
Thomas Carlyle

Introduction
by
Wulf Koepke

CAMDEN HOUSE

First Edition

ISBN: 0-938100-89-0

Printed by Thomson Shore, Inc.
Dexter, Michigan

Library of Congress Cataloging-in-Publication Data

Jean Paul, 1763-1825.
 [Des Feldpredigers Schmelzle Reise nach Flätz. English]
 Army-Chaplain Schmelzle's journey to Glaetz ; and, Life of Quintus Fixlein / Jean Paul Friedrich Richter ; translated by Thomas Carlyle ; introduction by Wulf Koepke. -- 1st ed.
      p. cm. -- (Studies in German literature, linguistics, and culture ; vol. 57)
 Translation of: Des Feldpredigers Schmelzle Reise nach Flätz; and of: Leben des Quintus Fixlein.
 "Reprint of the first edition of Carlyle's German romance, vol. III (1827)"--P.
 Includes bibliographical references.
 ISBN 0-9381000-89-0
 I. Carlyle, Thomas, 1795-1881. II. Jean Paul, 1763-1825. Leben des Quintus Fixlein. English. 1991. III. Title. IV. Title: Life of Quintus Fixlein. V. Series: Studies in German literature, linguistics, and culture ; v. 57.
PT2455.A3D47 1991
833'.6--dc20   90-28172
                                                                          CIP

Introduction

Wulf Koepke

Carlyle and Jean Paul Friedrich Richter

THOMAS CARLYLE'S PREOCCUPATION WITH German literature and the German spirit, which began in 1819, had acquainted him with two creative giants, Goethe and Schiller, and had motivated him to translate *Wilhelm Meister* (both the *Apprenticeship* and *Travels*) and to write his *Life of Schiller*. But then he discovered another great figure, even closer to his heart: the novelist Jean Paul Friedrich Richter (1763-1825). The study of Richter's works developed into a personal encounter. Not only did Carlyle claim that Jean Paul's writing was totally subjective and personal, he also adopted Jean Paul's mannerisms in his own style. He wrote on Jean Paul "in jeanpaulian terms"[1] and the figure of Jean Paul, somehow fused with Jean Paul's characters, especially the humorists, had a decisive impact on the content, structure, and style of *Sartor Resartus* (1833).[2] After the writing of *Sartor Resartus* and the creation of the figure of Teufelsdröckh, the fever of "jeanpaulism" seems to have passed through his system.

While it lasted, however, between 1825 and the early 1830s, Carlyle wrote two seminal articles on Jean Paul, translated several of Richter's works, and is credited with generating a short-lived popularity of Richter in England.

---

[1] J.W. Smeed, "Carlyle and Jean Paul Richter," *Comparative Literature* 16 (1964): 240.

[2] Cf. J.P. Vijn, *Carlyle and Jean Paul: Their Spiritual Optics*, Utrecht Publications in General and Comparative Literature, 18 (Amsterdam and Philadelphia: John Benjamin's Publishing Co., 1982); J.M. Smeed, "Carlyles Jean-Paul-Übersetzungen," *Deutsche Vierteljahrsschrift für Literatur und Geistesgeschichte* 35 (1961): 262-79; also "Carlyle and Jean Paul Richter," 230-40.

Carlyle did not discover Jean Paul Richter for England. Thomas de Quincey had published translations of Richter, two texts from *Flegeljahre*, and a dream from *Der Komet*, in 1821, and Carlyle said later that de Quincey had brought Jean Paul to his attention.[3] But as early as 1801, the *German Museum* had carried two excerpts from *Hesperus*,[4] and Henry Crabb Robinson had introduced him in *Amatonda* (1811). But Carlyle did not know about these fore-runners. As much as he was fascinated by what he perceived as Richter's personality, he did not know much about the facts of his life either. This is painfully apparent from the introduction to *German Romance* reproduced here. Jean Paul's father was not a clergyman in Wunsiedel, but a teacher; he then held posts as a minister, the latest being in Schwarzenbach where he died. Richter went to Leipzig in 1781 (close enough), and returned to his family, his widowed mother and brothers, living in abject poverty in Hof. He returned to Schwarzenbach to teach the children of his friends, between 1790 and 1794. After the death of his mother in 1797, Jean Paul moved to Leipzig, then to Weimar and Berlin where he met his wife. He had three, not two children. The title of Legationsrat came from Hildburghausen; the pension came first from the *Rheinbund* prince Karl Theodor von Dalberg, and after 1815, from the king of Bavaria. The major works including parts of *Flegeljahre* and *Die Vorschule der Ästhetik* had been written before Bayreuth where Jean Paul settled in 1804. Carlyle's characterization of Jean Paul's early career is totally inadequate. Carlyle does not know about the change from discursive satires to narrative prose, and he admits that he is not sure of the chronology of Richter's works. Strangely enough, Carlyle does not mention in his introduction *Siebenkäs*, which was one of his favorites and which contained

[3] Vijn, 196, cf. V. Stockley, *German Literature as Known in England 1750-1830* (London: George Routledge, 1929), 242-44 and 291-93; also Peter Michelsen, "Thomas de Quincey und Jean Paul," *Journal of English and Germanic Philology* 61 (1962): 736-55; Frederick Burwick, "The Dream Visions of Jean Paul and Thomas de Quincey," *Comparative Literature* 20 (1968): 1-26.

[4] Stockley, 241-42, also Smeed, "Carlyles Jean-Paul-Übersetzungen," 269-70.

Die Rede des toten Christus vom Weltgebäude herab, daß kein Gott sei (literally, The Speech of the Dead Christ from the Universe That there is no God), that he translated himself and that played a crucial role in the reception of Richter's works both in France and in England.[5] Carlyle's article on Jean Paul in the *Edinburgh Review*, 1827,[6] has more precise information on the biography, based on a spurious compilation by Heinrich Döring, Gotha, 1826.[7] Carlyle had learned that Richter's father was a teacher in Wunsiedel, that the wife's name was Caroline Mayer, and that the pension came from the king of Bavaria. (The year was still wrong.) The *Edinburgh Review* article repeats some of the formulations of the introduction, but goes to greater length to situate Jean Paul's rank and position in the history of great literature, associating him especially with Laurence Sterne, as could be expected, and with Cervantes, but also Rabelais, Montaigne, Swift, and Rousseau. Carlyle seems, at this point, to rely much more on his *own* readings of Richter's texts, whereas in the introduction, he had followed Franz Horn's *Poesie und Beredsamkeit der Deutschen*.[8] Also, *Siebenkäs* is

[5] Cf. on this the careful study of J.P. Vijn; for the French reception, Claude Pichois, *L'Image de Jean-Paul Richter dans les lettres françaises* (Paris: Corti, 1963). Carlyle also translated Jean Paul's masterful review of Madame de Staël's *De l'Allemagne* where he also comments on her treatment of his works, including the *Rede des toten Christus*.

[6] Reprinted in *The Reception of Classical German Literature in England 1760-1860: A Documentary History from Contemporary Periodicals*, ed. John Boening (New York and London: Garland, 1977), 6:19-27; Thomas Carlyle, *Collected Works* (London: Chapman and Hall, 1857-58), *Critical and Miscellaneous Essays* 1:1-29; "Jean Paul Friedrich Richter Again," 3:3-75; the translation of Jean Paul's review of *De l'Allemagne*, Appendix, 2:363-93.

[7] Eduard Berend, *Jean-Paul-Bibliographie*, neu bearbeitet von Johannes Krogoll (Stuttgart: Ernst Klett, 1963), 129 (No. 950 and 951), characterizes it as "bloße eilfertige Materialzusammenstellung." Carlyle has his fun with it as well, but it is still amazing that the curiosity about this unknown creative giant from Germany gave it a short-lived prominence in English letters that it could never achieve in Germany.

[8] 4 volumes, (Berlin: Enslin, 1822-1829); Franz Horn also reviewed several individual works by Richter, cf. *Jean-Paul-Bibliographie*, 9-11.

mentioned here, and he alludes to Madame de Staël, and the partial translation of *Die Rede des toten Christus* in her famous work, *De l'Allemagne* which leaves out the crucial conclusion, and thus results in the opposite meaning from what was intended.⁹

Carlyle continues to characterize Richter's two outstanding traits as imagination and humor, and he defends both structure and style of the works. He repeats the formula of the "intellectual Colossus" and makes the point that he is undeservedly unknown in England. He insists on the purity of Richter's personal character, and extols his "philosophy." Carlyle knows both of *Levana* and the *Vorschule*, and he also mentions the *Campaner Thal*, Richter's narrative work on the immortality of the soul, but apparently he never read it. Both humor and religious issues were of direct concern for Carlyle; his idealizing of "Jean Paul der Einzige"¹⁰ obviously is also designed to justify his own positions.

The *Foreign Review* 5, 1830, printed Carlyle's second article on Jean Paul, commonly cited as "Jean Paul Friedrich Richter Again," although Carlyle used no such title. It was ostensibly a review of the first three volumes of *Wahrheit aus Jean Pauls Leben*, containing the fragment of Jean Paul's *Selberlebensbeschreibung* (Description of My Own Life) and biographical materials, mostly short notes and aphorisms from the project of Jean Paul's autobiography. Later volumes of *Wahrheit* also contained letters. Carlyle was apparently quite disappointed; he had hoped for a real biography and a convincing portrait of the great man he so enthusiastically admired. Still, he went on, in this article, to present a perceptive analysis of the *Selberlebensbeschreibung* that covers the childhood and the years until Richter's confirmation, as well as a generally accurate biography, together with a critical evaluation of the works, quoting his own previous introduction, as well as offering various extended quotations and excerpts from Jean Paul's texts. In this article, his preference for *Siebenkäs* is directly acknowledged, whereas *Titan*

---

⁹ Cf. Pichois and J.P. Vijn on this issue.

¹⁰ Boening, 25; this was a common epithet for Jean Paul, also translated as *unicum*.

seems to have had less appeal. There are quotations from the *Vorschule* that indicate a real familiarity, as well as with *Levana*, the reading of which is also documented in his *Note Books*.[11] The stirring end of Carlyle's article consists of his translation of *Die Rede des toten Christus* where he tries to correct Madame de Staël's book as well as other English translations of that most provocative piece,[12] perhaps "his grandest, as undoubtedly, it is among his most celebrated."

The 1830 article is no mere rehash of the previous article and the introduction, nor is it limited to biographical matters. It is a better documented and more sober assessment of Jean Paul's character and achievement, a better synthesis, but less suggestive and enthusiastic. It is more the work of a critic than an enthusiast. Carlyle legitimized the high respect for Jean Paul Richter and the interest in his biography that characterizes the subsequent British reviews of works such as Richard Otto Spazier's biography, the translation of *Siebenkäs* (*Flower, Fruit, and Thorn Pieces*), and of *Flegeljahre* (*Walt and Vult; or, The Twins*).[13] Whereas for Carlyle it was only one episode in his life of hero worship, it determined the exalted image of Richter in England and among the New England transcendentalists.[14]

[11] *Two Note Books of Thomas Carlyle From 23d March 1822 to 16th May 1832*, ed. Charles Eliot Norton (Mamaroneck, NY: Paul P. Appel, 1972), 114, 123, 143.

[12] On the various French and English translations, their sources and interconnections, cf. Vijn: 53-90 who also documents subsequent reoccurrences of the *Rede* in Carlyle's texts.

[13] Cf. Boening, 60-204.

[14] Edward T. Brewer, *The New England Interest in Jean Paul Friedrich Richter*, University of California Publications in Modern Philology, vol. 27, no. 1 (Berkeley and Los Angeles: University of California Press, 1943). Brewer points to Carlyle as one of the two sources for American interest in Jean Paul, the other source is from the group of New England transcendentalists. Karl Follen's tenure at Harvard as the first professor of German literature was important, also Longfellow's enthusiasm.

Carlyle's Choice of Specimens

Carlyle reiterates the complaint of nearly all readers of Jean Paul, that his incessant allusions to the most diverse matters, his complex imagery and wit, make the texts almost inaccessible and untranslatable. He comes back to the abortive project of a man named Reinhold to provide a dictionary for Jean Paul's texts, of which only one volume appeared, a glossary to *Levana*. It would have been much easier, of course, to translate Jean Paul with the help of such glossaries. When looking for texts he might present to the British readers (and sell them, too), Carlyle, mindful of competition and market conditions,[15] opted for shorter and easier texts. It seems doubtful that he knew *Dr. Katzenbergers Badereise*, but he found a short narrative from the same period, *Des Feldpredigers Schmelzle Reise nach Flätz mit fortgehenden Noten; nebst Der Beichte des Teufels bei einem Staatsmanne*. The preface of this story is dated 1807, but it was published by Cotta in Tübingen only in early 1809, partly due to the bad economic conditions after 1807. Whereas Carlyle obviously liked this story, he was much less sure about his second choice, although it remained one of Richter's most popular texts: *Leben des Quintus Fixlein aus fünfzehn Zettelkästen gezogen; nebst einem Mußtheil und einigen Jus de tablette*, 1796 (actually in 1795). *Schmelzle* he presented "as one of the most finished, as it is at least one of the simplest, among his smaller humorous performances," whereas *Fixlein*, "no stepchild in his own country, seems nevertheless a much more immature, as it is a much earlier composition." Adding: "I select it not without reluctance, rather from necessity than preference." Carlyle keeps calling it a "novel" which may raise generic problems, but indicates that his definitions of "novel" were not very strict.

Although he writes that "both works I have endeavoured to present in their full dimensions," this applies only to the narrative texts in the narrow sense of the word. *Schmelzle* is followed by the

---

[15] On the various collections, cf. Stockley, 247-57.

Beichte des Teufels …, an independent and rather political text (as is *Schmelzle*) which Carlyle did not choose to include. He did, however, retain one of the jokes of the story, the "running commentary of notes," aphorisms on various matters pretending to be footnotes that have been placed in the wrong order, thus seem to have no connection with the body of the text. In the case of *Fixlein*, the omissions are more serious. Carlyle did not include any of the "Mußtheil für Mädchen" nor the "Jus de tablette für Mannspersonen" which include previously written sentimental stories, such as "Der Tod eines Engels" and "Der Mond"; narrative satires such as "Des Amts-Vogts Josua Freudel Klaglibell gegen seinen verfluchten Dämon" and "Des Rektors Florian Fälbels und seiner Primaner Reise nach dem Fichtelberg," as well as important essays as "Über die natürliche Magie der Einbildungskraft" and "Es gibt weder eine eigennützige Liebe noch eine Selbstliebe, sondern nur eigennützige Handlungen." Carlyle wanted to present Richter's texts as coherent, not only "riveted" together, and he would have had a hard time explaining the inner coherence with such a hodgepodge of texts. Although he acknowledged Richter's eccentricities and tried to justify them, he did what many of his defenders had done before him and would do after him: he toned them down to make his Jean Paul presentable. It is still a pity that he did not have the space to offer *Siebenkäs*; it could also be that he shied away from the insurmountable task of translating the more demanding texts. Thus, Carlyle presented the most accessible texts and, as he realized in the case of *Fixlein*, not the most significant or accomplished ones. *Siebenkäs* and *Flegeljahre* would present a much better picture, especially for a Victorian audience. E.T.A. Hoffmann, in contrast, is represented in *German Romance*, vol. 2, with *Der goldene Topf*, certainly not one of his most accessible stories.

Des Feldpredigers Schmelzle Reise nach Flätz

After completing such major works as *Titan*, *Flegeljahre*, *Vorschule der Ästhetik*, and *Levana*, Jean Paul Richter changed directions in his fictional writing. His late period is characterized by an even more fragmentary execution than before, of larger projects. The major project, *Der Komet*, remained unfinished, and so did his autobiography, the *Selberlebensbeschreibung*. But other works, such as *Leben Fibels* (1811) may be also called fragmentary.

During this period, political events became an immediate concern for Jean Paul. He was directly affected by the French occupation of Bayreuth, and he considered the end of the Holy Roman Empire and the devastating defeat of the Prussian army in 1806, a moral and political calamity for the Germans. It prompted him to speak out, first with a *Friedens-Predigt an Deutschland* (Sermon for Peace to Germany), then with *Dämmerungen für Deutschland* (1809, Twilights for Germany). Jean Paul, a persistent liberal, stood between the warring factions in Germany, and found a cold reception. Agreeing with his now deceased friend Johann Gottfried Herder, Jean Paul called for a moral, rather than military rearmament. He castigated vices, such as egotism and cowardice, not mistakes in military strategy. In addition to his essays, he wrote several satirical narratives. Both *Schmelzle* and *Dr. Katzenbergers Badereise* arise from this context, with an additional subtext (much more explicit in *Katzenberger*): a criticism of aestheticism, i.e., pursuit of the arts for their own sake. Aesthetics divorced from morality are decadent and destructive, such was Jean Paul's conviction, forcefully expressed since the nineties, and especially in *Titan*. One of the reasons is that such artists don't see reality as it is, but create their own artificial world. Subjectivism in its extreme can be morally dangerous.

Considered in this context, the funny story of the field chaplain Schmelzle, the exemplary coward, assumes a multi-dimensional meaning. On the surface, however, it is merely the character sketch of a poor man whose excessive imagination leads him to fear everything, lightning from a blue sky, and meteors raining down from space, and who thus becomes an object of laughter and pity. The other "normal" people around him, his wife and his brother-in-law in particular, like him and mean well, so the world of anxiety is shown to exist only in his head. It is a story that uses motifs of English narratives of the eighteenth century, Smollett in particular, with the stage coach ride, with nightly encounters with "ghosts," and other adventures, but also exhibits already some of the features of the post-1815 restoration world, especially the contrast between the anxiety-ridden individual and the quiet environment of the *Biedermeier*.

Schmelzle was not only more accessible in style and plot, it also exhibits instances of Jean Paul Richter's earlier English influences, Tobias Smollett in particular.[16] With a morally, if not aesthetically satisfying ending, Schmelzle earning what he deserves for his cowardice on the battlefield, the story could also appeal to Victorian readers. The humorous use of the uncanny could also fit into the period where Gothic novels had been superseded by Walter Scott's dark spaces. A satirical portrayal of a clergyman added some spice, without being too offensive. The juxtaposition of the two stories, with *Schmelzle* first — against the chronology — implies, intentionally or not, one more criticism of the *Fixlein* story.

Carlyle noted that *Schmelzle* had not had a warm reception in Germany, as opposed, for example, to *Katzenberger*. Katzenberger is, of course, a more imposing figure, and the interest is also sustained by a love story (of sorts). Jean Paul would never repeat the *Schmelzle* experiment which reminds one most of the early character sketches before Wutz, especially Freudel and Fälbel, published with *Fixlein*. Scholarly interest in the text has remained minimal,[17] and

---

[16] It seems that F. Holthausen, "Smollett und Jean Paul," *Archiv für das Studium der neueren Sprachen und Literaturen*, n.s. 34 (1916): 402-3, pointing to connections between *Humphrey Clinker* and *Katzenberger* is still the only special treatment; the *Vorschule* uses episodes from *Peregrine Pickle* for important points concerning humor (5:120, 155).

[17] There is a short study, "Des Feldpredigers Schmelzle Reise nach Flätz: Eine psychopathologische Skizze," *Hesperus*, no. 7 (March 1954): 31-39; the few studies on the late Jean Paul also mention *Schmelzle*, mostly in passing. The most illuminating contributions are those by J.W. Smeed, especially: "Jean Paul und die Tradition des theophrastischen Charakters," *Jahrbuch der Jean-Paul-Gesellschaft* 1 (1966): 53-77. Schmelzle is certainly a "character" in the tradition of Theophrastos and La Bruyère. Cf. also the introduction by Smeed to his edition of *Schmelzle*, Oxford University Press, 1966, especially 21-30.

xvi *Introduction*

indications are that it is not attracting many readers.[18] There is, however, good reason to echo Carlyle's judgment that it is a "finished story" — one of the gems in its genre — and that it provides a real insight into the mood of the Germans after 1807.

Leben des Quintus Fixlein

The title suggests an English parentage, and the overwhelming presence of English writers, notably Sterne and Swift, in Jean Paul's earlier works need not be belabored.[19] After Jean Paul had created his Schulmeisterlein Wutz, and appended his story to *Die unsichtbare Loge*, (1793; *The Invisible Lodge*) he would always come back to idyllic settings, a relaxation, as it were, from his efforts to create novels about German court society, such as *Hesperus*. *Fixlein* can be considered a contrasting story to *Hesperus*, written after its completion, and it also shared in the sudden fame of Jean Paul, beginning with the publication of *Hesperus* in 1795. Matzdorff, Jean Paul's publisher in Berlin, disappointed with the sales of the first novel, *Die unsichtbare Loge*, had hesitated to accept *Hesperus*, and was even less sure about *Fixlein*, so that Jean Paul published it with a publisher in Bayreuth by the name of Lübeck. *Fixlein*, also published in 1795, the imprint showing the year of 1796, sold well, and Jean Paul soon made plans for a revised edition. He wrote a preface for the second edition that attacked Weimar classicism, prefiguring *Titan* and numerous essays,[20] and he made copious notes for editorial changes. The second edition was delayed, how-

[18] Beside the edition by Smeed, cited above, there are editions in the Reclam-Universalbibliothek, Nr. 293 (1967), Nachwort Kurt Schreinert, and Insel Taschenbuch (Frankfurt am Main: Insel-Verlag, 1980). *Schmelzle* is of course also included in Jean Paul *Werke* (Munich: Hanser, 1967), 6:7-76, with notes 1239-46.

[19] Cf. my *Erfolglosigkeit: Zum Frühwerk Jean Pauls* (Munich: Fink, 1977) and *Jean-Paul-Bibliographie* for references.

[20] Cf. on this issue Kurt Wölfel, "Antiklassizismus und Empfindsamkeit: Jean Paul und die Weimarer Kunstdoktrin," in Kurt Wölfel, *Jean-Paul-Studien* (Frankfurt am Main: Suhrkamp, 1989), 238-58.

ever, and Jean Paul published the new preface separately — it is also absent from Carlyle's translation — and made few changes in the text. It appeared in 1800 with the date of 1801.

Fixlein continues the theme of the *Kauz* and the lovable yet frequently ridiculous parson that Jean Paul had initiated in *Hesperus* with the figure of Eymann. There are common traits of this type, both social and psychological, that remain constant in Jean Paul's texts: bookishness and scurrilous irrelevant scholarship, devotion to family and duties, dependence on the whims of powerful courtiers, lords of the manor, and rulers, a vivid imagination, and a fear of life, also poverty, yet a contented acceptance of hardship and enjoyment of life's pleasures. These teachers and Lutheran ministers, Jean Paul's own environment in his earlier days, are wretched people who survive only through the power of imagination, since a realistic view of their misery would call rather for suicide than for survival. Jean Paul's own *Selberlebensbeschreibung* contains late reflections on the consequences of poverty, and the motif of sudden, miraculous wealth, or the illusion thereof, runs through all of Jean Paul's works about this milieu, culminating in the invention of artificial diamonds by the protagonist of *Der Komet*, Nikolaus Marggraf. Fixlein will not inherit a fortune, like Walt in *Flegeljahre*, but he will obtain the ministry that assures him a meager existence, by mistake only. Deception and illusion are constant features of Jean Paul's texts. Fixlein, who firmly believes he will die at age thirty-five like his forebears, is deceived by a confusion of dates, and finally "healed" by a psychological cure of the narrator Jean Paul — who makes another of his inevitable appearances — himself. From the more realistic point of view of 1826, the plot, especially its ending, seemed unconvincing. But Carlyle may also have objected to the style, although he still used an excerpt from *Fixlein* as a specimen in his 1830 article. The style of *Fixlein*, close to *Hesperus*, is certainly much more sentimental, much less complex and concentrated, and much less masterfully crafted than *Schmelzle*. The sophistication of the later texts of Richter evidently appealed to Carlyle and his countrymen, given the relative success of *Flegeljahre*, *Siebenkäs* (in its second, more realistic version of 1818), and *Levana*. *Hesperus*, the

Introduction

one real success in Germany, never made it across the channel, and given the mood of the nineteenth century after 1815, with good reason. Thus Carlyle may have regarded *Fixlein* as a weak echo of Sterne's and Goldsmith's sentimentalism. Contrary to *Schmelzle*, it still attracts attention, and even more some of the pieces appended to it.[21]

The Translations

In the case of *Schmelzle*, Carlyle made a valiant effort to approximate the wit and multiple meanings of the original German text, yet it is evident that this was an impossible task. There is an obvious effort to be accurate. Only one example of Carlyle's problems:

> Der unnütze Necker hätte so gern den fast einfältigen Giganten — dem ers bald abgemerkt, daß dessen Gehirn kein schlauer Gast, sondern die negative Größe seines Rumpfes war — unter uns im bangen Postschrank und Notstall vor sich gesehen, zu einem Gießpuckel eingeknüllt und krumm geschlossen. (VI, 37)[22]

Which reads in Carlyle's translation:

> The unseasonable Banterer would willingly have seen the almost stupid Giant (of whom he had soon observed that his brain was no active substance, but in the inverse ratio of his trunk) squeezed in among us in the post-chest, and lying kneeled together like a sandbag before him.

---

[21] Cf. the recent bibliographies, the latest in the *Jahrbuch der Jean-Paul-Gesell-schaft* 19 (1984), by Sabine Müller. Ralph-Rainer Wuthenow offered a very interesting study on *Fälbel*. The notion of "Idylle" and, more recently, of narcissism has been debated in Jean Paul scholarship as well.

[22] Quoted from volume 6 of *Werke* (Munich: Hanser, 1967).

The word "einfältig" connotes also the folds into which his body is supposed to be compressed: the dragoon has just invited the giant, who travels with a dwarf for shows, to "sit down" with them in the coach — which frightens Schmelzle no end. However, it is physically not possible and will not take place. But fearing it Schmelzle makes a "Riese" into a "Giganten" which cannot be translated, nor can "schlauer Gast." Carlyle omits "Notstall," he makes no attempt at "Gießpuckel" and "krumm geschlossen," retaining only the basic idea, and who would blame him? "Krumm geschlossen" would be a prisoner in chains who cannot stand upright, and "Gießpuckel" is a word that really tests the knowledge of any German speaker.[23]

The "running notes" do not always correspond to those of the German original; they are fewer in number, especially toward the end, and not always in the same sequence, but that is certainly not a detriment to the translation.

The translation of *Fixlein* had to be much easier. One example has to suffice here. Fixlein takes a walk in the garden with his bride on their wedding night:

> Er ging mit seiner Braut in den Schloßgarten; sie eilte schnell durch das Schloß und vor dessen Gesindestube vorüber, wo die schönen Blumen des Jugendlebens unter einem langen Druckwerk breit und trocken gepresset wurden, und ihre Seele tat sich groß und atmend im freien offenen Garten auf, in dessen Blumenerde das Schicksal den ersten Blumensamen ihres heutigen Lebensflores ausgeworfen hatte. Stilles Eden! Grünes, mit Blüten zitterndes Helldunkel! — Der Mond ruhte unter der Erde wie ein Toter; aber jenseits des Gartens sind der Sonne helle rote Abendwolken wie Rosenblätter abgefallen, und der Abendstern, der Brautführer der Sonne,

---

[23] "Gießpuckel" or "Gießbuckel" is a round kettle used in the separation or alloying of metals, a vessel for melting. Jean Paul uses the comparison certainly for the shape of the vessel, like a ball, that would make a strange monster out of that giant. The association to alchemy makes this comparison more frightening for Schmelzle. This is clearly far-fetched. J.H. Campe, *Wörterbuch der deutschen Sprache* (Braunschweig, 1808), 2:374.

schwebt wie ein glänzender Schmetterling über dem Rosen-
rot und nimmt, bescheiden wie eine Braut, keinem einzigen
Sternchen sein Licht. (IV, 149-50)

He walked with his bride into the Castle-garden: she hastened quickly through the Castle, and past the servants'-hall,
where the flowers of her young life had been crushed broad
and dry, under a long dreary pressure; and her soul expanded
and breathed in the free open garden, on whose flowery soil
destiny had cast forth the first seeds of the blossoms which
today were gladdening her existence. Still Eden! green flower-chequered *chiaroscuro*! — The moon is sleeping under-
ground like a dead one; but beyond the garden the sun's red
evening-clouds have fallen down like rose-leaves; and the
evening-star, the brideman of the sun, hovers, like a glancing
butterfly, above the rosy red, and, modest as a bride, deprives no single starlet of its light.

Carlyle makes the pressing of the flowers of youth more explicitly
apply to Thienette, and the idea of the pressed and dried flowers (or
herbs) is less clear in the translation. "Blumenerde" may not be
quite the same as "flowery soil," and "Lebensflor" is obviously hard
to render. The glancing butterfly, instead of a shining, brilliant one,
must be a mistake (glancing = glänzend), but somehow makes
sense. The emotion comes through in the translation much more
clearly than the wit, which sounds far-fetched when deprived of its
linguistic habitat. All in all, the translation is certainly superior to
all others and very much worth reading.[24]

---

[24] For the virtues as well as the failings of these translations, cf. the very
careful study by J.W. Smeed, "Carlyles Jean-Paul-Übersetzungen." Smeed
points out that no other translator, before or after Carlyle, was congenial
enough to match the "echten Barockton Jean Paulscher Prosa" (268), and that
with all its limitations, this seems the best the English language can do with
Jean Paul. De Quincey who certainly empathized with Jean Paul, did not really
try to match the original and offered adaptations rather than translations
(270).

English Translations of Jean Paul Richter

Thomas Carlyle's *German Romance* contained the first translations of complete texts by Jean Paul into English. After a period of gestation, English interest peaked in the 1840s. There were translations of *Siebenkäs* (1845), *Flegeljahre* (1846), *Das Kampaner Thal* (1848), and *Levana* (1848). After that, interest shifted to the United States where the transcendentalists in New England had discovered the moral and stylistic qualities of Richter's texts.[25] Charles T. Brooks undertook translations of major novels: *Titan* (1862), *Hesperus* (1864), and *Die unsichtbare Loge* (1883). Other translations were not published.[26] The *Vorschule der Ästhetik*, a text whose significance was already recognized by Carlyle, had to wait till 1973 for a translation, and still awaits discovery as a seminal text of literary theory.[27]

As this list shows, the rediscovery of Jean Paul in the twentieth century which brought, among other things, a new reception and new translations of his texts in France, never reached the English-speaking world. He remains, as Carlyle said it in 1827, 0S"little known, except by name." This is reinforced even by curricula of German departments that exclude him, both because of the complexity of his texts and because of his eccentric position in the history of literature.

[25] Cf. Edward T. Brewer, note 14.

[26] Brewer, 20, lists unpublished manuscripts, among them the *Vorschule der Ästhetik*.

[27] Published as *Horn of Oberon: Jean Paul Richter's School for Aesthetics*, translated with a significant introduction by Margaret R. Hale (Detroit: Wayne State University Press, 1973). The list of previous translations is given in *Jean-Paul-Bibliographie*, 75-81, most of it short pieces and excerpts. After the translations of Charles T. Brooks, the last published being *The Invisible Lodge*, 1883, there is hardly any such activity until a translation of *Wutz* by John D. Grayson, in *Nineteenth-Century German Tales*, ed. Angel Flores (New York: Doubleday, 1959). It can therefore be stated that prior to this reprint none of Jean Paul's works were available in English translation.

It makes eminent sense, therefore, to start all over, and begin where Thomas Carlyle left off, offering, as it were, the first specimens of Richter's narrative texts for the first time in over one hundred years. In our postmodernist days, his texts should not be as bewildering as they were thought before, and it is hoped that these specimens will stimulate curiosity for others. This facsimile edition of the first edition of Carlyle's *German Romance*, vol. III makes available two works by an author, none of whose works are currently in print.

GERMAN ROMANCE:

SPECIMENS

OF

ITS CHIEF AUTHORS;

WITH

BIOGRAPHICAL AND CRITICAL

NOTICES.

BY THE TRANSLATOR OF WILHELM MEISTER, AND
AUTHOR OF THE LIFE OF SCHILLER.

IN FOUR VOLUMES.

VOL. III.

CONTAINING

JEAN PAUL FRIEDRICH RICHTER.

EDINBURGH:

WILLIAM TAIT, PRINCE'S STREET;
AND CHARLES TAIT, FLEET STREET, LONDON.
MDCCCXXVII.

EDINBURGH :

PRINTED BY JAMES BALLANTYNE AND CO.

JEAN PAUL FRIEDRICH RICHTER.

VOL. III.

JEAN PAUL FRIEDRICH RICHTER.

JEAN PAUL FRIEDRICH RICHTER, one of the chosen men of Germany and of the World, whom I hoped,
in my vanity, perhaps to gratify by this introduction
of him to a people whom he knew and valued, has
been called from his earthly sojourn since the com-
mencement of my little task, and no voice, either of
love or censure, shall any more reach his ear.
The circle of his existence is thus complete: his
works and himself have assumed their final shape and
combination, and lie ready for a judgment, which,
when it is just, must now be unalterable. To satisfy a
natural and rational curiosity respecting such a character, materials are not wanting; but to us in the
meantime they are inaccessible. I have inquired in
his own country, but without effect; having learned
only that two *Biographies* of Richter are in the press,
but that nothing on the subject has hitherto been published. For the present, therefore, I must content
myself with such meagre and transitory hints as were

in circulation in his lifetime, and compress into a few sentences a history which might be written in volumes. Richter was born at Wunsiedel in Bayreuth, on the 21st of March 1763. His father was clergyman of the place, and afterwards of Schwarzbach on the Saale. The young man also was destined for the clerical profession ; with a view to which, having finished his school studies in the Hof Gymnasium, he in 1780 proceeded to the University of Leipzig, with the highest testimonials from his former masters. Theology as a profession, however, he could not relish ; poetry, philosophy, and general literature, were his chief pursuits while at Leipzig ; from which, apparently after no long stay, he returned to Schwarzbach to his parents, uncertain what he should betake him to. In a little while, he attempted authorship ; publishing various short miscellaneous pieces, distinguished by intellectual vigour, copious fancy, the wildest yet truest humour, the whole concocted in a style entirely his own, which, if it betrayed the writer's inexperience, could not hide the existence in him of a highly-gifted, strong, and extraordinary mind. The reception of his first performances, or the inward felicity of writing, encouraged him to proceed : in the midst of an unsettled and changeful life, his pen was never idle, its productions never otherwise than new, fantastic, and powerful : he lived successively in Hof, in Weimar, Berlin, Meiningen, Coburg, " raying forth, wherever he might be

stationed, the wild light of his genius over all Germany." At last he settled in Bayreuth, having here,
in testimony of his literary merit, been honoured with
the title of Legations-Rath, and presented with a pension from his native Prince. In Bayreuth his chief
works were written; he had married, and been blessed with two children; his intellectual labours had
gained him esteem and love from all ranks of his countrymen, and chiefly from those whose suffrage was of
most value; a frank and original, yet modest, good,
and kind deportment, seems to have transferred these
sentiments to his private circle: with a heart at once of
he most earnest and most sportful cast; affectionate,
and encompassed with the objects of his affection; di-
ligent in the highest of all earthly tasks, the acquisition and the diffusion of Truth; and witnessing from
his sequestered home the working of his own mind on
thousands of fellow-minds, Richter seemed happy and
at peace; and his distant reader loved to fancy him as
in his calm privacy enjoying the fruit of past toils, or
amid the highest and mildest meditations, looking forward to long honourable years of future toil. For his
thoughts were manifold; thoughts of a moralist and a
sage, no less than of a poet and a wit. The last work
of his I saw advertised, was a little volume, entitled,
On the Ever-green of our Feelings; and in November
(1825), news came that Richter was dead; and a heart,
which we had figured as one of the truest, deepest,
and gentlest that ever lived in this world, was to beat
no more.

Of Richter's private character I have learned little ;
but that little was all favourable, and accordant with
the indications in his works. Of his public and intellectual character much might be said and thought ; for
the secret of it is by no means floating on the surface,
and it will reward some study. The most cursory inspection, even an external one, will satisfy us that he
neither was, nor wished to be considered as, a man who
wrote or thought in the track of other men, to whom
common practice is a law, and whose excellencies
and defects the common formulas of criticism will
easily represent. The very titles of his works are
startling. One of his earliest performances is named
Selection from the Papers of the Devil ; another is,
*Biographical Recreations under the Cranium of a
Giantess.* His novels are almost uniformly introduced
by some fantastic narrative accounting for his publication and obtainment of the story. *Hesperus,* his chief
novel, bears the secondary title of *Dog-post-days,* and
the chapters are named *Dog-posts,* as having been conveyed to him in a letter-bag, round the neck of a little
nimble Shock, from some unknown Island in the South
sea.

The first aspect of these peculiarities cannot prepossess us in his favour ; we are too forcibly reminded
of theatrical clap-traps and literary quackery ; nor on
opening one of the works themselves is the case much
mended. Piercing gleams of thought do not escape us ;
singular truths conveyed in a form as singular ; gro-

tesque and often truly ludicrous delineations ; pathetic,
magnificent, far-sounding passages ; effusions full of
wit, knowledge, and imagination, but difficult to bring
under any rubrick whatever ; all the elements, in short,
of a glorious intellect, but dashed together in such wild
arrangement, that their order seems the very ideal of
confusion. The style and structure of the book appear alike incomprehensible. The narrative is every
now and then suspended to make way for some " Ex-
tra-leaf," some wild digression upon any subject but the
one in hand ; the language groans with indescribable
metaphors and allusions to all things human and divine ; flowing onward, not like a river, but like an in-
undation ; circling in complex eddies, chafing and gur-
gling now this way, now that, till the proper current
sinks out of view amid the boundless uproar. We
close the work with a mingled feeling of astonishment,
oppression, and perplexity ; and Richter stands before us in brilliant cloudy vagueness, a giant mass of
intellect, but without form, beauty, or intelligible purpose.

To readers who believe that intrinsic is inseparable
from superficial excellence, and that nothing can be
good or beautiful which is not to be seen through in a
moment, Richter can occasion little difficulty. They
admit him to be a man of vast natural endowments,
but he is utterly uncultivated, and without command
of them ; full of monstrous affectation, the very High
Priest of bad taste ; knows not the art of writing,

scarcely that there is such an art ; an insane visionary
floating for ever among baseless dreams, which hide
the firm Earth from his view ; an intellectual Polyphe-
mus ; in short, a *monstrum horrendum, informe, in-
gens* (carefully adding) *cui lumen ademptum ;* and
they close their verdict reflectively, with his own
praiseworthy maxim: " Providence has given to the
English the empire of the sea, to the French that of
the land, to the Germans that of—the air."
In this way the matter is adjusted ; briefly, comfort-
ably, and wrong. The casket was difficult to open ;
did we know by its very shape that there was nothing
in it, that so we should cast it into the sea ? Affectation
is often singularity, but singularity is not always affectation. If the nature and condition of a man be really
and truly, not conceitedly and untruly, singular, so
also will his manner be, so also ought it to be. Affectation is the product of Falsehood, a heavy sin, and the
parent of numerous heavy sins ; let it be severely pu-
nished, but not too lightly imputed. Scarcely any mortal is absolutely free from it, neither most probably is
Richter ; but it is in minds of another substance than
his that it grows to be the ruling product. Moreover,
he is actually not a visionary ; but, with all his visions,
will be found to see the firm Earth in its whole figures
and relations much more clearly than thousands of
such critics, who too probably can see nothing else.
Far from being untrained or uncultivated, it will surprise these persons to discover that few men have stu-

died the art of writing, and many other arts besides,
more carefully than he; that his *Vorschule der Æs-
thetik* (Introduction to Æsthetics) abounds with deep
and sound maxims of criticism; in the course of which,
many complex works, his own among others, are rigid-
ly and justly tried, and even the graces and minutest
qualities of style are by no means overlooked or un-
wisely handled.

Withal, there is something in Richter that incites us
to a second, to a third perusal. His works are hard
to understand, but they always have a meaning, and
often a true and deep one. In our closer, more comprehensive glance, their truth steps forth with new distinctness, their error dissipates and recedes, passes
into venality, often even into beauty ; and at last the
thick haze which encircled the form of the writer melts
away, and he stands revealed to us in his own stead-
fast features, a colossal spirit, a lofty and original
thinker, a genuine poet, a high-minded, true, and most
amiable man.

I have called him a colossal spirit, for this impression continues with us : to the last we figure him as
something gigantic ; for all the elements of his structure are vast, and combined together in living and life-
giving, rather than in beautiful or symmetrical order:
His Intellect is keen, impetuous, far-grasping, fit to
rend in pieces the stubbornest materials, and extort
from them their most hidden and refractory truth. In
his Humour he sports with the highest and the lowest,

he can play at bowls with the sun and moon. His Imagination opens for us the Land of Dreams; we sail with him through the boundless abyss, and the secrets of Space, and Time, and Life, and Annihilation, hover round us in dim cloudy forms, and darkness, and immensity, and dread, encompass and overshadow us. Nay, in handling the smallest matter, he works it with the tools of a giant. A common truth is wrenched from its old combinations, and presented us in new, impassable, abysmal contrast with its opposite error. A trifle, some slender character, some weakling humourist, some jest, or quip, or spiritual toy, is shaped into most quaint, yet often truly living form; but shaped somehow as with the hammer of Vulcan, with three strokes that might have helped to forge an Ægis. The treasures of his mind are of a similar description with the mind itself; his knowledge is gathered from all the kingdoms of Art, and Science, and Nature, and lies round him in huge unwieldy heaps. His very language is Titanian; deep, strong, tumultuous, shining with a thousand hues, fused from a thousand elements, and winding in labyrinthic mazes.

Among Richter's gifts, perhaps the first that strikes us as truly great is his Imagination; for he loves to dwell in the loftiest and most solemn provinces of thought; his works abound with mysterious allegories, visions, and typical adumbrations; his Dreams, in particular, have a gloomy vastness, broken here and there by wild far-darting splendour, and shadowy forms of mean-

ing rise dimly from the bosom of the void Infinite.
Yet, if I mistake not, Humour is his ruling quality, the
quality which lives most deeply in his inward nature,
and most strongly influences his manner of being. In
this rare gift, for none is rarer than true humour, he
stands unrivalled in his own country ; and among late
writers, in every other. To describe humour is difficult
at all times, and would perhaps be still more difficult
in Richter's case. Like all his other qualities, it is
vast, rude, irregular ; often perhaps overstrained and
extravagant : yet fundamentally it is genuine humour,
the humour of Cervantes and Sterne, the product not
of Contempt but of Love, not of superficial distortion
of natural forms, but of deep though playful sympathy
with all forms of Nature. It springs not less from the
heart than from the head ; its result is not laughter,
but something far kindlier and better ; as it were, the
balm which a generous spirit pours over the wounds of
life, and which none but a generous spirit can give
forth. Such humour is compatible with tenderest and
sublimest feelings, or rather, it is incompatible with
the want of them. In Richter, accordingly, we find a
true sensibility ; a softness, sometimes a simple humble
pathos, which works its way into every heart. Some
slight incident is carelessly thrown before us : we smile
at it perhaps, but with a smile more sad than tears ;
and the unpretending passage in its meagre brevity
sinks deeper into the soul than sentimental volumes.
It is on the strength of this and its accompanying

endowments, that his main success as an artist depends. His favourite characters have always a dash of the ridiculous in their circumstances or their composition, perhaps in both : they are often men of no account ; vain, poor, ignorant, feeble ; and we scarcely know how it is that we love them ; for the author all along has been laughing no less heartily than we at their ineptitudes; yet so it is, his Fibel, his Fixlein, his Siebenkäs, even his Schmelzle, insinuate themselves into our affections ; and their ultimate place is closer to our hearts than that of many more splendid heroes. This is the test of true humour ; no wit, no sarcasm, no knowledge will suffice ; not talent but genius will accomplish the result. It is in studying these characters that we first convince ourselves of Richter's claim to the title of a poet, of a true creator. For with all his wild vagueness, this highest intellectual honour cannot be refused him. The figures and scenes which he lays before us, distorted, entangled, indescribable as they seem, have a true poetic existence ; for we not only *hear* of them, but we *see* them, afar off, by the wondrous light, which none but the Poet, in the strictest meaning of that word, can shed over them.

So long as humour will avail him, his management even of higher and stronger characters may still be pronounced successful ; but whenever humour ceases to be applicable, his success is more or less imperfect. In the treatment of heroes proper he is seldom completely happy. They shoot into rugged exaggeration

in his hands, their sensibility becomes too copious
and tearful, their magnanimity too fierce, abrupt, and
thorough-going. In some few instances they verge
towards absolute failure : compared with their less
ambitious brethren, they are almost of a vulgar cast;
with all their brilliancy and vigour, too like that posi-
tive, determinate, choleric, volcanic class of personages
whom we meet with so frequently in novels ; they call
themselves Men, and do their utmost to prove the as-
sertion, but they cannot make us believe it ; for after
all their vapouring and storming we see well enough
that they are but Engines, with no more life than the
Freethinkers' model in *Martinus Scriblerus*, the Nu-
remberg Man, who operated by a combination of pipes
and levers, and though he could breathe and digest
perfectly, and even reason as well as most country parsons, was made of wood and leather. In the general conduct of such histories and delineations, Richter seldom
appears to advantage : the incidents are often startling and extravagant ; the whole structure of the story
has a rugged, broken, huge, artificial aspect, and will
not assume the air of truth. Yet its chasms are strangely filled up with the costliest materials ; a world, a
universe of wit and knowledge and fancy and imagination has sent its fairest products to adorn the edifice ;
the rude and rent cyclopean walls are resplendent with
jewels and beaten gold ; rich stately foliage screens it,
the balmiest odours encircle it ; we stand astonished if
not captivated, delighted if not charmed, by the artist
and his art.

By a critic of his own country, Richter has been
named a Western Oriental, an epithet which Goethe
himself is at the pains to reproduce and illustrate in his
West-Östlichter Divan. The mildness, the warm all-
comprehending love attributed to Oriental poets, may
in fact be discovered in Richter ; not less their fantastic exaggeration, their brilliant extravagance ; above
all, their overflowing abundance, their lyrical diffuse-
ness, as if writing for readers who were altogether
passive, to whom no sentiment could be intelligible
unless it were expounded and dissected, and presented under all its thousand aspects. In this last point,
Richter is too much an Oriental : his passionate out-
pourings would often be more effective were they far
briefer. Withal, however, he is a Western Oriental :
he lives in the midst of cultivated Europe in the nineteenth century ; he has looked with a patient and piercing eye on its motley aspect; and it is this Europe,
it is the changes of its many-coloured life, that are held
up to us in his works. His subject is Life ; his chosen
study has been Man. Few have known the world
better, or taken at once a clearer and a kindlier view
of its concerns. For Richter's mind is at peace with
itself : a mild, humane, beneficent spirit breathes
through his works. His very contempt, of which he is
by no means incapable or sparing, is placid and tole-
rant ; his affection is warm, tender, comprehensive, not
dwelling among the high places of the world, not blind
to its objects when found among the poor and lowly.

Nature in all her scenes and manifestations he loves
with a deep, almost passionate love ; from the solemn
phases of the starry heaven to the simple floweret of
the meadow, his eye and his heart are open for her
charms and her mystic meanings. From early years,
he tells us, he may be said to have almost lived under the open sky : here he could recreate himself, here
he studied, here he often wrote. It is not with the
feeling of a mere painter and view-hunter that he
looks on Nature : but he dwells amid her beauties and
solemnities as in the mansion of a Mother; he finds
peace in her majestic peace; he worships, in this boundless Temple, the great original of Peace, to whom the
Earth and the fulness thereof belongs. For Richter
does not hide from us that he looks to the Maker of
of the Universe as to his Father ; that in his belief of
man's Immortality lies the sanctuary of his spirit, the
solace of all suffering, the solution of all that is mysterious in human destiny. The wild freedom with which
he treats the dogmas of religion must not mislead us
to suppose that he himself is irreligious or unbelieving.
It is Religion, it is Belief, in whatever dogmas expressed, or whether expressed in any, that has reconciled
for him the contradictions of existence, that has overspread his path with light, and chastened the fiery elements of his spirit by mingling with them Mercy and
Humility. To many of my readers it may be surpri-
sing, that in this respect Richter is almost solitary
among the great minds of his country. These men too,
with few exceptions, seem to have arrived at spiritual

peace, at full harmonious developement of being; but their path to it has been different. In Richter alone, among the great (and even sometimes truly moral) writers of his day,* do we find the Immortality of the Soul expressly insisted on, nay so much as incidentally alluded to. This is a fact well meriting investigation and reflection, but here is not the place for treating it.

Of Richter's Works I have left myself no room for speaking individually; nor, except with large details, could the criticism of them be attempted with any profit. His Novels, published in what order I have not accurately learned, are the *Unsichtbare Loge* (Invisible Lodge); *Flegeljahre* (Wild Oats); *Leben Fibels, Verfassers der Beinrodischen Fibel* (Life of Fibel; or to translate the spirit of it : Life of Primer, Author of the Christ-church Primer); *Leben des Quintus Fixlein,* and *Schmelzle's Reise,* here presented to the English reader; *Katzenberger's Badereise,* and the *Jubelsenior ;* with two of much larger and more ambitious structure, *Hesperus* and *Titan,* each of which I have in its turn seen rated as his masterpiece : the former only is

---

* The two venerable Jacobis belong, in character, if scarcely in date, to an older school; so also does Herder, from whom Richter learned much, both morally and intellectually, and whom he seems to have loved and reverenced beyond any other. Wieland is intelligible enough ; a sceptic in the style of Bolingbroke and Shaftesbury, what we call a French or Scotch sceptic, a rather shallow species. Lessing also is a sceptic, but of a much nobler sort ; a doubter who deserved to believe.

known to me.   His work on Criticism has been mentioned already : he has also written on Education, a
volume named *Levana*; the *Campanerthal* (Campa-
nian Vale) I understand to turn upon the Immortality
of the Soul.   His miscellaneous and fugitive writings
were long to enumerate.   Essays, fantasies, apologues,
dreams, have appeared in various periodicals : the best
of these performances, collected and revised by himself,
were published some years ago, under the title of
Herbst-Blumine (Autumnal Flora).   There is also a
Chrestomathie (what we should call Beauties) of Richter, in four volumes.

To characterize these works would be difficult after
the fullest inspection : to describe them to English
readers would be next to impossible.   Whether poetical, philosophical, didactic, or fantastic, they seem all
to be emblems, more or less complete, of the singular
mind where they originated.   As a whole, the first
perusal of them, more particularly to a foreigner, is
almost infallibly offensive ; and neither their meaning,
nor their no-meaning, is to be discerned without long
and sedulous study.   They are a tropical wilderness,
full of endless tortuosities ; but with the fairest flowers,
and the coolest fountains ; now overarching us with
high umbrageous gloom, now opening in long gorgeous
vistas.   We wander through them enjoying their wild
grandeur ; and by degrees, our half-contemptuous wonder at the Author passes into reverence and love.   His
face was long hid from us : but we see him at length,
in the firm shape of spiritual manhood ; a vast and

most singular nature, but vindicating his singular nature by the force, the beauty, and benignity which per-
vade it.   In fine, we joyfully accept him for what he
is, and was meant to be.   The graces, the polish, the
sprightly elegancies which belong to men of lighter
make, we cannot look for or demand from him.   His
movement is essentially slow and cumbrous, for he ad-
vances not with one faculty, but with a whole mind;
with intellect, and pathos, and wit, and humour, and
imagination, moving onward like a mighty host, motley, ponderous, irregular, and irresistible.   He is not
airy, sparkling, and precise; but deep, billowy, and
vast.   The melody of his nature is not expressed in
common note-marks, or written down by the critical
gamut; for it is wild and manifold; its voice is like
the voice of cataracts and the sounding of primeval
forests.   To feeble ears it is discord, but to ears that
understand it deep majestic music.
    In his own country, we are told,* " Richter has

---

* Franz Horn's *Poesie und Beredsamkeit der Deutschen*
(Poetry and Eloquence of the Germans, from Luther's time to
the present); a work which I am bound to recommend to all
students of German literature, as a valuable guide and indicator.
Bating a certain not altogether erroneous sectarianism in regard
to religion; and a certain janty priggishness of style, nay, it
must be owned, a corresponding priggishness of character, they
will find in Horn a lively, fair, well-read, and on the whole interesting and instructive critic.   The work is in three volumes; to
which a prior publication, entitled *Umrisse* (Outlines), forms a
fourth; bringing down the History, or rather Sketch, to the bor-
ders of the year 1819.

been in fashion, then out of fashion, then in it again ;
till at last he has been raised far above all fashion,"
which indeed is his proper place. What his fate will
be in England is now to be decided. Could much re-
spected counsels from admirers of Richter have avail-
ed with me, he had not at present been put upon his
trial. Predictions are unanimous that here he will be
condemned or even neglected. Of my countrymen, in
this small instance, I have ventured to think otherwise.
To those, it is true, " the space of whose Heaven does
not extend more than three ells," and who understand
and perceive that with these three ells the Canopy of
the Universe terminates, Richter will justly enough appear a monster, from without the verge of warm three-
ell Creation ; and their duty, with regard to him, will
limit itself to chasing him forth of the habitable World,
back again into his native Chaos. If we judge of works
of art, as the French do of language, with a *Cela ne se
dit pas*, Richter will not escape his doom ; for it is too
true that he respects not the majesty of Use and Wont,
and has said and thought much which is by no means
usually said and thought. In England, however, such
principles of literary jurisprudence are rarer. To many,
I may hope, even this dim glimpse of a spirit like
Richter's will be gratifying ; and if it can hardly be expected that their first judgment of him will be favourable, curiosity may be awakened, and a second and a
truer judgment, on ampler grounds and maturer reflection, may follow. His larger works must ultimately

become known to us; they deserve it better than
thousands which have had that honour.

Of the two Works here offered to the reader, little
special explanation is required. *Schmelzle's Journey*
I have not found noticed by any of his German critics;
and must give it on my own responsibility, as one of
the most finished, as it is at least one of the simplest,
among his smaller humorous performances. *The Life
of Fixlein*, no stepchild in its own country, seems nevertheless a much more immature, as it is a much earlier composition. I select it not without reluctance;
rather from necessity than preference. Its faults, I am
too sure, will strike us much sooner than its beauties;
and even by the friendliest and most patient critic, it
must be admitted that among the latter, many of our
Author's highest qualities are by no means exhibited
in full concentration, nay, that some of them are wanting altogether, or at best, indicated rather than evinced.
Let the reader accept it with such allowances; not as
Richter's best novel, which it is far from being, but
simply as his shortest complete one; not as a full impress of him, but as a faint outline, intended rather to
excite curiosity than to satisfy it. On the whole, Richter's is a mind peculiarly difficult to represent by specimen; for its elements are complex and various, and
it is not more by quality than by quantity that it im-
presses us.

Both Works I have endeavoured to present in their
full dimensions, with all their appurtenances, strange as

some of these may appear. If the language seem rugged, heterogeneous, perplexed, the blame is not wholly mine. Richter's style may be pronounced the most untranslateable, not in German only, but in any other modern literature.* Let the English reader fancy a Burton writing, not an *Anatomy of Melancholy*, but a foreign romance, through the scriptory organs of a Jeremy Bentham ! Richter exhausts all the powers of his own most ductile language : what in him was overstrained and rude, would naturally become not less but more so in the hands of his translator.

For this, and many other offences of·my Author, apologies might be attempted ; but much as I wish for a favourable sentence, it is not meet that Richter, in the Literary Judgment-hall, should appear as a culprit ;

---

* The following long title of a little German Book I may quote by way of premunition : " K. REINHOLD's *Lexicon for* JEAN PAUL'S *Works, or Explanation of all the foreign Words and unusual Modes of Speech which occur in his Writings ; with short Notices of the historical Persons and Facts therein alluded to ; and plain German Versions of the most difficult Passages in the Context. A necessary Assistant for all who would read those Works with Profit. First volume, containing* LEVANA. Leipzig, 1808." Unhappily, with this First Volume, K. Reinhold seems to have stopped short. More than once, in the following pages, have I longed for his help ; and been forced at last to rest satisfied with *a* meaning, and too imperfect a conviction that it was the right one.

or solicit suffrages, which, if he cannot claim them, are unavailing. With the hundred real, and the ten thousand seeming weaknesses of his cause, a fair trial is a thing he will court rather than dread.

ARMY-CHAPLAIN SCHMELZLE'S

JOURNEY TO FLÆTZ;

WITH

A RUNNING COMMENTARY OF NOTES.

BY

JEAN PAUL.

PREFACE.

This, I conceive, may be managed in two words.

The *first* word must relate to the Circular Letter of Army-chaplain Schmelzle, wherein he describes to his friends his Journey to the metropolitan city of Flätz; after having, in an Introduction, premised some proofs and assurances of his valour. Properly speaking, the *Journey* itself has been written purely with a view that his courageousness, impugned by rumour, may be fully evinced and demonstrated by the plain facts which he therein records. Whether, in the meantime, there shall not be found certain quick-scented readers, who may infer, directly contrariwise, that his breast is not everywhere bomb-proof, especially in the left side: on this point I keep my judgment suspended.

For the rest, I beg the judges of literature, as well as their satellites, the critics of literature, to regard this *Journey*, for whose literary contents I, as Editor, am answerable, solely in the light of a Portrait (in the French sense), a little Sketch of Character. It is a voluntary or involuntary comedy-piece, at which I have

laughed so often, that I purpose in time coming to
paint some similar Pictures of Character myself. And,
for the present, when could such a little comic toy be
more fitly imparted and set forth to the world, than in
these very days, when the sound both of heavy money
and of light laughter has died away from among us;
when, like the Turks, we count and pay merely with
sealed *purses*, and the coin within them has vanished?

Despicable would it seem to me, if any clownish
squire of the goose-quill should publicly and censori-
ously demand of me, in what way this self-cabinet-
piece of Schmelzle's has come into my hands? I know
it well, and do not disclose it. This comedy-piece, for
which I, at all events, as my Bookseller will testify,
draw the profit myself, I got hold of so unblameably, that
I await, with unspeakable composure, what the Army-
chaplain shall please to say against the publication of
it, in case he say anything at all. My conscience bears
me witness, that I acquired this article, at least by more
honourable methods than are those of the learned persons who steal with their ears, who, in the character of
spiritual auditory-thieves, and classroom cutpurses and
pirates, are in the habit of disloading their plundered
Lectures, and vending them up and down the country
as productions of their own. Hitherto, in my whole
life, I have stolen little, except now and then in youth
some—glances.

The *second* word must explain or apologize for the
singular form of this little Work, standing as it does on

a substratum of Notes. I myself am not contented with
it. Let the World open, and look, and determine, in
like manner. But the truth is, this line of demarcation,
stretching through the whole book, originated in the
following accident: certain thoughts (or digressions)
of my own, with which it was not permitted me to
disturb those of the Army-chaplain, and which could
only be allowed to fight behind the lines, in the shape
of Notes, I, with a view to conveniency and order, had
written down in a separate paper ; at the same time, as
will be observed, regularly providing every Note with
its Number, and thus referring it to the proper page
of the main Manuscript. But, in the copying of the
latter, I had forgotten to insert the corresponding numbers in the Text itself. Therefore, let no man, any
more than I do, cast a stone at my worthy Printer, in
as much as he (perhaps in the thought that it was my
way, that I had some purpose in it) took these Notes,
just as they stood, pellmell, without arrangement of
Numbers, and clapped them under the Text; at the
same time, by a praiseworthy artful computation, taking care at least, that, at the bottom of every page in
the Text, there should some portion of this glittering
Note-precipitate make its appearance. Well, the thing
at any rate is done, nay perpetuated, namely printed.
After all, I might almost partly rejoice at it. For, in
good truth, had I meditated for years (as I have done
for the last twenty) how to provide for my digression-
comets new orbits, if not focal suns, for my episodes

new epopees,—I could scarce possibly have hit upon
a better or more spacious Limbo for such Vanities
than Chance and Printer here accidentally offer me
ready-made. I have only to regret, that the thing
has been printed, before I could turn it to account.
Heavens! what remotest allusions (had I known it before printing) might not have been privily introduced
in every Text-page and Note-number; and what apparent incongruity in the real congruity between this
upper and under side of the cards! How vehemently
and devilishly might one not have cut aloft, and to the
right and left, from these impregnable casemates and
covered-ways; and what *læsio ultra dimidium* (injury beyond the half of the Text) might not, with these
satirical injuries, have been effected and completed!

But Fate meant not so kindly with me: of this
golden harvest-field of satire, I was not to be informed
till three days before the Preface.

Perhaps, however, the writing world, by the little
blue flame of this accident, may be guided to a weigh-
tier acquisition, to a larger subterranean treasure, than
I, alas, have dug up! For, to the writer, there is now a
way pointed out of producing in one marbled volume
a group of altogether different works; of writing in
one leaf, for both sexes at the same time, without con-
founding them, nay, for the five faculties all at once,
without disturbing their limitations; since now, instead
of boiling up a vile fermenting shove-together, fit for
nobody, he has nothing to do but draw his note-lines

or partition-lines; and so on his five-story leaf give
board and lodging to the most discordant heads. Perhaps one might then read many a book for the fourth
time, simply because every time one had read but a
fourth part of it.

On the whole, this Work has at least the property of
being a short one; so that the reader, I hope, may
almost run through it, and read it at the bookseller's
counter, without, as in the case of thicker volumes,
first needing to buy it. And why, indeed, in this world
of Matter should anything whatever be great, except
only what belongs not to it, the world of Spirit?

JEAN PAUL FR. RICHTER.

Bayreuth, in the Hay and Peace Month, 1807.

SCHMELZLE'S

JOURNEY TO FLÆTZ.

Circular Letter of the proposed Catechetical Professor
ATTILA SCHMELZLE, *to his Friends; containing*
some Account of a Holidays Journey to Flätz, with
an Introduction, touching his Flight, and his Cou-
rage as former Army-chaplain.

NOTHING can be more ludicrous, my esteemed Friends,
than to hear people stigmatising a man as cowardly and
hare-hearted, who perhaps is struggling all the while
with precisely the opposite faults, those of a lion;
though indeed the African lion himself, since the time

---

103. Good princes easily obtain good subjects; not so easily
good subjects good princes: thus Adam, in the state of innocence, ruled over animals all tame and gentle, till simply through
his means they fell and grew savage.

of Sparrmann's Travels, passes among us for a pol-
troon. Yet this case is mine, worthy Friends ; and I
purpose to say a few words thereupon, before describing my Journey.

You in truth are all aware that, directly in the teeth
of this calumny, it is courage, it is desperadoes (provided they be not braggarts and tumultuous persons),
whom I chiefly venerate ; for example, my brother-in-
law, the Dragoon, who never in his life bastinadoed
one man, but always a whole social circle at the same
time. How truculent was my fancy, even in childhood, when I, as the parson was toning away to the
silent congregation, used to take it into my head :
" How now, if thou shouldst start up from thy pew,
and shout aloud : I am here too, Mr Parson !" and to
paint out this thought in such glowing colours, that for
very dread, I have often been obliged to leave the
church ! Anything like Rugenda's battle-pieces ; horrid murder-tumults, seafights or Stormings of Toulon,
exploding fleets ; and, in my childhood, Battles of
Prague on the harpsichord ; nay, in short, every map
of any remarkable scene of war : these are perhaps
too much my favourite objects ; and I read—and purchase nothing sooner ; and doubtless, they might lead
me into many errors, were it not that my circumstances restrain me. Now, if it be objected that true cou-

_____

5. For a good Physician saves, if not always from the disease,
at least from a bad Physician.

rage is something higher than mere thinking and willing, then you, my worthy friends, will be the first to
recognise mine, when it shall break forth into, not bar-
ren and empty, but active and effective words, while I
strengthen my future Catechetical Pupils, as well as
can be done in a course of College Lectures, and steel
them into Christian heroes.

It is well known that, out of care for the preserva-
tion of my life, I never walk within at least ten fields
of any shore full of bathers or swimmers ; merely because I foresee to a certainty, that in case one of them
were drowning, I should that moment (for the heart
overbalances the head) plunge after the fool to save
him, into some bottomless depth or other, where we
should both perish.   And if dreaming is the reflex of
waking, let me ask you, true Hearts, if you have forgotten my relating to you dreams of mine, which no
Cæsar, no Alexander or Luther, need have felt ashamed of ?   Have I not, to mention a few instances, taken Rome by storm ; and done battle with the Pope
and the whole elephantine body of the Cardinal College, at one and the same time ?   Did I not once on
horseback, while simply looking at a review of military,
dash headlong into a *bataillon quarré ;* and then cap-
ture, in Aix-la-Chapelle, the Peruke of Charlemagne,
for which the town pays yearly ten reichsthalers of

---

100. In books lie the Phœnix-ashes of a past Millenium and
Paradise ; but War blows, and much ashes are scattered away.

barber-money; and carrying it off to Halberstadt von
Gleim, there in like manner seize the Great Frederick's
Hat; put both Peruke and Hat on my head, and yet return home, after I had stormed their batteries and turned the cannon against the cannoneers themselves?
Did I not once submit to be made a Jew of, and then
be regaled with hams; though they were ape-hams on
the Orinocco (see Humboldt)? And a thousand such
things: for I have thrown the Consistorial President of
Flätz out of the Palace window; those alarm-fulmina-
tors, sold by Heinrich Backofen in Gotha, at six groschen the dozen, and each going off like a cannon, I
have listened to so calmly that the fulminators did not
even awaken me; and more of the like sort.

But enough! It is now time briefly to touch that
farther slander of my chaplainship, which unhappily has
likewise gained some circulation in Flätz, but which, as
Cæsar did Alexander, I shall now by my touch dissi-
pate into dust.   Be what truth in it there can, it is
still little or nothing.   Your great Minister and General in Flätz (perhaps the very greatest in the world,
for there are not many Schabackers) may indeed, like
any other great man, be turned against me; but not
with the Artillery of Truth; for this Artillery I here
set before you, my good Hearts, and do you but fire it

---

102. Dear Political or Religious Inquisitor! Art thou aware
that Turin tapers never rightly begin shining, till thou breakest
them, and then they take fire?

1

off for my advantage! The matter is this : Certain foolish rumours are afloat in the Flätz country, that I, on occasion of some important battles, took leg-bail (such is their plebeian phrase), and that afterwards, on the chaplain's being called for to preach a Thanksgiving sermon for the victory, no chaplain whatever was to be found. The ridiculousness of this story will best appear, when I tell you that I never was in any action ; but have always been accustomed, several hours prior to such an event, to withdraw so many miles to the rear, that our men, so soon as they were beaten, would be sure to find me. A good retreat is reckoned the masterpiece in the art of war ; and at no time can a retreat be executed with such order, force, and security, as just before the battle, when you are not yet beaten.

It is true, I might perhaps, as expectant Professor of Catechetics, sit still and smile at such nugatory speculations on my courage ; for if by Socratic questioning I can hammer my future Catechist Pupils into the habit of asking questions in their turn, I shall thereby have tempered *them* into heroes, seeing they have nothing to fight with but children—(Catechists at all events, though dreading fire, have no reason to dread light, since in our days, as in London illuminations, it is only the *unlighted* windows that are battered in ;

---

86. Very true ! In youth we love and enjoy the most ill-assorted friends, perhaps more than, in old age, the best-assorted,

whereas, in other ages, it was with nations and light, as it is with dogs and water; if you give them none for a long time, they at last get a horror at it) ;—and on the whole, for Catechists, any park looks kindlier, and smiles more sweetly, than a sulphurous park of artillery; and the Warlike Foot, which the age is placed on, is to them the true Devil's cloven-foot of human nature.

But for my part I think not so : almost as if the party spirit of my christian name, Attila, had passed into me more strongly than was proper, I feel myself impelled still farther to prove my courageousness ; which, dearest Friends ! I shall here in a few lines again do. This proof I could manage by mere inferences and learned citations. For example, if Galen remarks that animals with large hind-quarters are timid, I have nothing to do but turn round, and show the enemy my back, and what is under it, in order to convince him that I am not deficient in valour, but in flesh. Again, if by well-known experiences it has been found that flesh-eating produces courage, I can evince, that in this particular I yield to no officer of the service ; though it is the habit of these gentlemen not only to run up long scores of roastmeat with their landlords, but also to leave them unpaid, that so at every hour they may have an open document in the

---

128. In Love there are Summer Holidays ; but in Marriage also there are Winter Holidays, I hope.

hands of the enemy himself (the landlord), testifying that they have eaten their own share (with some of other people's too), and so put common butcher-meat on a War-footing, living not like others *by* bravery, but *for* bravery. As little have I ever, in my character of chaplain, shrunk from comparison with any officer in the regiment, who may be a true lion, and so snatch every sort of plunder, but yet, like this King of the Beasts, is afraid of *fire ;* or who,—like King James of England,* that scampered off at sight of drawn swords, yet so much the more gallantly, before all Europe, went out against the storming Luther with book and pen,—does, from a similar idiosyncrasy, attack all war-like armaments, both by word and writing. And here I recollect with satisfaction, a brave sub-lieutenant, whose confessor I was (he still owes me the confes-sion-money), and who, in respect of stout-heartedness, had in him perhaps something of that Indian dog which Alexander had presented to him, as a sort of Dog-Alexander. By way of trying this crack dog, the Macedonian made various heroic or heraldic beasts be let loose against him : first a stag ; but the dog lay still : then a sow ; he lay still : then a bear ; he lay still. Alexander was on the point of condemning him ;

---

143. Women have weekly at least one active and passive day of glory, the holy day, the Sunday. The higher ranks alone have more Sundays than work-days ; as in great towns, you can

---

* The good Professor of Catechetics is out here *Indignor* *quandoque bonus dormitat Schmelzle.*—ED.

when a lion was let forth : the dog rose, and tore the lion in pieces. So likewise the sub-lieutenant. A challenger, a foreign enemy, a Frenchman, are to him only stag, and sow, and bear, and he lies still in his place : but let his oldest enemy, his creditor, come and knock at his gate, and demand of him actual smart-money for long bygone pleasures, thus presuming to rob him both of past and present : the sub-lieutenant rises, and throws his creditor down stairs. I, alas, am still standing by the sow ; and thus, naturally enough, misunderstood.

Quo, says Livy, xii. 5, and with great justice, *quo timoris minus est, eo minus ferme periculi est,* The less fear you have, the less danger you are likely to be in. With equal justice I invert the maxim, and say : The less the danger, the smaller the fear ; nay, there may be situations, in which one has absolutely no knowledge of fear ; and, among these, mine is to be reckoned. The more hateful, therefore, must that calumny about hare-heartedness appear to me.

To my Holidays' Journey, I shall prefix a few facts, which prove how easily foresight—that is to say, when a person would not resemble the stupid marmot, that will even attack a man on horseback—may pass for cowardice. For the rest, I wish only that I could with equal ease wipe away a quite different reproach, that of being a foolhardy desperado ; though I trust, in the

celebrate your Sunday on Friday with the Turks, on Saturday with the Jews, and on Sunday with yourself.

sequel, I shall be able to advance some facts which in-
validate it.

What boots the heroic arm, without a hero's eye ?
The former readily grows stronger and more nervous ;
but the latter is not so soon ground sharper, like glasses.
Nevertheless, the merits of foresight obtain from the
mass of men less admiration (nay, I should say, more
ridicule) than those of courage. Whoso, for instance,
shall see me walking under quite cloudless skies, with
a wax-cloth umbrella over me, to him I shall probably appear ridiculous, so long as he is not aware that
I carry this umbrella as a thunder-screen, to keep off
any bolt out of the blue heaven (whereof there are
several examples in the history of the Middle Ages)
from striking me to death. My thunder-screen, in fact,
is exactly that of Reimarus : on a long walking-stick,
I carry the wax-cloth roof; from the peak of which,
depends a string of gold-lace as a conductor ; and this,
by means of a key fastened to it, which it trails along
the ground, will lead off every possible bolt, and easily
distribute it over the whole superficies of the Earth.
With this *Paratonnerre Portatif* in my hand, I can
walk about for weeks, under the clear sky, without
the smallest danger. This Diving-bell, moreover, pro-
tects me against something else ; against shot. For
who, in the latter end of Harvest, will give me black
on white that no lurking ninny of a sportsman some-

21. Schiller and Klopstock are Poetic Mirrors held up to the
Sun-god : the Mirrors reflect the Sun, with such dazzling bright-

where, when I am out enjoying Nature, shall so fire off his piece, at an angle of 45°, that in falling down again, the shot needs only light directly on my crown, and so come to the same as if I had been shot through the brain from a side?

It is bad enough, at any rate, that we have nothing to guard us from the Moon; which at present is bombarding us with stones like a very Turk: for this paltry little Earth's-train-bearer and errand-maid thinks, in these rebellious times, that she too must begin, forsooth, to sling somewhat against her Mother! In good truth, as matters stand, any young Catechist of feeling may go out o' nights, with whole limbs, into the moonshine, a-meditating; and ere long (in the midst of his meditation the villainous Satellite hits him) come home a pounded jelly. By Heaven! new proofs of courage are required of us on every hand! No sooner have we, with great effort, got thunder-rods manufactured, and comet-tails explained away, than the enemy opens new batteries in the Moon, or somewhere else in the Blue!

Suffice one other story to manifest how ludicrous the most serious foresight, with all imaginable inward courage, often externally appears in the eyes of the many. Equestrians are well acquainted with the dangers of a horse that runs away. My evil star would have it, that I should once in Vienna get upon a hack-horse; a pretty enough honey-coloured nag, but old

ness, that you cannot find the Picture of the World imaged forth in them.

and hard-mouthed as Satan ; so that the beast, in the
next street, went off with me ; and this in truth—only
at a *walk*.   No pulling, no tugging, took effect ; I, at
last, on the back of this Self-riding-horse, made signals
of distress, and cried : " Stop him, good people, for
God's sake stop him, my horse is off !" But these
simple persons seeing the beast move along as slowly
as a Reichshofrath law-suit, or the Daily Postwagen,
could not in the least understand the matter, till I cried
as if possessed : " Stop him then, ye blockheads and
joltheads ; don't you see that I cannot hold the nag ?"
But now, to these noodles, the sight of a hard-mouthed
horse going off with its rider step by step, seemed
ridiculous rather than otherwise : half Vienna gathered
itself like a comet-tail behind my beast and me.   Prince
Kaunitz, the best horseman of the century (the last),
pulled up to follow me.   I myself sat and swam like a
perpendicular piece of drift-ice on my honey-coloured
nag, which stalked on, on, step by step : a many-cor-
nered, red-coated letter-carrier, was delivering his letters, to the right and left, in the various stories, and he
still crossed over before me again, with satirical features, because the nag went along too slowly.   The
Schwanzschleuderer, or Train-dasher (the person, as
you know, who drives along the streets with a huge
barrel of water, and besplashes them with a leathern

---

34. Women are like precious carved works of ivory ; nothing
is whiter and smoother, and nothing sooner grows *yellow.*

pipe of three ells long from an iron trough), came
across the haunches of my horse, and, in the course of
his duty, wetted both these and myself in a very cool-
ing manner, though, for my part, I had too much cold
sweat on me already, to need any fresh refrigeration.
On my infernal Trojan Horse (only I myself was Troy,
not beridden but riding to destruction), I arrived at
Malzlein (a suburb of Vienna), or perhaps, so confused were my senses, it might be quite another range
of streets. At last, late in the dusk, I had to turn into
the Prater; and here, long after the Evening Gun, to my
horror, and quite against the police-rules, keep riding
to and fro on my honey-coloured nag; and possibly I
might even have passed the night on him, had not my
brother-in-law, the Dragoon, observed my plight, and
so found me still sitting firm as a rock on my runaway steed. He made no ceremonies; caught the
brute; and put the pleasant question: Why I had not
vaulted, and come off by ground-and-lofty tumbling?
though he knew full well, that for this a wooden-horse,
which stands still, is requisite. However, he took me
down; and so, after all this riding, horse and man got
home with whole skins and unbroken bones.

But now at last to my Journey!

---

72. The Half-learned is adored by the Quarter-learned; the
latter by the Sixteenth-part-learned; and so on; but not the
Whole-learned by the Half-learned.

Journey to Flätz.

You are aware, my friends, that this Journey to
Flätz was necessarily to take place in Vacation time :
not only because the Cattle-market, and consequently
the Minister and General von Schabacker, was there
then ; but more especially, because the latter (as I had
it positively from a private hand) did annually, on the
23d of July, the market-eve, about five o'clock, become so full of gaudium and graciousness, that in many
cases he did not so much snarl on people, as listen to
them, and grant their prayers. The cause of this gaudium I had rather not trust to paper.   In short, my
Petition, praying that he would be pleased to indemnify and reward me, as an unjustly deposed Army-chaplain, by a Catechetical Professorship, could plainly be
presented to him at no better season, than exactly about
five o'clock in the evening of the first dog-day. In less
than a week, I had finished writing my Petition. As
I spared neither summaries nor copies of it, I had soon
got so far as to see the relatively best lying completed
before me ; when, to my terror, I observed, that, in this
paper, I had introduced above thirty *dashes*, or breaks,
in the middle of my sentences ! Nowadays, alas, these
stings shoot forth involuntarily from learned pens, as

---

35. *Bien écouter c'est presque répondre,* says Marivaux justly of social circles : but I extend it to round Councillor-tables

from the tails of wasps. I debated long within myself whether a private scholar could justly be entitled to approach a minister with dashes,—greatly as this level interlineation of thoughts, these horizontal note-marks of poetical *music*-pieces, and these rope-ladders or Achilles'-tendons of philosophical *see*-pieces, are at present fashionable and indispensable : but, at last, I was obliged (as erasures may offend people of quality) to write my best proof-petition over again ; and then to afflict myself for another quarter of an hour over the name Attila Schmelzle, seeing it is always my principle that this and the address of the letter, the two cardinal points of the whole, can never be written legibly enough.

First Stage ; from Neusattel to Vierstädten.

THE 22d of July, or Wednesday, about five in the afternoon, was now, by the way-bill of the regular Post-coach, irrevocably fixed for my departure. I had still half a day to order my house ; from which, for two nights and two days and a half, my breast, its breast-work and palisado, was now, along with my Self, to be withdrawn. Besides this, my good wife Bergelchen, as I call my Teutoberga, was immediately to tra-

---

and Cabinet-tables, where reports are made, and the Prince listens.

vel after me, on Friday the 24th, in order to see and
to make purchases at the yearly Fair ; nay, she was
ready to have gone along with me, the faithful spouse.
I therefore assembled my little knot of domestics, and
promulgated to them the Household Law and Vale-
dictory Rescript, which, after my departure, in the
first place *before* the outset of my wife, and in the
second place *after* this outset, they had rigorously to
obey ; explaining to them especially whatever, in case
of conflagrations, house-breakings, thunder-storms, or
transits of troops, it would behove them to do. To my
wife I delivered an inventory of the best goods in our
little Register-ship ; which goods she, in case the house
took fire, had, in the first place, to secure. I ordered
her, in stormy nights (the peculiar thief-weather), to
put our Eolian harp in the window, that so any villainous prowler might imagine I was fantasying on my
instrument, and therefore awake : for like reasons, also,
to take the house-dog within doors by day, that he
might sleep then, and so be livelier at night. I farther counselled her to have an eye on the focus of
every knot in the panes of the stable-window, nay, on
every glass of water she might set down in the house ;
as I had already often recounted to her examples of

---

17. The Bed of Honour, since so frequently whole regiments
lie on it, and receive their last unction, and last honour but one,
really ought from time to time to be new-filled, beaten, and
sunned.

such accidental burning-glasses having set whole build-
ings in flames. I then appointed her the hour when she
was to set out on Friday morning to follow me ; and
recapitulated more emphatically the household pre-
cepts, which, prior to her departure, she must afresh
inculcate on her domestics. My dear, heart-sound,
blooming Berga, answered her faithful lord, as it seemed very seriously : " Go thy ways, little old one ; it
shall all be done as smooth as velvet. Wert thou but
away! There is no end of thee!" Her brother my
brother-in-law the Dragoon, for whom, out of com-
plaisance, I had paid the coach-fare, in order to have
in the vehicle along with me a stout swordsman and
hector, as spiritual relative and bully-rock, so to speak ;
the Dragoon, I say, on hearing these my regulations,
puckered up (which I easily forgave the wild soldier
and bachelor) his sun-burnt face considerably into ridicule, and said : " Were I in thy place, sister, I should
do what I liked, and then afterwards take a peep into
these regulation papers of his."

" Oh!" answered I, " misfortune may conceal itself like a scorpion in any corner : I might say, we are
like children, who, looking at their gaily painted toy-
box, soon pull off the lid, and, pop ! out springs a
mouse who has young ones."

" Mouse, mouse !" said he, stepping up and down.

---

120. Many a one becomes a free-spoken Diogenes, not when
he dwells in the Cask, but when the Cask dwells in him.

" But, good brother, it is five o'clock ; and you will
find, when you return, that all looks exactly as it does
to-day ; the dog like the dog, and my sister like a
pretty woman : *allons donc !*" It was purely his blame
that I, fearing his misconceptions, had not previously
made a sort of testament.

I now packed in two different sorts of medicines,
heating as well as cooling, against two different possi-
bilities ; also my old splints for arm or leg breakages,
in case the coach overset ; and (out of foresight) two
times the money I was likely to need.   Only here I
could have wished, so uncertain is the stowage of such
things, that I had been an Ape with cheek-pouches, or
some sort of Oppossum with a natural bag, that so I
might have reposited these necessaries of existence in
pockets which were sensitive.   Shaving is a task I always go through before setting out on journeys ; having a rational mistrust against stranger blood-thirsty
barbers : but, on this occasion, I retained my beard ;
since, however close shaved, it would have grown again
by the road to such a length that I could have fronted
no Minister and General with it.

With a vehement emotion, I threw myself on the
pith-heart of my Berga, and, with a still more vehement
one, tore myself away : in her, however, this our first
marriage-separation seemed to produce less lamenta-

---

3. Culture makes whole lands, for instance Germany, Gaul,
and others, physically warmer, but spiritually colder.

tion than triumph, less consternation than rejoicing ;
simply because she turned her eye not half so much
on the parting, as on the meeting, and the journey
after me, and the wonders of the Fair. Yet she threw
and hung herself on my somewhat long and thin neck
and body, almost painfully, being, indeed, a too fleshy
and weighty load, and said to me : " Whisk thee off
quick, my charming Attel (Attila), and trouble thy
head with no cares by the way, thou singular man !
A whiff or two of ill luck we can stand, by God's help,
so long as my father is no beggar. And for thee,
Franz," continued she, turning with some heat to her
brother, " I leave my Attel on thy soul : thou well
knowest, thou wild fly, what I will do, if thou play the
fool, and leave him anywhere in the lurch." Her meaning here was good, and I could not take it ill : to you
also, my Friends, her wealth and her open-heartedness
are nothing new.

Melted into sensibility, I said : " Now, Berga, if
there be a reunion appointed for us, surely it is either
in Heaven or in Flätz ; and I hope in God, the latter."
With these words, we whirled stoutly away. I looked
round through the back-window of the coach at my
good little village of Neusattel, and it seemed to me,
in my melting mood, as if its steeples were rising aloft
like an epitaphium over my life, or over my body,

1. The more Weakness the more Lying : Force goes straight ;
any cannon-ball with holes or cavities in it goes crooked.

perhaps, to return a lifeless corpse. " How will it all
be," thought I, " when thou at last, after two or three
days, comest back ?" And now I noticed my Bergelchen looking after us from the garret-window. I lean-
ed far out from the coach-door, and her falcon eye instantly distinguished my head ; kiss on kiss she threw
with both hands after the carriage, as it rolled down
into the valley. " Thou true-hearted wife," thought I,
" how is thy lowly birth, by thy spiritual new-birth,
made forgettable, nay, remarkable !"

I must confess, the assemblage and conversational
picnic of the stagecoach was much less to my taste :
the whole of them suspicious, unknown rabble, whom
(as markets usually do) the Flätz cattle-market was
alluring by its scent. I dislike becoming acquainted
with strangers : not so my brother-in-law, the Dragoon ; who now, as he always does, had in a few minutes elbowed himself into close quarters with the
whole ragamuffin posse of them. Beside me sat a person, who, in all human probability, was a Harlot ; on
her breast, a Dwarf intending to exhibit himself at the
Fair ; on the other side was a Ratcatcher gazing at me ;
and a Blind Passenger,* in a red mantle, had joined us
down in the valley. No one of them, except my brother-in-law, pleased me. That rascals among these

---

38. Epictetus advises us to travel, because our old acquaintances by the influence of shame impede our transition to higher

---

* Passenger so placed in the huge German Postwagen, that he
cannot look out.—ED.

people would not study me and my properties and
accidents, to entangle me in their snares, no man could
be my surety.   In strange places, I even, out of prudence, avoid looking long up at any jail-window ; because some losel, sitting behind the bars, may in a moment call down out of mere malice : " How goes it,
comrade Schmelzle ?" or farther, because any lurking
catchpole may fancy I am planning a rescue for some
confederate above.   From another sort of prudence,
little different from this, I also make a point of never
turning round when any booby calls, Thief! after me.

As to the Dwarf himself, I had no objection to his travelling with me whithersoever he pleased ; but he thought
to raise a particular delectation in our minds, by promi-
sing that his Pollux and Brother in Trade, an extraordinary Giant, who was also making for the Fair to exhibit himself, would by midnight, with his elephantine
pace, infallibily overtake the coach, and plant himself
among us, or behind on the outside.   Both these noodles, it appeared, are in the habit of going in company
to fairs, as reciprocal exaggerators of opposite magni-
tudes : the Dwarf is the convex magnifying-glass of
the Giant, the Giant the concave diminishing-glass of
the Dwarf.   Nobody expressed much joy at the pros-
pective arrival of this Anti-dwarf, except my brother-

---

virtues ; as a bashful man will rather lay aside his provincial
accent in some foreign quarter, and then return wholly purified
to his own countrymen : in our days, people of rank and virtue

in-law, who (if I may venture on a play of words)
seems made, like a clock, solely for the purpose of
striking, and once actually said to me: " That if in
the Upper world he could not get a soul to curry and
towzle by a time, he would rather go to the Under,
where most probably there would be plenty of cuffing
and to spare." The Ratcatcher, besides the circumstance that no man can prepossess us much in his favour, who lives solely by poisoning, like this Destroying Angel of rats, this mouse-Atropos ; and also, which
is still worse, that such a fellow bids fair to become an
increaser of the vermin kingdom, the moment he may
cease to be a lessener of it ; besides all this, I say, the
present Ratcatcher had many baneful features about
him : first, his stabbing look, piercing you like a sti-
letto ; then the lean sharp bony visage, conjoined with
his enumeration of his considerable stock of poisons ;
then (for I hated him more and more) his sly stillness,
his sly smile, as if in some corner he noticed a mouse,
as he would notice a man ! To me, I declare, though
usually I take not the slightest exception against people's looks, it seemed at last as if his throat were a
Dog-grotto, a *Grotta del cane*, his cheek-bones cliffs
and breakers, his hot breath the wind of a calcining
furnace, and his black hairy breast a kiln for parching
and roasting.

---

follow this advice, but inversely ; and travel because their old
acquaintances, by the influence of shame, would too much deter
them from new sins.

Nor was I far wrong, I believe; for soon after this,
he began quite coolly to inform the company, in which
were a dwarf and a female, that, in his time, he had,
not without enjoyment, run ten men through the body;
had with great convenience hewed off a dozen men's
arms; slowly split four heads, torn out two hearts, and
more of the like sort; while none of them, otherwise
persons of spirit, had in the least resisted: "but why?"
added he, with a poisonous smile, and taking the hat
from his odious baldpate; "I am invulnerable. Let any
one of the company that chooses lay as much fire on my
bare crown as he likes, I shall not mind it."

My brother-in-law, the Dragoon, directly kindled his
tinder-box, and put a heap of the burning matter on the
Ratcatcher's pole; but the fellow stood it, as if it had
been a mere picture of fire, and the two looked ex-
pectingly at one another; and the former smiled very
foolishly, saying: "It was simply pleasant to him, like
a good warming-plaster; for this was always the wintry
region of his body."

Here the Dragoon groped a little on the naked scull,
and cried with amazement, that "it was as cold as a
knee-pan."

But now the fellow, to our horror, after some pre-
parations, actually lifted off the quarter-scull and held

32. Our Age (by some called the Paper Age, as if it were
made from the rags of some better dressed one) is improving in
so far, as it now tears its rags rather into Bandages than into
Papers; although, or because, the Rag-hacker (the Devil as they

it out to us, saying: " He had sawed it off a murderer, his own having accidentally been broken;" and
withal explained, that the stabbing and arm-cutting he
had talked of was to be understood as a jest, seeing he
had merely done it in the character of Famulus at an
Anatomical Theatre. However, the jester seemed to
rise little in favour with any of us ; and for my part, as
he put his brain-lid and sham-scull on again, I thought
to myself ; " This dungbed-bell has changed its place,
indeed, but not the hemlock it was made to cover."

Farther, I could not but reckon it a suspicious circumstance, that he as well as all the company (the
Blind Passenger too) were making for this very Flätz,
to which I myself was bound : much good I could not
expect of this ; and, in truth, turning home again would
have been as pleasant to me as going on, had I not rather felt a pleasure in defying the future.

I come now to the red-mantled Blind Passenger ;
most probably an *Emigré* or *Refugié;* for he speaks
German not worse than he does French ; and his name,
I think, was *Jean Pierre* or *Jean Paul*, or some such
thing, if indeed he had any name. His red cloak, notwithstanding this his identity of colour with the Hangman, would in itself have remained heartily indifferent to

---

call it) will not altogether be at rest. Meanwhile, if Learned
Heads transform themselves into Books, Crowned Heads transform and coin themselves into Government-paper : in Norway,
according to the *Universal Indicator*, the people have even pa-

me ; had it not been for this singular circumstance, that
he had already five times, contrary to all expectation,
come upon me in five different towns (in great Berlin, in
little Hof, in Coburg, Meiningen, and Bayreuth), and
each of these times, had looked at me significantly
enough, and then gone his ways.   Whether this *Jean
Pierre* is dogging me with hostile intent or not, I cannot say ; but to our fancy, at any rate, no object can
be gratifying that thus, with corps of observation, or
out of loop-holes, holds and aims at us with muskets,
which for year after year it shall move to this side
and that, without our knowing on whom it is to fire.
Still more offensive did Redcloak become to me, when
he began to talk about his soft mildness of soul ; a thing
which seemed either to betoken pumping you or un-
dermining you.

I replied : " Sir, I am just come, with my brother-
in-law here, from the field of battle (the last affair
was at Pimpelstadt), and so perhaps am too much of
a humour for fire, pluck, and war-fury ; and to many
a one, who happens to have a roaring waterspout of a
heart, it may be well if his clerical character (which is
mine) rather enjoins on him mildness than wildness.
However, all mildness has its iron limit. If any thought-

---

per-houses ; and in many good German States, the Exchequer
Collegium (to say nothing of the Justice Collegium) keeps its
own paper-mills, to furnish wrappage enough for the meal of its
wind-mills. I could wish, however, that our Collegiums would

less dog chance to anger me, in the first heat of rage
I kick my foot through him ; and after me, my good
brother here will perhaps drive matters twice as far,
for he is the man to do it. Perhaps it may be singular ; but I confess, I regret to this day, that once when
a boy I received three blows from another, without
tightly returning them ; and I often feel as if I must still
pay them to his descendants. In sooth, if I but chance
to see a child running off like a dastard from the weak
attack of a child like himself, I cannot for my life understand his running, and can scarcely keep from in-
terfering to save him by a decisive knock."

The Passenger meanwhile was smiling, not in the
best fashion. He gave himself out for a Legations-
Rath, and seemed fox enough for such a post ; but a
mad fox will, in the long run, bite me as rabidly as a
mad wolf will. For the rest, I calmly went on with
my eulogy on courage ; only that, instead of ludicrous
gasconading, which directly betrays the coward, I purposely expressed myself in words at once cool, clear,
and firm.

" I am altogether for Montaigne's advice," said I :
" Fear nothing but fear."

" I again," replied the Legations-man, with useless
wiredrawing, " I should fear again that I did not sufficiently fear fear, but continued too dastardly."

---

take pattern from that Glass Manufactory at Madrid, in which
(according to Baumgärtner) there were indeed nineteen clerks stationed, but also eleven workmen

" To this fear also," replied I coldly, " I set limits.
A man, for instance, may not in the least believe in,
or be afraid of ghosts ; and yet by night may bathe
himself in cold sweat, and this purely out of terror at
the dreadful fright he should be in (especially with
what whiffs of epilepsies, falling-sicknesses, and so forth,
he might be visited), in case simply his own too vivid
fancy should create any wild fever-image, and hang it
up in the air before him."

" One should not, therefore," added my brother-in-
law the Dragoon, contrary to his custom, moralizing a
little, " one should not bamboozle the poor sheep, man,
with any ghost-tricks ; the henheart may die on the
spot."

A loud storm of thunder, overtaking the stagecoach,
altered the discourse. You, my Friends, knowing me
as a man not quite destitute of some tincture of Natural Philosophy, will easily guess my precautions against
thunder. I place myself on a chair in the middle of the
room (often, when suspicious clouds are out, I stay
whole nights on it), and by careful removal of all con-
ductors, rings, buckles, and so forth, I here sit thun-
der-proof, and listen with a cool spirit to this elemen-

---

2. In his Prince, a soldier reverences and obeys at once his
Prince and his Generalissimo ; a Citizen only his Prince.

45. Our present writers shrug their shoulders most at those
on whose shoulders they stand ; and exalt those most, who crawl
up along them.

tal music of the cloud-kettledrum. These precautions have never harmed me, for I am still alive at this date : and to the present hour, I congratulate myself on once hurrying out of church, though I had confessed but the day previous ; and running, without more ceremony, and before I had received the sacrament, into the char-nel-house, because a heavy thunder-cloud (which did, in fact, strike the churchyard lindentree) was hovering over it. So soon as the cloud had disloaded itself, I returned from the charnel-house into the church, and was happy enough to come in after the Hangman (usually the last), and so still participate in the Feast of Love.

Such, for my own part, is my manner of proceeding : but in the full stagecoach, I met with men to whom Natural Philosophy was no philosophy at all. For when the clouds gathered dreadfully together over our coach-canopy, and sparkling, began to play through the air, like so many fire-flies, and I at last could not but request that the sweating coach-conclave would at least bring out their watches, rings, money, and such like, and put them all into one of the carriage-pockets, that none of us might have a conductor on his body ; not only would no one of them do it ; but my own

103. The Great perhaps take as good charge of their posterity as the Ants : the eggs once laid, the male and female Ants fly about their business, and confide them to the trusty *working-Ants.*

brother-in-law the Dragoon even sprang out, with naked drawn sword, to the coach-box, and swore that he
would conduct the thunder all away himself. Nor do
I know whether this desperate mortal was not acting
prudently; for our position within was frightful, and
any one of us might every moment be a dead man. At
last, to crown all, I got into a half altercation with two
of the rude members of our leathern household, the
Poisoner and the Harlot ; seeing, by their questions,
they almost gave me to understand, that, in our conversational picnic, especially with the Blind Passenger,
I had not always come off with the best share. Such
an imputation wounds your honour to the quick ; and
in my breast there was a thunder louder than that
above us : however, I was obliged to carry on the needful exchange of sharp words as quietly and slowly as
possible ; and I quarrelled softly, and in a low tone,
lest in the end a whole coachful of people, set in arms
against each other, might get into heat and perspira-
tion ; and so, by vapour steaming through the coach-
roof, conduct the too near thunderbolt down into the
midst of us. At last, I laid before the company the
whole theory of Electricity, in clear words, but low
and slow (striving to avoid all emission of vapour) ; and

---

10. And does Life offer us, in regard to our ideal hopes and
purposes, anything but a prosaic. unrhymed. unmetrical Translation ?

especially endeavoured to frighten them away from
fear. For, indeed, through fear, the stroke—nay, two
strokes, the electric or the apoplectic—might hit any
one of us ; since in Erxleben and Reimarus, it is sufficiently proved, that violent fear, by the transpiration it
causes, may attract the lightning. I accordingly, in
some fear of my own and other people's fear, represented to the passengers that now, in a coach so hot and
crowded, with a drawn sword on the coachbox piercing
the very lightning, with the thunder-cloud hanging over
us, and even with so many transpirations from incipient
fear ; in short, with such visible danger on every hand,
they must absolutely fear nothing, if they would not,
all and sundry, be smitten to death in a few minutes.

" O Heaven !" cried I, " Courage ! only courage !
No fear, not even fear of fear ! Would you have Providence to shoot you here sitting, like so many hares
hunted into a pinfold ? Fear, if you like, when you are
out ef the coach ; fear to your heart's content, in other
places, where there is less to be afraid of ; only not
here, not here !"

I shall not determine—since among millions scarcely
one man dies by thunder-clouds, but millions perhaps

---

78. Our German frame of Government, cased in its harness,
had much difficulty in moving, for the same reason why Beetles
cannot fly, when their *wings* have *wing-shells*, of very sufficient
strength, and—grown together.

by snow-clouds, and rain-clouds, and thin mist—whether my Coach-sermon could have made any claim to a prize for man-saving ; however, at last, all uninjured, and driving towards a rainbow, we entered the town of Vierstädten, where dwelt a Postmaster, in the only street which the place had.

Second Stage, from Vierstädten to Niedherschöna.

THE Postmaster was a churl and a striker ; a class of mortals whom I inexpressibly detest, as my fancy always whispers to me, in their presence, that by accident or dislike I might happen to put on a scornful or impertinent look, and hound these mastiffs on my own throat ; and so, from the very first, I must incessantly watch them. Happily, in this case (supposing I even had made a wrong face), I could have shielded myself with the Dragoon ; for whose giant force such matters are a tidbit. This brother-in-law of mine, for example, cannot pass any tavern where he hears a sound of battle, without entering, and, as he crosses the thresh-

---

8. Constitutions of Government are like highways : on a new and quite untrodden one, where every carriage helps in the process of bruising and smoothing, you are as much jolted and pitched, as on an old worn-out one, full of holes. What is to be done then ? Travel on.

old, shouting: " Peace, dogs !"—and therewith, under show of a peace-deputation, he directly snatches
up the first chair-leg in his hand, as if it were an American peace-calumet, and cuts to the right and left
among the belligerent powers, or he gnashes the hard
heads of the parties together (he himself takes no side),
catching each by the hind-lock : in such cases, the
rogue is in Heaven !

I, for my part, rather avoid discrepant circles than
seek them ; as I likewise avoid all dead or killed people : the prudent man easily foresees what is to be got
by them ; either vexatious and injurious witnessing, or
often even (when circumstances conspire) painful investigation, and suspicions of your being an accomplice.

In Vierstädten, nothing of importance presented itself, except—to my horror—a dog without tail, which
came running along the town or street. In the first fire
of passion at this sight, I pointed it out to the passengers, and then put the question, Whether they could
reckon a system of Medical Police well arranged, which,
like this of Vierstädten, allowed dogs openly to scour
about, when their tails were wanting ? " What am I
to do," said I, " when this member is cut away, and
any such beast comes running towards me, and I cannot, either by the tail being cocked up or being drawn

---

3. In Criminal Courts, murdered children are often represented
as still-born ; in Anticritiques, still-born as murdered.

in, since the whole is snipt off, come to any conclusion
whether the vermin is mad or not? In this way, the
most prudent man may be bit, and become rabid, and
so make shipwreck purely for want of a tail-compass."
The Blind Passenger (he now got himself inscribed
as a Seeing one, God knows for what objects) had
heard my observation; which he now spun out in my
presence almost into ridicule, and at last awakened in
me the suspicion, that by an overdone flattery in imitating my style of speech, he meant to banter me.
" The Dog-tail," said he, " is, in truth, an alarm-bea-
con, and finger-post for us, that we come not even into
the outmost precincts of madness: cut away from
Comets their tails, from Bashaws theirs, from Crabs
theirs (outstretched it denotes that they are burst);
and in the most dangerous predicaments of life, we are
left without clew, without indicator, without hand *in
margine;* and we perish not so much as knowing
how."
For the rest, this stage passed over without quarrel-
ling or péril. About ten o'clock, the whole party, including even the Postilion, myself excepted, fell asleep.
I indeed pretended to be sleeping, that I might observe
whether some one, for his own good reasons, might not

---

101. Not only were the Rhodians, from their Colossus, called
Colossians; but also innumerable Germans are. from their Luther, called Lutherans.

also be pretending it; but all continued snoring; the moon threw its brightening beams on nothing but down-pressed eyelids.

I had now a glorious opportunity of following La-vater's counsel, to apply the physiognomical ellwand specially to sleepers, since sleep, like death, expresses the genuine form in coarser lines. Other sleepers not in stagecoaches I think it less advisable to mete with this ellwand; having always an apprehension lest some fellow, but pretending to be asleep, may, the instant I am near enough, start up as in a dream, and deceit-fully plant such a knock on the physiognomical men-surator's own facial structure, as to exclude it for ever from appearing in any Physiognomical Fragments (it-self being reduced to one), either in the stippled or line style. Nay, might not the most honest sleeper in the world, just while you are in hand with his physiog-nomical dissection, lay about him, spurred on by ho-nour in some cudgelling-scene he may be dreaming; and in a few instants of clapperclawing, and kicking, and trampling, lull you into a much more lasting sleep than that out of which he was awakened?

In my *Adumbrating Magic-lantern*, as I have named the Work, the whole physiognomical contents of this

_____

88. Hitherto I have always regarded the Polemical writings of our present philosophic and æsthetic Idealist Logic-buffers,—in which, certainly, a few contumelies, and misconceptions, and misconclusions do make their appearance,—rather on the fair side;

same sleeping stagecoach will be given to the world :
there I shall explain to you at large how the Poisoner,
with the murder-cupola, appeared to me devil-like ;
the Dwarf old-child-like ; the Harlot languidly shame-
less ; my Brother-in-law peacefully satisfied, with re-
venge or food ; and the Legations-Rath, *Jean Pierre*,
Heaven only knows why, like a half angel,—though,
perhaps, it might be because only the fair body, not
the other half, the soul, which had passed away in
sleep, was affecting me.

I had almost forgotten to mention, that in a little
village, while my Brother-in-law and the Postilion
were sitting at their liquor, I happily fronted a small
terror, Destiny having twice been on my side.   Not
far from a Hunting Box, beside a pretty clump of
trees, I noticed a white tablet, with a black inscription
on it.   This gave me hopes that perhaps some little
monumental piece, some pillar of honour, some battle
memento, might here be awaiting me.   Over an untrodden flowery tangle, I reach the black on white ; and to
my horror and amazement, I decypher in the moonshine : *Beware of Spring-guns !* Thus was I standing
perhaps half a nail's breadth from the trigger, with
which, if I but stirred my heel, I should shoot myself

---

observing in it merely an imitation of classical Antiquity, in particular of the ancient Athletes, who (according to Schöttgen) be-
smeared their bodies with *mud*, that they might not be laid hold
of ; and filled their hands with *sand*, that they might lay hold of
their antagonists.

off, like a forgotten ramrod, into the other world, beyond the verge of Time ! The first thing I did was to
slutch down my toe-nails, to bite, and, as it were, eat
myself into the ground with them ; since I might at
least continue in warm life so long as I pegged my
body firmly in beside the Atropos-scissars and hangman's block, which lay beside me ; then I endeavoured
to recollect by what steps the Fiend had led me hither
unshot, but in my agony I had perspired the whole of
it, and could remember nothing. In the Devil's village
close at hand, there was no dog to be seen and called
to, who might have plucked me from the water ; and
my Brother-in-law and the Postilion were both ca-
rousing with full can. However, I summoned my courage and determination ; wrote down on a leaf of my
pocket-book my last will, the accidental manner of my
death, and my dying remembrance of Berga ; and then,
with full sails, flew helterskelter through the midst of
it the shortest way ; expecting at every step to awaken
the murderous engine, and thus to clap over my still
long candle of life the *bonsoir*, or extinguisher, with
my own hand. However, I got off without shot. In
the tavern, indeed, there was more than one fool to
laugh at me ; because, forsooth, what none but a fool

---

103. Or are all Mosques, Episcopal-churches, Pagodas, Cha-
pels-of-Ease, Tabernacles, and Pantheons, anything else than the
Ethnic Forecourt of the Invisible Temple and its Holy of
Holies ?

could know, this Notice had stood there for the last ten years, without any gun, as guns often do without any notice. But so it is, my Friends, with our game-police, which warns against all things, only not against warnings.

For the rest, throughout the whole stage, I had a constant source of altercation with the coachman, because he grudged stopping perhaps once in the quarter of an hour, when I chose to come out for a natural purpose. Unhappily, in truth, one has little reason to expect water-doctors among the postilion class, since Physicians themselves have so seldom learned from Haller's large *Physiology*, that a postponement of the above operation will precipitate devilish stoneware, and at last precipitate the proprietor himself; this stone-manufactory being generally concluded, not by the Lithotomist, but by Death. Had postilions read that Tycho Brahe died like a bombshell by bursting, they would rather pull up for a moment; with such unlooked-for knowledge, they would see it to be reasonable that a man, though expecting some time to carry his death-stone *on* him, should not incline, for the time being, to carry it *in* him. Nay, have I not often, at Weimar, in the longest concluding scenes of Schiller, run out with tears in my eyes; purely that, while his Minerva was melting me on the whole, I might not

---

40. The common man is copious only in narration, not in reasoning; the cultivated man is brief only in the former, not in the latter: because the common man's reasons are a sort of sensations, which, as well as things visible, he merely *looks at* ;

SCHMELZLE'S JOURNEY TO FLÆTZ. 65

by the Gorgon's head on her breast be partially turned to stone? And did I not return to the weeping play-house, and fall into the general emotion so much the more briskly, as now I had nothing to give vent to but my heart? Deep in the dark we arrived at Neiderschöna.

Third Stage, from Niederschöna to Flätz.

WHILE I am standing at the Posthouse musing, with my eye fixed on my portmanteau, comes a beast of a watchman, and bellows and brays in his night-tube so close by my ear, that I start back in trepidation, I whom even a too hasty accosting will vex. Is there no medical police, then, against such efflated hour-fulmi-nators and alarm-cannon, by which notwithstanding no gunpowder cannon are saved? In my opinion, nobody should be invested with the watchman-horn but some reasonable man, who had already blown himself into an asthma, and who would consequently be in case to sing out his hour-verse so low, that you could not hear it.

---

by the cultivated man, again, both reasons and things visible are rather *thought* than looked at.

9. In any national calamity, the ancient Egyptians took re-venge on the god Typhon, whom they blamed for it, by hurling

VOL. III.   E

What I had long expected, and the Dwarf predicted, now took place : deeply stooping, through the high Posthouse door, issued the Giant, and raised, in the open air, a most unreasonably high figure, heightened by the ell-long bonnet and feather on his huge jobbernowl. My Brother-in-law, beside him, looked but like his son of fourteen years ; the Dwarf like his lap-dog waiting for him on its two hind legs. " Good friend," said my bantering Brother-in-law, leading him towards me and the stagecoach, " just step softly in, we shall all be happy to make room for you. Fold yourself neatly together, lay your head on your knee, and it will do." The unseasonable banterer would willingly have seen the almost stupid Giant (of whom he had soon observed that his brain was no active substance, but in the inverse ratio of his trunk) squeezed in among us in the post-chest, and lying kneaded together like a sand-bag before him. " Won't do ! Won't do !" said the Giant, looking in. " The gentleman perhaps does not know," said the Dwarf, " how big the Giant is ; and so he thinks that because *I* go in—But that is another story ; *I,* will creep into any hole, do but tell me where."

In short, there was no resource for the Postmaster

---

his favourites, the Asses, down over rocks. In similar wise, have countries of a different religion now and then taken their revenge.

70. Let Poetry veil itself in Philosophy, but only as the latter

and the Giant, but that the latter should plant himself behind, in the character of luggage, and there lie
bending down like a weeping willow over the whole
vehicle. To me such a back-wall and rear-guard could
not be particularly gratifying : and I may refer it (I
hope) to any one of you, ye Friends, if with such ware
at your back, you would not, as clearly and earnestly
as I, have considered what manifold murderous projects
a knave of a Giant behind you, a *pursuer* in all senses,
might not maliciously attempt ; say, that he broke in
and assailed you by the back-window, or with Titanian
strength laid hold of the coach-roof and demolished
the whole party in a lump. However, this Elephant
(who indeed seemed to owe the similarity more to his
overpowering mass than to his quick light of inward
faculty), crossing his arms over the top of the vehicle,
soon began to sleep and snore above us ; an Elephant,
of whom, as I more and more joyfully observed, my
brother-in-law, the Dragoon, could easily be the tamer
and bridle-holder, nay, had already been so.

As more than one person now felt inclined to sleep,
but I, on the contrary, as was proper, to wake, I freely
offered my seat of honour, the front place in the coach

---

does in the former. Philosophy in poetized Prose resembles
those tavern drinking-glasses, encircled with party-coloured
wreaths of figures, which disturb your enjoyment both of the
drink, and (often awkwardly eclipsing and covering each other)
of the carving also.

(meaning thereby to abolish many little flaws of envy in my fellow-passengers), to such persons as wished to take a nap thereon. The Legations-man accepted the offer with eagerness, and soon fell asleep there sitting, under the Titan.* To me this sort of coach-sleeping of a diplomatic *chargé d' affaires*, remained a thing incomprehensible. A man, that in the middle of a stranger and often barbarously-minded company, permits himself to slumber, may easily, supposing him to talk in his sleep and coach, (think of the Saxon minister† before the Seven Years War!) blab out a thousand secrets, and crimes, some of which, perhaps, he has not committed. Should not every minister, ambassador, or other man of honour and rank, really shudder at the thought of insanity or violent fevers; seeing no mortal can be his surety that he shall not in such cases publish the greatest scandals, of which, it may be, the half are lies?

At last, after the long July night, we passengers, together with Aurora, arrived in the precincts of Flätz.

---

158. Governments should not too often change the penny-trumps and child's-drums of the Poets for the regimental trumpet and fire-drum : on the other hand, good subjects should regard many a princely drum-tendency simply as a disease, in

---

* *Titan* is also the title of this Legations-Rath Jean Pierre or Jean Paul (Friedrich Richter)'s chief novel.—ED.

† Brühl, I suppose ; but the historical edition of the matter is, that Brühl's treasonable secrets were come at by the more ordinary means of wax impressions of his keys.—ED.

I looked with a sharp yet moistened eye at the steeples :
I believe, every man who has any thing decisive to seek
in a town, and to whom it is either to be a judgment-
seat of his hopes, or their anchoring-station, either a
battle-field or a sugar-field, first and longest directs his
eye on the steeples of the town, as upon the indexes and
balance-tongues of his future destiny ; these artificial
peaks, which, like natural ones, are the thrones of our
Future. As I happened to express myself on this point
perhaps too poetically to *Jean Pierre*, he answered,
with sufficient want of taste : " The steeples of such
towns are indeed the Swiss Alpine peaks, on which we
milk and manufacture the Swiss cheese of our Future."
Did the Legations-Peter mean with this style to make
me ridiculous, or only himself ? Determine !

" Here is the place, the town," said I in secret,
" where to-day much and for many years is to be determined, where thou, this evening, about five o'clock,
art to present thy petition and thyself : May it pros-
per ! May it be successful ! Let Flätz, this arena of
thy little efforts among the rest, become a building-
space for fair castles and air-castles to two hearts, thy
own and thy Berga's !"

At the Tiger Inn, I alighted.

---

which the patient, by air insinuating under the skin, has got
dreadfully swoln.

89. In great towns, a stranger, for the first day or two after
his arrival, lives purely at his own expense in an inn : afterwards,

First Day in Flätz.

No mortal, in my situation at this Tiger-hotel, would have triumphed much in his more immediate prospects. I, as the only man known to me, especially in the way of love (of the runaway Dragoon anon!), looked out from the windows of the overflowing Inn, and down on the rushing sea of marketers, and very soon began to reflect, that except Heaven and the rascals and murderers, none knew how many of the latter two classes were floating among the tide; purposing perhaps to lay hold of the most innocent strangers, and in part cut their purses, in part their throats. My situation had a special circumstance against it. My brother-in-law, who still comes plump out with everything, had mentioned that I was to put up at the Tiger: O Heaven, when will such people learn to be secret, and to cover even the meanest pettinesses of life under mantles and veils, were it only that a silly mouse may as often give birth to a mountain, as a mountain to a mouse! The whole

---

in the houses of his friends, without expense : on the other hand, if you arrive at the Earth, as for instance I have done, you are courteously maintained, precisely for the first few years, free of charges ; but in the next and longer series—for you often stay sixty—you are actually obliged (I have the documents in my hands) to pay for every drop and morsel, as if you were in the great Earth Inn, which indeed you are.

rabble of the stagecoach stopped at the Tiger; the Harlot, the Ratcatcher, *Jean Pierre*, the Giant, who had dismounted at the Gate of the town, and carrying the huge block-head of the Dwarf on his shoulders as his own (cloaking over the deception by his cloak), had thus, like a ninny, exhibited himself gratis by half a dwarf more gigantic, than he could be seen for money.

And now for each of the Passengers, the question was how he could make the Tiger, the heraldic emblem of the Inn, his prototype; and so, what lamb he might suck the blood of, and tear in pieces, and devour. My brother-in-law too left me, having gone in quest of some horse-dealer; but he retained the chamber next mine for his sister: this, it appeared, was to denote attention on his part. I remained solitary, left to my own intrepidity and force of purpose.

Yet among so many villains, encompassing if not even beleaguering me, I thought warmly of one far distant, faithful soul, of my Berga in Neusattel; a true heart of pith, which perhaps with many a weak marriage-partner might have given protection rather than sought it.

" Appear, then, quickly to-morrow at noon, Berga," said my heart; " and if possible before noon, that I may lengthen thy market paradise so many hours as thou arrivest earlier!"

A clergyman, amid the tempests of the world, readily makes for a free harbour, for the church: the church-

---

107. Germany is a long lofty mountain—under the sea.

wall is his casemate-wall and fortification; and behind
are to be found more peaceful and more accordant
souls than on the market-place : in short, I went into
the High Church. However, in the course of the psalm,
I was somewhat disturbed by a Heiduc, who came up
to a well-dressed young gentleman sitting opposite me,
and tore the double opera-glass from his nose, it being
against rule in Flätz, as it is in Dresden, to look at the
Court with glasses which diminish and approximate.
I myself had on a pair of spectacles, but they were
magnifiers. It was impossible for me to resolve on taking them off; and here again, I am afraid, I shall pass
for a fool-hardy person and a desperado ; so much only
I reckoned fit, to look invariably into my psalm-book ;
not once lifting my eyes while the Court was rustling
and entering, thereby to denote that my glasses were
ground convex. For the rest, the sermon was good,
if not always finely conceived for a Court-church ; it
admonished the hearers against innumerable vices, to
whose counterparts, the virtues, another preacher might

---

144. The Reviewer does not in reality employ his pen for
writing ; but he burns it, to awaken weak people from their
swoons, with the smell ; he tickles with it the throat of the pla-
giary, to make him render back ; and he picks with it his own
teeth. He is the only individual in the whole learned lexicon
that can never exhaust himself, never write himself out, let him
sit before the ink-glass for centuries or tens of centuries. For
while the Scholar, the Philosopher, and the Poet, produce their
new book solely from new materials and growth, the Reviewer

so readily have exhorted us. During the whole service, I made it my business to exhibit true deep reverence, not only towards God, but also towards my illustrious Prince. For the latter reverence I had my private reason : I wished to stamp this sentiment strongly and openly as with raised letters on my countenance, and so give the lie to any malicious imp about Court, by whom my contravention of the *Panegyric on Nero,* and my free German satire on this real tyrant himself, which I had inserted in the *Flätz Weekly Journal,* might have been perverted into a secret characteristic portrait of my own Sovereign. We live in such times at present, that scarcely can we compose a pasquinade on the Devil in Hell but some human Devil on Earth will apply it to an angel.

When the Court at last issued from church, and were getting into their carriages, I kept at such a distance that my face could not possibly be noticed, in case I had happened to assume no reverent look, but an indifferent or even proud one. God knows, who has kneaded into me those mad desperate fancies and crotchets, which perhaps would sit better on a Hero Scha-

---

merely lays his old gage of taste and knowledge on a thousand new works ; and his light, in the ever-passing, ever-differently-cut glass-world, which he *elucidates*, is still refracted into new colours.

71. The Youth is singular from caprice, and takes pleasure in it ; the Man is so from constraint, unintentionally, and feels pain in it.

backer than on an Army-chaplain under him. I cannot here forbear recording to you, my Friends, one of
the maddest among them, though at first it may throw
too glaring a light on me. It was at my ordination to be
Army-chaplain, while about to participate in the Sacrament, on the first day of Easter. Now, here while I was
standing, moved into softness, before the balustrade of
the altar, in the middle of the whole male congregation,—nay, I perhaps more deeply moved than any
among them, since, as a person going to war, I might
consider myself a half-dead man, that was now parta-
king in the last Feast of Souls, as it were like a person
to be hanged on the morrow,—here, then, amid the
pathetic effects of the organ and singing, there rose
something—were it the first Easter-day which awoke
in me what primitive Christians called their Easter-
laughter, or merely the contrast between the most
devilish predicaments and the most holy,—in short
there rose something in me (for which reason, I have
ever since taken the part of every simple person, who
might ascribe such things to the Devil), and this something started the question : " Now, could there be
aught more diabolical than if thou, just in receiving the
Holy Supper, wert madly and blasphemously to begin

198. The Populace and Cattle grow giddy on the edge of no
abyss ; with the Man it is otherwise.

11. The Golden Calf of Self-love soon waxes to be a burning
Phalaris' Bull, which reduces its father and adorer to ashes.

laughing ?" Instantly I took to wrestling with this hell-dog of a thought; neglected the most precious feelings, merely to keep the dog in my eye, and scare him away; yet was forced to draw back from him, exhausted and unsuccessful, and arrived at the step of the altar with the mournful certainty that in a little while I should, without more ado, begin laughing, let me weep and moan inwardly as I liked. Accordingly, while I and a very worthy old Bürgermeister were bowing down together before the long parson, and the latter (perhaps kneeling on the low cushion, I fancied him too long) put the wafer in my clenched mouth, I felt all the muscles of laughter already beginning sardonically to contract; and these had not long acted on the guiltless integument, till an actual smile appeared there; and as we bowed the second time, I was grinning like an ape. My companion the Bürgermeister justly expostulated with me, in a low voice, as we walked round behind the altar : " In Heaven's name, are you an ordained Preacher of the Gospel, or a Merry-Andrew ? Is it Satan that is laughing out of you ?"

" Ah, Heaven ! who else ?" said I ; and this being over, I finished my devotions in a more becoming fashion.

---

103. The male Beau-crop which surrounds the female Roses and Lilies, must (if I rightly comprehend its flatteries) most probably presuppose in the fair the manners of the Spaniards and Italians, who offer any valuable, by way of present, to the man who praises it excessively.

From the church (I now return to the Flätz one),
I proceeded to the Tiger Inn, and dined at the *table-
d'hôte*, being at no time shy of encountering men. Previous to the second course, a waiter handed me an
empty plate, on which, to my astonishment, I noticed
a French verse scratched in with a fork, containing nothing less than a lampoon on the Commandant of Flätz.
Without ceremony, I held out the plate to the company; saying, I had just, as they saw, got this lam-
pooning cover presented to me, and must request them
to bear witness that I had nothing to do with the matter. An officer directly changed plates with me. During the fifth course, I could not but admire the che-
mico-medical ignorance of the company; for a hare,
out of which a gentleman extracted and exhibited several grains of shot, that is to say, therefore, of lead
alloyed with arsenic, and then cleaned by hot vinegar,
did, nevertheless, by the spectators (I expected) continue to be pleasantly eaten.

In the course of our table-talk, one topic seized me
keenly by my weak side, I mean by my honour. The
law custom of the city happened to be mentioned, as
it affects natural children; and I learned that here a
loose girl may convert any man she pleases to select

---

199. But not many existing Governments, I believe, do be-
head under pretext of trepanning; or sew (in a more choice alle-
gory) the people's lips together, under pretence of sewing the
harelips in them.

into the father of her brat, simply by her oath. "Horrible!" said I, and my hair stood on end. " In this way may the worthiest head of a family, with a wife and children, or a clergyman lodging in the Tiger, be stript of honour and innocence, by any wicked chambermaid whom he may have seen, or who may have seen him, in the course of her employment!"

An elderly officer observed: " But will the girl swear herself to the Devil so readily?"

What logic! " Or suppose," continued I, without answer, " a man happened to be travelling with that Vienna Locksmith, who afterwards became a mother, and was brought to bed of a baby son; or with any disguised Chevalier d'Eon, who often passes the night in his company, whereby the Locksmith or the Chevalier can swear to their private interviews : no delicate man of honour will in the end risk travelling with another ; seeing he knows not how soon the latter may pull off his boots, and pull on his women's-pumps, and swear his companion into fatherhood, and himself to the Devil!"

Some of the company, however, misunderstood my

---

67. Hospitable Entertainer, wouldst thou search into thy Guest? Accompany him to another Entertainer, and listen to him. Just so : Wouldst thou become better acquainted with Mistress in an hour, than by living with her for a month? Accompany her among her female friends and female enemies (if that is no pleonasm), and look at her !

oratorical fire so much, that they, sheep-wise, gave
some insinuations as if I myself were not strict in this
point, but lax. By Heaven! I no longer knew what
I was eating or speaking. Happily, on the opposite
side of the table, some lying story of a French defeat
was started : now, as I had read on the street corners
that French and German Proclamation, calling before
the Court Martial any one who had heard war rumours (disadvantageous, namely), without giving notice of them,—I, as a man not willing ever to forget
himself, had nothing more prudent to do in this case,
than to withdraw with empty ears, telling none but the
landlord why.

It was no improper time; for I had previously determined to have my beard shaven about half past four,
that so, towards five, I might present myself with a
chin just polished by the razor smoothing-iron, and
sleek as wove-paper, without the smallest root-stump
of a hair left on it. By way of preparation, like Pitt
before Parliamentary debates, I poured a devilish deal
of Pontac into my stomach, with true disgust, and contrary to all sanitary rules ; not so much for fronting
the light stranger Barber, as the Minister and General
von Schabacker, with whom I had it in view to exchange perhaps more than one fiery statement.

---

80. In the Summer of life, men keep digging and filling ice-
pits as well as circumstances will admit; that so, in their Winter, they may have something in store to give them coolness.

28. It is impossible for me, amid the tendril-forest of allu-

The common Hotel Barber was ushered in to me ; but at first view you noticed in his polygonal zigzag visage, more of a man that would finally go mad, than of one growing wiser. Now, madmen are a class of persons whom I hate incredibly; and nothing can take me to see any madhouse, simply because the first maniac among them may clutch me in his giant fists if he like ; and because, owing to infection, I cannot be sure that I shall ever get out again with the sense which I brought in. In a general way, I sit (when once I am lathered) in such a posture on my chair as to keep both my hands (the eyes I fix intently on the barbering countenance) lying clenched along my sides, and pointed directly at the midriff of the barber ; that so, on the smallest ambiguity of movement, I may dash in upon him, and overset him in a twinkling.

I scarce know rightly how it happened ; but here, while I am anxiously studying the foolish twisted visage of the shaver, and he just then chanced to lay his long whetted weapon a little too abruptly against my bare throat, I gave him such a sudden bounce on the abdominal viscera, that the silly varlet had well nigh suicidally slit his own windpipe. For me, truly, no-

sions (even this again is a tendril-twig), to state and declare on the spot whether all the Courts or Heights, the (Bougouer) *Snow-line* of Europe, have ever been mentioned in my Writings or not ; but I could wish for information on the subject, that if not, I may try to do it still.

thing remained but to indemnify the man ; and then, contrary to my usual principles, to tie round a broad stuffed cravat, by way of cloak to what remained unshorn.

And now at last I sallied forth to the General, drinking out the remnant of the Pontac, as I crossed the threshold. I hope, there were plans lying ready within me for answering rightly, nay for asking. The Petition I carried in my pocket, and in my right hand. In the left, I had a duplicate of it. My fire of spirit easily helped over the living fence of ministerial obstructions ; and soon I unexpectedly found myself in the ante-chamber, among his most distinguished lackeys ; persons, so far as I could see, not inclined to change flour for bran with any one. Selecting the most respectable individual of the number, I delivered him my paper request, accompanied with the verbal one that he would hand it in. He took it, but ungraciously : I waited in vain till far in the sixth hour, at which season alone the gay General can safely be applied to. At last I pitch upon another lackey, and repeat my request : he runs about seeking his runaway brother, or my Pe-

---

36. And so I should like, in all cases, to be the First, especially in Begging. The first prisoner-of-war, the first cripple, the first man ruined by burning (like him who brings the first fire-engine) gains the head-subscription and the heart ; the next comer finds nothing but Duty to address ; and at last, in this melodious *mancando* of sympathy, matters sink so far, that the last

tition; to no purpose, neither of them could be found.
How happy was it that in the midst of my Pontac,
before shaving, I had written out the duplicate of this
paper; and therefore—simply on the principle that you
should always keep a second wooden leg packed into
your knapsack when you have the first on your body—
and out of fear that if the original petition chanced to
drop from me in the way between the Tiger and Schabacker's, my whole journey and hope would melt into
water—and therefore, I say, having stuck the repeating work of that original paper into my pocket, I had,
in any case, something to hand in, and that something
truly a Ditto. I handed it in.

Unhappily six o'clock was already past. The lackey,
however, did not keep me long waiting; but returned
with—I may say, the text of this whole Circular—the
almost rude answer (which you, my Friends, out of
regard for me and Schabacker, will not divulge) that:
"In case I were the Attila Schmelzle of Schabacker's
Regiment, I might lift my pigeon-liver flag again, and
fly to the Devil, as I did at Pimpelstadt." Another
man would have dropt dead on the spot: I, however,
walked quite stoutly off, answering the fellow: "With

(if the last but one may at least have retired laden with a rich
" God help you!") obtains from the benignant hand nothing
more than its fist. And as in Begging the first, so in Giving I
should like to be the last : one obliterates the other, especially
the last the first. So, however, is the world ordered.

great pleasure indeed, I fly to the Devil; and so Devil
a fly I care." On the road home, I examined myself
whether it had not been the Pontac that spoke out of
me (though the very examination contradicted this, for
Pontac never examines); but I found that nothing but
I, my heart, my courage perhaps, had spoken: and
why, after all, any whimpering? Does not the patri-
mony of my good wife endow me better than ten Catechetical Professorships? And has she not furnished
all the corners of my book of Life with so many golden
clasps, that I can open it for ever without wearing it?
Let henhearts cackle and pip; I flapped my pinions,
and said: " Dash boldly through it, come what may!"
I felt myself excited and exalted; I fancied Republics,
in which I, as a hero, might be at home; I longed to be
in that noble Grecian time, when one hero readily put
up with bastinadoes from another, and said: " Strike,
but hear!" and out of this ignoble one, where men
will scarcely put up with hard words, to say nothing
of more. I painted out to my mind how I should feel,
if, in happier circumstances, I were uprooting hollow
Thrones, and before whole nations mounting on mighty
deeds as on the Temple-steps of Immortality; and in

---

136. If you mount too high above your time, your ears (on
the side of Fame) are little better off than if you sink too deep
below it: in truth, Charles up in his Balloon, and Halley down
in his Diving-bell, felt equally the same strange pain in their
ears.

gigantic ages, finding quite other men to outman and
outstrip, than the mite-populace about me, or, at the
best, here and there a Vulcanello. I thought and
thought, and grew wilder and wilder, and intoxicated
myself (no Pontac intoxication therefore, which, you
know, increases more by continuance than cessation of
drinking), and gesticulated openly, as I put the question to myself: " Wilt thou be a mere state-lapdog ?
A dog's-dog, a *pium desiderium* of an *impium desiderium*, an Ex-Ex, a Nothing's-Nothing ?—Fire and
Fury !" With this, however, I dashed down my hat
into the mud of the market. On lifting and cleaning
this old servant, I could not but perceive how worn
and faded it was ; and I therefore determined instantly
to purchase a new one, and carry the same home in
my hand.

I accomplished this ; I bought one of the finest cut.
Strangely enough, by this hat, as if it had been a Gra-
duation-hat, was my head tried and examined, in the
Ziegengasse or Goat-gate of Flätz.   For as General
Schabacker came driving along that street in his car-
riage, and I (it need not be said) was determined to

---

25. In youth, like a blind man just couched, (and what is
birth but a couching of the sight ?) you take the Distant for the
Near, the starry heaven for tangible room-furniture, pictures for
objects ; and, to the young man, the whole world is sitting on
his very nose, till repeating bandaging and unbandaging have at
last taught him, like the blind patient, to estimate *Distance* and
Appearance.

avenge myself, not by vulgar clownishness, but by courtesy, I had here got one of the most ticklish problems
imaginable to solve on the spur of the instant. You
observe, if I swung only the fine hat which I carried in
my hand, and kept the faded one on my head,—I might
have the appearance of a perfect clown, who does not
doff at all: if, on the other hand, I pulled the old hat
from my head, and therewith did my reverence, then
two hats, both in play at once (let me swing the other
at the same time or not), brought my salute within the
verge of ridicule. Now do you, my Friends, before
reading farther, bethink you how a man was to extri-
cate himself from such a plight, without losing his presence of mind! I think, perhaps, by this means : by
merely losing his hat. In one word, then, I simply
dropped the new hat from my hand into the mud, to
put myself in a condition for taking off the old hat by
itself, and swaying it in needful courtesy, without any
shade of ridicule.

Arrived at the Tiger,—to avoid misconstructions, I
first had the glossy, fine, and superfine hat cleaned, and
some time afterwards the mud-hat or rubbis-hat.

---

125. In the long run, out of mere fear and necessity, we shall
become the warmest cosmopolites I know of ; so rapidlly do ships
shoot to and fro, and, like shuttles, weave Islands and Quarters
of the World together. For let but the political weatherglass fall
to-day in South America : to-morrow we in Europe have storm
and thunder.

And now, weighing my momentous Past in the adjusting balance within me, I walked in fiery mood to and fro. The Pontac must—I know that there is no unadulterated liquor here below—have been more than usually adulterated ; so keenly did it chase my fancy out of one fire into the other. I now looked forth into a wide glittering life, in which I lived without post, merely on money ; and which I beheld, as it were, sowed with the Delphic caves, and Zenonic walks, and Muse-hills of all the Sciences, which I might now cultivate at my ease. In particular, I should have it in my power to apply more diligently to writing Prize-essays for Academies ; of which (that is to say, of the Prize-essays) no author need ever be ashamed, since, in all cases, there is a whole crowning Academy to stand and blush for the crownee. And even if the Prize-marksman does not hit the crown, he still continues more unknown and more anonymous (his Device not being unsealed) than any other author, who indeed can publish some nameless Long-ear of a book, but not hinder it from being, by a Literary Ass-burial (*sepultura asinina*), publicly interred, in a short time, before half the world.

---

19. It is easier, they say, to climb a hill when you ascend back foremost. This, perhaps, might admit of application to political eminences ; if you still turned towards them that part of the body on which you sit, and kept your face directed down to the people ; all the while, however, removing and mounting.

Only one thing grieved me by anticipation; the sorrow of my Berga, for whom, dear tired wayfarer, I on the morrow must overcloud her arrival, and her shortened market-spectacle, by my negatory intelligence. She would so gladly (and who can take it ill of a rich farmer's daughter?) have made herself somebody in Neusattel, and overshone many a female dignitary! Every mortal longs for his parade-place, and some earlier living honour than the last honours. Especially so good a lowly-born housewife as my Berga, conscious perhaps rather of her metallic than of her spiritual treasure, would still wish at banquets to be mistress of some seat or other, and so in place to overtop this or that plucked goose of the neighbourhood.

It is in this point of view that husbands are so indispensable. I therefore resolved to purchase for myself, and consequently for her, one of the best of those titles, which our Courts in Germany (as in a Leipzig saleroom) stand offering to buyers, in all sizes and sorts, from Noble and Half-noble down to Rath or Councillor; and once invested therewith, to reflect from my own Quarter-nobility such an Eighth-part-nobility on this true soul, that many a Neusattelitess (I hope) shall

---

26. Few German writers are not original, if we may ascribe originality (as is at least the conversational practice of all people) to a man, who merely dishes out his own thoughts without foreign admixture. For as, between their Memory, where their reading or foreign matter dwells, and their Imagination or Pro-

half burst with envy, and say and cry: " Pooh, the stupid farmer thing ! See how it wabbles and bridles ! It has forgot how matters stood when it had no money-bag, and no Hofrath !" For to the Hofrathship I shall before this have attained.

But in the cold solitude of my room, and the fire of my remembrances, I longed unspeakably for my Bergelchen : I and my heart were wearied with the foreign busy day ; no one here said a kind word to me, which he did not hope to put in the bill. Friends ! I languished for my friend, whose heart would pour out its blood as a balsam for a second heart ; I cursed my over-prudent regulations, and wished, that, to have the good Berga at my side, I had given up the stupid house-ware to all thieves and fires whatsoever : as I walked to and fro, it seemed to me easier and easier to become all things, an Exchequer-Rath, an Excise-Rath, any Rath in the world, and whatever she required when she came.

" See thou take thy pleasure in the town !" had Bergelchen kept saying the whole week through. But how, without her, can I take any ? Our tears of sorrow friends dry up, and accompany with their own :

---

ductive Power, where their writing or own peculiar matter originates, a sufficient space intervenes, and the boundary-stones are fixed in so conscientiously and firmly that nothing foreign may pass over into their own, or inversely, so that they may really read a hundred works without losing their own primitive flavour, but our tears of joy we find most readily repeated in the eyes of our wives. Pardon me, good Friends, these libations of my sensibility; I am but showing you my heart and my Berga. If I need an Absolution-merchant, the Pontac-merchant is the man.

First Night in Flätz.

YET the wine did not take from me the good sense to look under the bed, before going into it, and examine whether any one was lurking there; for example, the Dwarf, or the Ratcather, or the Legations-Rath; also to shove the key under the latch (which I reckon the best bolting arrangement of all), and then, by way of farther assurance, to bore my night-screws into the door, and pile all the chairs in a heap behind it; and, lastly, to keep on my breeches and shoes, wishing absolutely to have no care upon my mind.

But I had still other precautions to take in regard to sleep-walking. To me it has always been incomprehensible how so many men can go to bed, and lie down their ease there, without reflecting that perhaps, in

---

or even altering it,—their individuality may, I believe, be considered as secured; and their spiritual nourishment, their pancakes, loaves, fritters, caviare, and meat-balls, are not assimilated to their system, but given back pure and unaltered. Often in my own mind, I figure such writers as living but thousandfold more

the first sleep, they may get up again as Somnambu-
lists, and crawl over the tops of roofs and the like ;
awakening in some spot where they may fall in a moment and break their necks.   While at home, there is
little risk in my sleep : because, my right toe being
fastened every night with three ells of tape (I call it
in jest our marriage tie) to my wife's left hand, I feel
a certainty that, in case I should start up from this
bed-arrest, I must with the tether infallibly awaken
her, and so by my Berga, as by my living bridle, be
again led back to bed.   But here in the Inn, I had nothing for it but to knot myself once or twice to the
bed-foot, that I might not wander ; though in this way,
an irruption of villains would have brought double peril
with it.—Alas ! so dangerous is sleep at all times, that
every man, who is not lying on his back a corpse, must
be on his guard lest with the general system some limb
or other also fall asleep ; in which case the sleeping
limb (there are not wanting examples of it in Medical
History) may next morning be lying ripe for amputa-
tion.   For this reason, I have myself frequently awakened, that no part of me fall asleep.

Having properly tied myself to the bed-posts, and

---

artificial Ducklings from Vaucasson's Artificial Duck of Wood.
For in fact they are not less cunningly put together, than this
timber Duck, which will gobble meat and apparently void it
'again, under show of having digested it, and derived from it blood
and juices ; though the secret of the business is, the artist has

at length got under the coverlid, I now began to be
dubious about my Pontac Fire-bath, and apprehensive
of the valorous and tumultuous dreams too likely to en-
sue; which, alas, did actually prove to be nothing better
than heroic and monarchic feats, castle-stormings, rock-
throwings, and the like. This point also I am sorry to
see so little attended to in medicine. Medical gentlemen, as well as their customers, all stretch themselves
quietly in their beds, without one among them considering whether a furious rage (supposing him also directly after to drink cold water in his dream), or a
heart-devouring grief, all which he may undergo in
vision, does harm to life or not.

Shortly before midnight, I awoke from a heavy dream,
to encounter a ghost-trick much too ghostly for my fancy. My brother-in-law, who manufactured it, deserves
for such vapid cookery to be named before you without reserve, as the maltmaster of this washy brewage.
Had suspicion been more compatible with intrepidity, I
might perhaps, by his moral maxim about this matter,
on the road, as well as by his taking up the side-room,
at the middle door of which stood my couch, have easily divined the whole. But now, on awakening, I felt

---

merely introduced an ingenious compound ejective matter behind,
with which concoction and nourishment have nothing to do, but
which the Duck illusorily gives forth and publishes to the world.

15. After the manner of the fine polished English folding-
knives, there are now also folding-war-swords, or in other words
—Treaties of Peace.

myself blown upon by a cold ghost-breath, which I
could nowise deduce from the distant bolted window ;
a point I had rightly decided, for the Dragoon was
producing the phenomenon, through the key-hole, by a
pair of bellows. Every sort of coldness, in the night-
season, reminds you of clay-coldness and spectre-cold-
ness. I summoned my resolution, however, and abode
the issue : but now the very coverlid began to get in
motion ; I pulled it towards me ; it would not stay ;
sharply I sit upright in my bed, and cry : " What is
that ?" No answer ; everywhere silence in the Inn ; the
whole room full of moonshine. And now my drawing-
plaster, my coverlid, actually rose up, and let in the
air ; at which I felt like a wounded man whose cataplasm you suddenly pull off. In this crisis, I made
a bold leap from this Devil's-torus, and, leaping, snap-
ped asunder my somnambulist tether. " Where is the
silly human fool," cried I, " that dares to ape the unseen sublime world of Spirits, which may, in the instant, open before him ?" But on, above, under the
bed, there was nothing to be heard or seen. I looked
out of the window : everywhere spectral moonlight and
street-stillness ; nothing moving except (probably from

---

13. *Omnibus una* SALUS *Sanctis, sed* GLORIA *dispar :* that
is to say (as Divines once taught) according to Saint Paul, we
have all the same Beatitude in Heaven, but different degrees of
Honour. Here, on Earth, we find a shadow of this in the writing world ; for the Beatitude of authors once beatified by Cri-

92   SCHMELZLE'S JOURNEY TO FLÆTZ.

the wind), on the distant Gallows-hill, a person lately hanged.

Any man would have taken it for self-deception as well as I : therefore I again wrapped myself in my passive *lit de justice* and air-bed, and waited with calmness to see whether my fright would subside or not.

In a few minutes, the coverlid, the infernal Faust's-mantle, again began flying and towing ; also, by way of change, the invisible bed-maker again lifted me up. Accursed hour !—I should beg to know whether, in the whole of cultivated Europe, there is one cultivated or uncultivated man, who, in a case of this kind, would not have lighted on ghost-devilry ? I lighted on it, under my piece of (self) moveable property, my coverlid : and thought Berga had died suddenly, and was now, in spirit, laying hold of my bed. However, I could not speak to her, nor as little to the Devil, who might well be supposed to have a hand in the game ; but I turned myself solely to Heaven, and prayed aloud : " To thee I commit myself ; thou alone heretofore hast cared for thy weak servant ; and I swear that I will turn a new leaf,"—a promise which shall be kept nevertheless, though the whole was but stupid treachery and trick.

---

ticism, whether they be genial, good, mediocre, or poor, is the same throughout ; they all obtain the same pecuniary Felicity, the same slender profit. But, Heavens ! in regard to the degrees of Fame, again, how far (in spite of the same emolument and sale) will a Dunce, even in his lifetime, be put below a Genius !

My prayer had no effect with the unchristian Dragoon, who now, once for all, had got me prisoner in
the dragnet of a coverlid; and heeded little whether a
guest's bed were, by his means, made a state-bed and
death-bed or not. He span out my nerves, like gold-
wire through smaller and smaller holes, to utter inani-
tion and evanition; for the bed-clothes at last literally
marched off to the door of the room.

Now was the moment to rise into the sublime; and
to trouble myself no longer about aught here below,
but softly to devote myself to death. "Snatch me
away," cried I, and, without thinking, cut three crosses; "quick, dispatch me, ye ghosts: I die more innocent than thousands of tyrants and blasphemers, to
whom ye yet appear not, but to unpolluted me." Here
I heard a sort of laugh, either on the street or in the
side-room: at this warm human tone, I suddenly bloomed up again, as at the coming of a new Spring, in every
twig and leaf. Wholly despising the winged coverlid, which was not now to be picked from the door, I
laid myself down uncovered, but warm and perspiring
from other causes, and soon fell asleep. For the rest,
I am not the least ashamed, in the face of all refined

Is not a shallow writer frequently forgotten in a single Fair, while
a deep writer, or even a writer of genius, will blossom through
fifty Fairs, and so may celebrate his Twenty-five Years' Jubilee,
before, late forgotten, he is lowered into the German Temple of
Fame; a Temple imitating the peculiarity of the *Padri Lucchesi*

capital cities,—though they were standing here at my hand,—that by this Devil-belief and Devil-address, I have attained some likeness to our great German Lion, to Luther.

Second Day in Flätz.

EARLY in the morning, I felt myself awakened by the well-known coverlid ; it had laid itself on me like a night-mare : I gaped up ; quiet, in a corner of the room, sat a red, round, blooming, decorated girl, like a full-blown tulip in the freshness of life, and gently rustling with gay ribbons as with leaves.

" Who's there—how came you in ?" cried I, half-blind.

" I covered thee softly, and thought to let thee sleep," said Bergelchen; " I have walked all night to be here early ; do but look !"

She showed me her boots, the only remnant of her travelling-gear, which, in the moulting process of the toilette, she had not stript at the gate of Flätz.

" Is there," said I, alarmed at her coming six hours sooner, and the more, as I had been alarmed all night

---

churches in Naples, which (according to Volkmann) permit *burials* under their roofs, but no *tombstone.*

79. Weak and wrong heads are the hardest to change ; and their inward man acquires a scanty covering : thus capons never moult.

and was still so, at her mysterious entrance : " is there some fresh woe come over us, fire, murder, robbery ?"

She answered : " The old Rat thou hast chased so long died yesterday ; farther, there was nothing of importance."

" And all has been managed rightly, and according to my Letter of Instructions, at home ?" inquired I.

" Yes, truly," answered she ; " only I did not see the Letter ; it is lost ; thou hast packed it among thy clothes."

Well, I could not but forgive the blooming brave pedestrian all omissions. Her eye, then her heart was bringing fresh cool morning air and morning red into my sultry hours. And yet, for this kind soul, looking into life with such love and hope, I must in a little while overcloud the merited Heaven of to-day, with tidings of my failure in the Catechetical Professorship ! I dallied and postponed to the utmost. I asked how she had got in, as the whole *chevaux-de-frise* barricado of chairs was still standing fast at the door. She laughed heartily, curtseying in village fashion, and said, she had planned it with her brother the day before yesterday, knowing my precautions in locking, that he should admit her into my room, that so she might

---

89. In times of misfortune, the Ancients supported themselves with Philosophy or Christianity ; the moderns again (for example in the reign of Terror) take to Pleasure ; as the wounded Buffalo, for bandage and salve, rolls himself in the mire.

cunningly awaken me. And now bolted the Dragoon
with loud laughter into the apartment, and cried:
" Slept well, brother ?"
In this wise, truly the whole ghost-story was now
solved and expounded, as if by the pen of a Biester or
a Hennings ; I instantly saw through the entire ghost-
scheme, which our Dragoon had executed. With some
bitterness I told him my conjecture, and his sister my
story. But he lied and laughed ; nay, attempted shame-
lessly enough to palm spectre-notions on me a second
time, in open day. I answered coldly, that in me he had
found the wrong man, granting even that I had some
similiarity with Luther, with Hobbes, with Brutus, all
of whom had seen and dreaded ghosts. He replied,
tearing the facts away from their originating causes :
" All he could say was, that last night he had heard
some poor sinner creaking and lamenting dolefully
enough ; and from this he had inferred, it must be an
unhappy brother set upon by goblins."
In the end, his sister's eyes also were opened to the
low character which he had tried to act with me : she
sharply flew at him, pushed him with both hands out
of his and my door, and called after him : " Wait, thou
villain, I will mind it !"

---

181. God be thanked that we live nowhere for ever except in
Hell or Heaven ; on Earth otherwise we should grow to be the ve-
riest rascals, and the World a House of Incurables, for want of the
dog-doctor (the Hangman), and the issue-cord (on the Gallows),

3

Then hastily turning round, she fell on my neck, and (at the wrong place) into laughter, and said : "" The wild fool ! But I could not keep my laugh another minute, and he was not to see it. Forgive the ninny, thou a learned man, his ass pranks : what can one expect?"

I inquired whether she, in her nocturnal travelling, had not met with any spectral persons ; though I knew that to her, a wild beast, a river, a half abyss, are nothing : No, she had not ; but the gay-dressed town's-people, she said, had scared her in the morning. O ! How I do love these soft Harmonica-quiverings of female fright !

At last, however, I was forced to bite or cut the colpquinta-apple, and give her the half of it ; I mean the news of my rejected petition for the Catechetical Professorship. Wishing to spare this joyful heart the rudeness of the whole truth, and to subtract something from a heavy burden, more fit for the shoulders of a man, I began : " Bergelchen, the Professorship affair is taking another, though still a good enough course : the General, whom may the Devil and his Grandmother teach sense, will not be taken except by

---

and the sulphur and chalybeate medicines (on Battle-fields). So that we too find our gigantic moral force dependent on the *Debt of Nature* which we have to pay, exactly as your politicians (for example, the Author of the *New Leviathan*) demonstrate that the English have their *National Debt* to thank for their superiority.

storm; and storm he shall have, as certainly as I have
on my nightcap."

"Then, thou art nothing yet?" inquired she.

"For the moment, indeed, not!" answered I.

"But before Saturday night?" said she.

"Not quite," said I.

"Then am I sore stricken, and could leap out of
the window," said she, and turned away her rosy face,
to hide its wet eyes, and was silent very long. Then,
with painfully quivering voice, she began: "Good
Christ stand by me at Neusattel on Sunday, when these
high-prancing prideful dames look at me in church, and
I grow scarlet for shame!"

Here in sympathetic woe I sprang out of bed to the
dear soul, over whose brightly blooming cheeks warm
tears were rolling, and cried: "Thou true heart, do
not tear me in pieces so! May I die, if yet in these
dog-days I become not all and everything that thou
wishest! Speak, wilt thou be Mining-räthin, Build-rä-
thin, Court-räthin, War-räthin, Chamber-räthin, Commerce-räthin, Legations-räthin, or Devil and his Dam's
räthin: I am here, and will buy it, and be it. To-morrow I send riding posts to Saxony and Hessia, to Prussia and Russia, to Friesland and Katzenellenbogen,

---

63. To apprehend danger from the Education of the People,
is like fearing lest the thunderbolt strike into the house because
it has *windows*; whereas the lightning never comes through these,
but through their *lead* framing, or down by the *smoke* of the
chimney.

and demand patents. Nay, I will carry matters farther
than another, and be all things at once, Flachsenfing-
en Court-rath, Scheerau Excise-rath, Haarhaar Build-
ing-rath, Pestitz * Chamber-rath (for we have the cash);
and thus, alone and single-handed, represent with one
podex and *corpus* a whole Rath-session of select Raths ;
and stand, a complete Legion of Honour, on one single pair of legs : the like no man ever did."

" O ! Now thou art angel-good !" said she, and gladder tears rolled down ; " thou shalt counsel me thyself which are the finest Raths, and these we will be."

" No," continued I, in the fire of the moment, " neither shall this serve us : to me it is not enough that to
Mrs Chaplain thou canst announce thyself as Building-
räthin, to Mrs Town-parson as Legations-räthin, to
Mrs Burgermister as Court-rathin, to Mrs Road-and-
toll-surveyor as Commerce-räthin, or how and where
thou pleasest——"

" Ah! my own too good Attelchen !" said she.

" —But," continued I, " I shall likewise become
corresponding member of the several Learned Socie-
ties in the several best capital cities (among which I
have only to choose) ; and truly no common actual
member, but a whole honorary member ; then thee, as

76. Your economical, preaching Poetry, apparently supposes
that a surgical Stone-cutter is an Artistical one ; and a Pulpit or
a Sinai a Hill of the Muses.

* Cities of Richter's romance kingdom. Flachsenfingen he
sometimes calls *Klein-Wien*, Little Vienna.—ED.

another honorary member, growing out of my honorary-membership, I uplift and exalt."

Pardon me, my Friends, this warm cataplasm, or deception-balsam for a wounded breast, whose blood is so pure and precious, that one may be permitted to endeavour, with all possible stanching-lints and spider-webs, to drive it back into the fair heart, its home.

But now came bright and brightest hours. I had conquered Time, I had conquered myself and Berga : seldom does a conqueror, as I did, bless both the victorious and the vanquished party. Berga called back her former Heaven, and pulled off her dusty boots, and on her flowery shoes. Precious morning beverage, intoxicating to a heart that loves ! I felt (if the low figure may be permitted) a double-beer of courage in me, now that I had one being more to protect. In general it is my nature—which the honourable Premier seems not to be fully aware of—to grow bolder not among the bold, but fastest among poltroons, the bad example acting on me by the rule of contraries. Little touches may in this case shadow forth man and wife, without casting them into the shade : When the trim waiter with his green silk apron brought up cracknels for breakfast, and I told him : " Johann, for two !" Berga said : " He would oblige her very much," and called him Herr Johann.

---

113. According to Smith, the universal measure of economical value is *Labour.* This fact, at least in regard to spiritual and poetical value, we Germans had discovered before Smith ;

Bergelchen, more familiar with rural burghs than
capital cities, felt a good deal amazed and alarmed at the
coffee-trays, dressing-tables, paper-hangings, sconces,
alabaster inkholders, with Egyptian emblems, as well
as at the gilt bell-handle, lying ready for any one to
pull out or to push in. Accordingly, she had not courage to walk through the hall, with its lustres, purely because a whistling, whiffling Cap-and-feather was
gesturing up and down in it. Nay, her poor heart was
like to fail when she peeped out of the window at so
many gay promenading town's-people (I was briskly
that in a little while, at my side, she must break into
whistling a Gascon air down over them); and thought
the middle of this dazzling courtly throng. In a case
like this, reasons are of less avail than examples. I
tried to elevate my Bergelchen, by reciting some of
my nocturnal dream-feats; for example, how, riding
on a whale's back, with a three-pronged fork, I had
pierced and eaten three eagles; and by more of the
like sort: but I produced no effect; perhaps, because
to the timid female heart the battle-field was presented
rather than the conqueror, the abyss rather than the
overleaper of it.

At this time a sheaf of newspapers was brought me,
full of gallant decisive victories. And though these

---

and to my knowledge, we have always preferred the learned poet
to the poet of genius, and the heavy book full of labour, to the
light one full of sport.

happen only on one side, and on the other are just so
many defeats, yet the former somehow assimilate more
with my blood than the latter, and inspire me (as
Schiller's *Robbers* used to do) with a strange inclination to lay hold of some one, and thrash and curry him
on the spot. Unluckily for the waiter, he had chanced
even now, like a military host, to stand a triple bell-
order for march, before he would leave his ground and
come up. " Sir," began I, my head full of battle-fields,
and my arm of inclination to baste him ; and Berga fear-
ed the very worst, as I gave her the well-known anger
and alarm signal, namely, shoved up my cap to my
hindhead—" Sir, is this your way of treating guests ?
Why don't you come promptly ? Don't come so again ;
and now be going, friend !" Although his retreat was
my victory, I still kept briskly cannonading on the field
of action, and fired the louder (to let him hear it), the
more steps he descended in his flight. Bergelchen,—
who felt quite horrorstruck at my fury, particularly in
a quite strange house, and at a quality waiter with silk
apron, mustered all her soft words against the wild ones
of a man-of-war, and spoke of dangers that might follow. " Dangers," answered I, " are just what I seek ;
but for a man there are none ; in all cases he will either

---

4. The Hypocrite does not imitate the old practice, of cutting
fruit by a knife poisoned only on the one side, and giving the
poisoned side to the victim, the cutter eating the sound side himself ; on the contrary, he so disinterestedly inverts this practice.

conquer or evade them, either show them front or back."

I could scarcely lay aside this indignant mood, so sweet was it to me, and so much did I feel refreshed by the fire of rage, and quickened in my breast as by a benignant stimulant. It belongs certainly to the class of Unrecognised Mercies (on which, in ancient times, special sermons were preached), that one is never more completely in his Heaven and *Monplaisir* (a pleasure-palace), than while in the midst of right hearty storm-ing and indignation. Heavens! what might not a man of weight accomplish in this new walk of charity! The gall bladder is for us the chief swimming-bladder and Montgolfier; and the filling of it costs us nothing but a contumelious word or two from some bystander. And does not the whirlwind Luther, with whom I no-wise compare myself, confess, in his *Table-talk*, that he never preached, sung, or prayed so well, as while in a rage? Truly, he was a man sufficient of himself to rouse many others into rage.

The whole morning till noon now passed in viewing sights, and trafficking for wares; and indeed, for the greatest part, in the broad street of our Hotel. Berga needed but to press along with me into the market throng; needed but to look, and see that she was de-

---

that to others he shows and gives the sound moral half, or side, and retains for himself the poisoned one. Heavens! compared with such a man, how wicked does the Devil seem!

corated more according to the fashion than hundreds
like her. But soon, in her care for household gear, she
forgot that of dress, and in the potter-market the toi-
lette-table faded from her thoughts.

I, for my share, full of true tedium, while gliding
after her through her various marts, with their long
cheapenings and chafferings, merely acted the Philosopher hid within me : I weighed this empty Life, and
the heavy value which is put upon it, and the daily
anxiety of man lest it, this lightest down-feather of the
Earth, fly off, and feather him, and take him with it.
These thoughts, perhaps, I owe to the street-fry of
boys, who were turning their market-freedom to account, by throwing stones at one another all round
me : for, in the midst of this tumult, I vividly figured
myself to be a man, who had never seen war ; and
who, therefore, never having experienced that often of
a thousand bullets not one will hit, feels apprehensive
of these few silly stones lest they beat in his nose and
eyes. O ! It is the battle-field alone that sows, ma-
nures, and nourishes true courage, courage even for
daily, domestic, and smallest perils. For not till he
comes from the battle-field can a man both sing and
cannonade ; like the canary-bird, which, though so melodious, so timid, so small, so tender, so solitary, so soft-

67. Individual Minds, nay, Political Bodies, are like organic
bodies : extract the *interior* air from them, the atmosphere
crushes them together; pump off under the bell the *exterior* resist-

feathered, can yet be trained to fire off cannon, though cannon of smaller calibre.

After dinner (in our room), we issued from the Purgatory of the market-tumult,—where Berga, at every booth, had something to order, and load her attendant maid with,—into Heaven, into the Dog Inn, as the best Flätz public and pleasure-house without the gates is named, where, in market time, hundreds turn in, and see thousands going by. On the way thither, my little wife, my elbow-tendril, as it were, had extracted from me such a measure of courage, that, while going through the Gate (where I, aware of the military order that you must not pass *near* the sentry, threw myself over to the other side), she quietly glided on, close by the very guns and fixed bayonets of the City Guard. Outside the wall, I could direct her with my finger, to the bechained, begrated, gigantic Schabacker-Palace, mounting up even externally on stairs, where I last night had called and (it may be) stormed: " I had rather take a peep at the Giant," said she, " and the Dwarf : why else are we under one roof with them ?"

In the pleasure-house itself we found sufficient pleasure ; encircled, as we were, with blooming faces and meadows.   In my secret heart, I all along kept look-

---

ing air, the interior inflates and bursts them.   Therefore, let every State keep up its internal and its external resistance both at once.

ing down, with success, on Schabacker's refusal; and till midnight made myself a happy day of it: I had deserved it, Berga still more. Nevertheless, about one in the morning, I was destined to find a windmill to tilt with; a windmill, which truly lays about it with somewhat longer, stronger, and more numerous arms than a giant, for which Don Quixote might readily enough have taken it. On the market-place, for reasons more easily fancied than specified in words, I let Berga go along some twenty paces before me; and I myself, for these foresaid reasons, retire without malice behind a covered booth, the tent most probably of some rude trader; and linger there a moment according to circumstances: lo! steering hither with dart and spear, comes the Booth-watcher, and coins and stamps me, on the spot, into a filcher and housebreaker of his Booth-street; though the simpleton sees nothing but that I am standing in the corner, and doing anything but—taking. A sense of honour without callosity is never blunted for such attacks. But how in the dead of night was a man of this kind, who had nothing in his head—at the utmost beer, instead of brains—to be enlightened on the truth of the matter?

I shall not conceal my perilous resource: I seized

---

8. In great Saloons, the real stove is masked into a pretty ornamented sham stove; so, likewise, it is fit and pretty that a virgin *Love* should always hide itself in an interesting virgin *Friendship*.

the fox by the tail, as we say ; in other words, I made
as if I had been muddled, and knew not rightly, in my
liquor, what I was about : I therefore mimicked everything I was master of in this department ; staggered
hither and thither ; splayed out my feet like a dancing-
master ; got into zigzag in spite of all efforts at the
straight line ; nay, I knocked my good head (perhaps
one of the clearest and emptiest of the night) like a
full one, against real posts.

However, the Booth-bailiff, who probably had been
oftener drunk than I, and knew the symptoms better,
or even felt them in himself at this moment, looked
upon the whole exhibition as mere craft, and shouted
dreadfully : " Stop, rascal ; thou art no more drunk
than I ! I know thee of old. Stand, I say, till I speak
to thee ! Wouldst' have thy long finger in the market,
too ? Stand, dog, or I'll make thee !"

You see the whole *nodus* of the matter : I whisked
away zigzag among the booths as fast as possible, from
the claws of this rude Tosspot ; yet he still hobbled
after me. But my Teutoberga, who had heard somewhat of it, came running back ; clutched the tipsy
market-warder by the collar, and said (shrieking, it is
true, in village wise) : " Stupid sot, go sleep the drink
out of thy head, or I'll teach thee ! Dost' know, then,
whom thou art speaking to ? My husband, Army-

---

12. Nations—unlike rivers, which precipitate their impurities
in level places and when at rest—drop their baseness just whilst

chaplain Schmelzle under General and Minister von
Schabacker at Pimpelstadt, thou blockhead!—Fye!
Take shame, fellow!" The watchman mumbled: "Meant
no harm," and reeled about his business. " O thou
Lioness!" said I, in the transport of love, " why hast
thou never been in any deadly peril, that I might show
thee the Lion in thy husband."

Thus lovingly we both reached home ; and perhaps
in the sequel of this Fair day might still have enjoyed
a glorious after-midnight, had not the Devil led my
eye to the ninth volume of Lichtenberg's Works, and
the 206th page, where this passage occurs : " It is not
impossible that at a future period, our Chemists may
light on some means of suddenly decomposing the Atmosphere by a sort of Ferment. In this way the world
may be destroyed."   Ah !   True indeed !   Since the
Earth-ball is lapped up in the larger Atmospheric ball,
let but any chemical scoundrel, in the remotest scoun-
drel-island, say in New Holland, devise some decomposing substance for the Atmosphere, like what a spark
of fire would be for a powder-waggon : in a few seconds, the monstrous devouring world-storm catches
me and you in Flätz by the throat ; my breathing, and
the like, in this choak-air is over, and the whole game
ended ! The Earth becomes a boundless gallows, where
the very cattle are hanged : worm-powder, and bug-

---

in the most violent motion ; and become the dirtier the farther
they flow along through lazy flats.

liquor, Bradly ant-ploughs, and rat-poison, and wolf-traps are, in this universal world-trap and world-poison, no longer specially needful; and the Devil takes the whole, in the Bartholomew-night, when this cursed " Ferment" is invented.

From the true soul, however, I concealed these deadly Night Thoughts; seeing she would either painfully have sympathized in them, or else mirthfully laughed at them. I merely gave orders that next morning (Saturday) she was to be standing booted and ready, at the outset of the returning coach; if so were she would have me speedily fulfil her wishes in regard to that stock of Rathships which lay so near her heart. She rejoiced in my purpose, gladly surrendering the market for such prospects. I too slept sound, my great toe tied to her finger, the whole night through.

The Dragoon, next morning, twitched me by the ear, and secretly whispered into it that he had a pleasant fairing to give his sister; and so would ride off somewhat early, on the nag he had yesterday purchased of the horse-dealer. I thanked him beforehand.

At the appointed hour, all gaily started from the Staple, I excepted; for I still retained, even in the fairest daylight, that nocturnal Devil's-Ferment and Decomposition (of my cerebral globe as well as of the

---

28. When Nature takes the huge old Earth-round, the Earth-loaf, and kneads it up again, for the purpose of introducing under this pie-crust, new stuffing and Dwarfs—she then, for most part,

Earth-globe) fermenting in my head ; a proof that the
night had not affected me, or exaggerated my fear. The
Blind Passenger, whom I liked so ill, also mounted
along with us, and looked at me as usual, but without
effect ; for on this occasion, when the destruction not
of myself only, but of worlds, was occupying my
thoughts, the Passenger was nothing to me but a joke
and a show : as a man, while his leg is a-sawing off,
does not feel the throbbing of his heart ; or amid the
humming of cannon, does not guard himself from that of
wasps ; so to me any Passenger, with all the fire-brands
he might throw into my near or distant Future, could
appear but ludicrous, at a time when I was reflecting
that the " Ferment" might, even in my journey between
Flätz and Neusattel, be, by some American or European man of science, quite guiltlessly experimenting
and decomposing, lighted upon by accident and let
loose. The question, nay prize-question now, however,
were this : " In how far, since Lichtenberg's threatening, it may not appear world-murderous and self-mur-
derous, if enlightened Potentates of chemical nations
do not enjoin it on their chemical subjects, who in their
decompositions and separations may so easily separate
the soul from their body and unite Heaven with Earth,—
not in future to make any other chemical experiments

---

as a mother when baking will do to her daughters, gives in jest
a little fraction of the dough (two or three thousand square
leagues of such dough are enough for a child) to some Poetical

than those already made, which hitherto have profited
the State rather than harmed it ?"

Unfortunately, I continued sunk in this Domsday
of the Ferment with all my thoughts and meditations,
without, in the whole course of our return from Flätz
to Neusattel, suffering or observing anything, except
that I actually arrived there, and at the same time saw
the Blind Passenger once more go his ways.

My Bergelchen alone had I constantly looked at by
the road, partly that I might still see her, so long as
life and eyes endured ; partly that, even at the smallest danger to her, be it a great, or even all-over-sweep-
ing Deluge and World's-doom, I might die, if not *for*
her, at least *by* her, and so united with that staunch true
heart, cast away a plagued and plaguing life, in which,
at any rate, not half of my wishes for her have been
fulfilled.

So then were my Journey over—crowned with some
Historiola ; and in time coming, perhaps, still more rewarded through you, ye Friends about Flätz, if in these
pages you shall find any well-ground pruning-knives,
whereby you may more readily outroot the weedy
tangle of Lies, which for the present excludes me from
the gallant Schabacker—Only this cursed Ferment still
sits in my head.   Farewell then, so long as there are

---

or Philosophical, or Legislative polisher, that so the little elf
may have something to be shaping and manufacturing beside its
mother.   And when the other young ones get a taste of sister-

Atmospheres left us to breathe. I wish I had that
Ferment out of my head.

Yours always,

ATTILA SCHMELZLE.

P. S.—My brother-in-law has kept his promise well,
and Berga is dancing.   Particulars in my next !

------

kin's baking, they all clap hands, and cry : " Aha, Mother ! canst
bake like *Suky* here ?"

LIFE

OF

QUINTUS FIXLEIN.

EXTRACTED FROM

FIFTEEN LETTER-BOXES,

BY

JEAN PAUL.

LETTER TO MY FRIENDS,

INSTEAD OF PREFACE.

———

MERCHANTS, Authors, young Ladies, and Quakers, call all persons, with whom they have any business, Friends; and my readers accordingly are my table and college Friends. Now, at this time, I am about presenting so many hundred Friends with just as many hundred gratis copies; and my Bookseller has orders to supply each on request, after the Fair, with his copy—in return for a trifling consideration and *don gratuit* to printers, pressmen, and other such persons. But as I could not, like the French authors, send the whole Edition to the binder, the blank leaf in front was necessarily wanting; and thus to write a complimentary word or two upon it was out of my power. I have therefore caused a few white leaves be inserted directly after the title-page: on these we are now printing.

My Book contains the Life of a Schoolmaster, extracted and compiled from various public and private documents. With this Biography, dear Friends, it is the purpose of the Author not so much to procure you a pleasure, as to teach you how to enjoy one. In truth,

King Xerxes should have offered his prize-medals not for the invention of new pleasures, but for a good methodology and directory to use the old ones.

Of ways for becoming happier (not happy) I could never inquire out more than three. The first, rather an elevated road, is this: To soar away so far above the clouds of life, that you see the whole external world, with its wolf-dens, charnel-houses, and thunder-rods, lying far down beneath you, shrunk into a little child's garden. The second is: Simply to sink down into this little garden; and there to nestle yourself so snugly, so homewise, in some furrow, that in looking out from your warm lark-nest, you likewise can discern no wolf-dens, charnel-houses, or thunder-rods, but only blades and ears, every one of which, for the nest-bird, is a tree, and a sun-screen, and rain-screen. The third finally, which I look upon as the hardest and cunningest, is that of alternating between the other two.

This I shall now satisfactorily expound to men at large.

The Hero, the Reformer, your Brutus, your Howard, your Republican, he whom civic storm, or genius poetic storm, impels; in short, every mortal with a great Purpose, or even a perennial Passion (were it but that of writing the largest folios), all these men fence themselves in by their internal world against the frosts and heats of the external, as the madman in a worse sense does: every *fixed* idea, such as rules every genius, every enthusiast, at least periodically, separates and elevates a man above the bed and board of this

Earth, above its Dog's-grottoes, buckthorns and De-vil's-walls ; like the Bird of Paradise, he slumbers fly-ing ; and on his outspread pinions, oversleeps uncon-sciously the earthquakes and conflagrations of Life, in his long fair dream of his ideal Mother-land.—Alas ! To few is this dream granted ; and these few are so often awakened by Flying Dogs !*

This skyward track, however, is fit only for the winged portion of the human species, for the smallest. What can it profit poor quill-driving brethren, whose souls have not even wing-shells, to say nothing of wings ? Or these tethered persons with the best back breast and neck fins, who float motionless in the wicker Fish-box of the State, and are not allowed to swim, because the Box or State, long ago tied to the shore, itself swims in the name of the Fishes ? To the whole standing and writing host of heavy-laden State-domes-tics, Purveyors, Clerks of all departments, and all the lobsters packed together heels over head into the Lob-ster-basket of the Government office-rooms, and for refreshment, sprinkled over with a few nettles ; to these persons, what way of becoming happy *here*, can I pos-sibly point out ?

My *second* merely ; and that is as follows : To take a compound microscope, and with it to discover, and convince themselves, that their drop of Burgundy is properly a Red Sea, that butterfly-dust is peacock-feathers, mouldiness a flowery-field, and sand a heap

* So are the Vampyres called.

of jewels. These microscopic recreations are more lasting than all costly watering-place recreations.—But I must explain these metaphors by new ones. The purpose, for which I have sent *Fixlein's Life* into the Messrs Lübeks' Warehouse, is simply that in this same *Life*—therefore in this Preface it is less needful—I may show to the whole Earth that we ought to value little joys more than great ones, the nightgown more than the dress-coat; that Plutus' heaps are worth less than his handfuls, the plum than the penny for a rainy day; and that not great, but little good-haps can make us happy.—Can I accomplish this, I shall, through means of my Book, bring up for Posterity, a race of men finding refreshment in all things; in the warmth of their rooms and of their night-caps; in their pillows; in the three High Festivals; in mere Apostles' days; in the Evening Moral Tales of their wives, when these gentle persons have been forth as ambassadresses visiting some Dowager Residence, whither the husband could not be persuaded; in the bloodletting-day of these their newsbringers; in the day of slaughtering, salting, potting against the rigour of grim winter; and in all such days. You perceive, my drift is that man must become a little Tailor-bird, which, not amid the crashing boughs of the storm-tost, roaring, immeasureable tree of Life, but on one of its leaves, sews itself a nest together, and there lies snug. The most essential sermon one could preach to our century, were a sermon on the duty of staying at home.

The *third* skyward road is the alternation between the other two. The foregoing *second* way is not good enough for man, who here on Earth should take into his hand not the Sickle only, but also the Plough. The *first* is too good for him. He has not always the force, like Rugendas, in the midst of the Battle to compose Battle-pieces; and, like Backhuisen in the Shipwreck, to clutch at no board but the drawing-board to paint it on. And then his *pains* are not less lasting than his *fatigues*. Still oftener is Strength denied its Arena: it is but the smallest portion of life that, to a working soul, offers Alps, Revolutions, Rhine-falls, Worms Diets, and Wars with Xerxes; and for the whole it is better so: the longer portion of life is a field beaten flat as a threshing-floor, without lofty Gothard Mountains; often it is a tedious ice-field, without a single glacier tinged with dawn.

But even by walking, a man rests and recovers himself for climbing; by little joys and duties, for great. The victorious Dictator must contrive to plough down his battle Mars-field into a flax and carrot field; to transform his theatre of war into a parlour theatre, on which his children may enact some good pieces from the *Children's Friend*. Can he accomplish this, can he turn so softly from the path of poetical happiness into that of household happiness,—then is he little different from myself, who even now, though modesty might forbid me to disclose it—who even now, I say, amid the creation of this Letter, have been enabled to re-

flect, that when it is done, so also will the Roses and
Elder-berries of pastry be done, which a sure hand is
seething in butter for the Author of this Work.

As I purpose appending to this Letter a Postcript
(at the end of the Book), I reserve somewhat which I
had to say about the Third* half-satirical half-philoso-
phical part of the Work, till that opportunity.

Here, out of respect for the rights of a Letter, the
Author drops his half anonymity,† and for the first
time subscribes himself with his *whole* true name,

JEAN PAUL FRIEDRICH RICHTER.

Hof in Voigtland, 29*th June* 1795.

---

* *Fixlein* stands in the middle of the volume ; preceded by
Einer Mustheil für Mädchen (A Jelly-course for young Ladies) ; and followed by *Some* JUS DE TABLETTE *for Men.* A
small portion of the Preface relating to the first I have already
omitted. Neither of the two have the smallest relation to *Fixlein.*—ED.

† *J. P. H.*, *Jean Paul* HASUS, *Jean Paul,* &c. have in succession been Richter's signatures. At present even, his German
designation, either in writing or speech, is never *Richter,* but
Jean Paul.—ED.

LIFE OF QUINTUS FIXLEIN,

DOWN TO OUR OWN TIMES.

IN FIFTEEN LETTER-BOXES.

FIRST LETTER-BOX.

Dog-days Vacation. Visits. An Indigent of Quality.

EGIDIUS ZEBEDÆUS FIXLEIN had just for eight days
been Quintus,* and fairly commenced his teaching du-

---

* For understanding many little hints which occur in this
Life of Fixlein, it will be necessary to bear in mind the following particulars : A German *Gymnasium*, in its complete state,
appears to include eight Masters ; Rector, Conrector, Subrector,
Quintus, Quartus, Tertius, &c., to the *first* or lowest. The
forms, or classes, again, are arranged in an inverse order ; the
Primaner (boys of the *Prima*, or first form) being the most
advanced, and taught by the Rector ; the *Secundaner*, by the
Conrector, &c. ; and therefore the *Quartaner* by the Quintus. In
many cases, it would seem, the number of Teachers is only six ;
but, in this Flachsenfingen Gymnasium, we have express evidence that there was no curtailment.—ED.

ties, when Fortune tabled out for him four refreshing
courses and collations, besprinkled with flowers and
sugar. These were the four canicular weeks. I could
find in my heart, at this hour, to pat the cranium of
that good-man who invented the Dog-days Vacation :
I never go to walk in that season, without thinking
how a thousand down-pressed pedagogic persons are
now erecting themselves in the open air ; and the stiff
knapsack is lying unbuckled at their feet, and they can
seek whatsoever their soul desires ; butterflies,—or
roots of numbers,—or roots of words,—or herbs,—or
their native villages.

The last did our Fixlein. He moved not, however,
till Sunday,—for you like to know how holidays taste
in the city ; and then, in company with his Shock and
a Quintaner, or Fifth-Form boy, who carried his Green
nightgown, he issued through the gate in the morning. The dew was still lying ; and as he reached the
back of the gardens, the children of the Orphan Hos-
pital were uplifting with clear voices their morning
hymn. The city was Flachsenfingen, the village Hukelum, the dog Schil, and the year of Grace 1791.

" Mannikin," said he to the Quintaner, for he liked
to speak, as Love, children, and the people of Vienna
do, in diminutives, " Mannikin, give me the bundle
to the village : run about, and seek thee a little bird, as
thou art thyself, and so have something to pet too in
vacation-time." For the mannikin was at once his page,
lackey, room-comrade, train-bearer, and gentleman in
waiting : and the Shock also was his mannikin.

He stept slowly along, through the crisped cole-
beds, overlaid with coloured beads of dew ; and looked
at the bushes, out of which, when the morning wind
bent them asunder, there seemed to start a flight of
jewel-colibri, so brightly did they glitter. From time to
time he drew the bell-rope of his—whistle, that the
mannikin might not skip away too far ; and he shortened his league and half of road, by measuring it not in
leagues, but in villages. It is more pleasant for pedes-
trians—for geographers it is not—to count by wersts
than by miles.   In walking, our Quintus furthermore
got by heart the few fields, on which the grain was
already reaped.

But now roam slower, Fixlein, through His Lordship's garden of Hukelum ; not, indeed, lest thy coat
sweep away any tulip-stamina, but that thy good mother may have time to lay her Cupid's-band of black
taffeta about her smooth brow.   I am grieved to think
my fair readers take it ill of her, that she means first
to iron this same band : they cannot know that she has
no maid ; and that to-day the whole Preceptorial dinner—the money purveyances the guest has made over
to her three days before—is to be arranged and prepared by herself, without the aid of any Mistress of
the Household whatever ; for indeed she belongs to the
Tiers Etat, being neither more nor less than a gardener's widow.

You can figure how this true, warm-hearted mother,
may have lain in wait all morning for her Schoolman.

whom she loved as the apple of her eye ; since, on the
whole populous Earth, she had not (her first son, as
well as her husband, was dead) any other for her soul,
which indeed overflowed with love ; not any other but
her Zebedäus. Could she ever tell you aught about
him, I mean aught joyful, without ten times wiping her
eyes ? Nay, did she not once divide her solitary Kirmes
(or Churchale) cake between two mendicant students,
because she-thought Heaven would punish her for so
feasting, while her boy in Leipzig had nothing to feast
on, and must pass the cake-garden like other gardens,
merely smelling at it ?

" Dickens ! Thou already, Zebedäus !" said the mother, giving an embarrassed smile, to keep from weeping, as the son, who had ducked past the window, and
crossed the grassy threshold without knocking, suddenly entered. For joy she forgot to put the heater
into the smoothing-iron, as her illustrious scholar, amid
the loud boiling of the soup, tenderly kissed her brow,
and even said Mamma ; a name which lighted on her
breast like downy silk. All the windows were open ;
and the garden, with its flower-essences, and bird-
music, and butterfly-collections, was almost half within
the room : but I suppose I have not yet mentioned
that the little garden-house, rather a chamber than a
house, was situated on the western cape of the Castle
garden. The owner had graciously allowed the widow
to retain this dowager-mansion ; as indeed the mansion
would otherwise have stood empty, for he now kept
no gardener.

But Fixlein, in spite of his joy, could not stay long with her; being bound for the Church, which, to his spiritual appetite, was at all times a king's kitchen; a mother's. A sermon pleased him simply because it was a sermon, and because he himself had once preached one. The mother was contented he should go : these good women think they enjoy their guests, if they can only give them aught to enjoy.

In the choir, this Free-haven and Ethnic Forecourt of stranger church-goers, he smiled on all parishioners; and, as in his childhood, standing under the wooden wing of an archangel, he looked down on the coifed *parterre.* His young years now inclosed him like children in their smiling circle ; and a long garland wound itself in rings among them, and by fits they plucked flowers from it, and threw them in his face : Was it not old Senior Astman that stood there on the pulpit Parnassus, the man by whom he had been so often flogged, while acquiring Greek with him from a grammar written in Latin, which he could not explain, yet was forced to walk by the light of ? Stood there not behind the pulpit-stairs the sacristy-cabin, and in this was there not a church-library of consequence— no schoolboy could have buckled it wholly in his book-strap—lying under the minever cover of pastil dust ? And did it not consist of the Polyglott in folio, which he, spurred on by Pfeiffer's *Critica Sacra,* had turned up leaf by leaf, in his early years, excerpting there-from the *literæ inversæ, majusculæ, minusculæ,* and

so forth, with an immensity of toil? And could he
not at present, the sooner the more readily, have wished to cast this alphabetic soft-fodder into the Hebrew
letter-trough, whereto your Oriental Rhizophagi (Root-
eaters) are tied, especially as here they get so little
vowel hard-fodder to keep them in heart?—Stood there
not close by him the organ-stool, the throne to which,
every Apostle-day, the Schoolmaster had by three nods
elevated him, thence to fetch down the sacred hyssop,
the sprinkler of the Church?

My readers themselves will gather spirits when they
now hear that our Quintus, during the outshaking of
the poor-bag, was invited by the Senior to come over
in the afternoon; and to them, it will be little less gratifying, than if he had invited themselves. But what
will they say, when they get home with him to mother
and dinner-table, both already clad in their white Sunday dress; and behold the large cake which Fraülein
Thiennette (Stephanie) has rolled from her peel? In
the first place, however, they will wish to know who
she is?

She is—for if (according to Lessing) in the very
excellence of the Iliad, we neglect the personalities of
its author; the same thing will apply to the fate of
several authors, for instance to my own; but an au-
thoress of cakes must not be forgotten in the excellence
of her baking—Thiennette is a poor, indigent, insol-
vent young lady; has not much, except years, of
which she counts five-and-twenty; no near relations

living now ; no acquirements (for in literature she does
not even know *Werter*) except economical ; reads no
books, not even mine ; inhabits, that is, watches like
a wardeness, quite alone, the thirteen void disfurnish-
ed chambers of the Castle of Hukelum, which belongs
to the Dragoon Rittmeister Aufhammer, at present
resident in his other mansion of Schadeck : on occasion, she commands and feeds his soccagers and hand-
maids ; and can write herself By the grace of God—
which, in the thirteenth century, the country nobles
did as well as princes,—for she lives by the grace of
man, at least of woman, the Lady Rittmeisterinn Aufhammer's grace, who, at all times, blesses those vassals
whom her husband curses. But, in the breast of the
orphaned Thiennette, lay a sugared marchpane heart,
which, for very love, you could have devoured : her
fate was hard, but her soul was soft ; she was modest,
courteous, and timid, but too much so ;—cheerfully and
coldly she received the most cutting humiliations in
Schadeck, and felt no pain, and not till some days after
did she see it all clearly, and then these cuts began
sharply to bleed, and she wept in her loneliness over
her lot.

It is hard for me to give a light tone, after this deep
one, and to add, that Fixlein had been almost brought
up beside her, and that she, his school-moiety over
with the Senior, while the latter was training him for
the dignities of the Third Form, had learned the *Verba
Anomala* along with him,

The Achilles'-shield of the cake, jagged and embossed with carved work of brown scales, was whirling round in the Quintus like a swing-wheel of hungry and thankful ideas. Of that philosophy which despises eating, and of that high breeding which wastes it, he had not so much about him as belongs to the ungratefulness of such cultivated persons ; but for his platter of meat, for his dinner of herbs, he could never give thanks enough.

Innocent and contented, the quadruple dinner-party —for the Shock with his cover under the stove cannot be omitted—now began their Feast of Sweet Bread, their Feast of Honour for Thiennette, their Grove-feast in the garden. It may truly be a subject of wonder how a man who has not, like the King of France, four hundred and forty-eight persons (the hundred and sixty-one *Garçons de la Maison-bouche* I do not reckon) in his kitchen, nor a *Fruiterie* of thirty-one human bipeds, nor a Pastry-cookery of three-and-twenty, nor a daily expenditure of 387 Livres 21 Sous,—how such a man, I say, can eat with any satisfaction. Nevertheless, to me, a cooking mother is as dear as a whole royal cooking household, given rather to feed upon me than to feed me.—The most precious fragments which the Biographer and the World can gather from this meal, consist of here and there an edifying piece of table-talk. The mother had much to tell. Thiennette is this night, she mentions, for the first time, to put on her morning promenade-dress of white

muslin, as also a satin girdle and steel buckle : but,
adds she, it will not sit her ; as the Rittmeisterinn (for
this lady used to hang her cast clothes on Thiennette,
as Catholics do their cast crutches and sores on their
patron Saints) was much thicker. Good women grudge
each other nothing, save only clothes, husbands, and
flax. In the fancy of the Quintus, by virtue of this
apparel, a pair of angel pinions were sprouting forth
from the shoulder-blades of Thiennette : for him a
garment was a sort of hollow half-man, to whom only
the nobler parts and the first principles were wanting :
he honoured these wrappages and hulls of our interior,
not as an Elegant, or a Critic of Beauty, but because it
was not possible for him to despise aught which he
saw others honouring. Farther, the good mother read
to him, as it were, the monumental inscription of his
father, who had sunk into the arms of Death in the
thirty-second year of his age, from a cause which I explain not here, but in a future Letter-box, having too
much affection for the reader. Our Quintus could not
sate himself with hearing of his father.

The fairest piece of news was, that Fräulein Thiennette had sent word to-day : " he might visit Her
Ladyship to-morrow, as My Lord, his godfather, was
to be absent in town." This, however, I must explain.
Old Aufhammer was called *Egidius*, and was Fixlein's
godfather : but he—though the Rittmeisterinn duly
covered the cradle of the child with nightly offerings,
with flesh-tithes and grain-tithes—had frugally made

him no christening present, except that of his name,
which proved to be the very balefullest. For, our
Egidius Fixlein, with his Shock, which, by reason of
the French convulsions, had, in company with other
emigrants, run off from Nantes, was but lately returned from college—when he and his dog, as ill luck
would have it, went to walk in the Hukelum wood.
Now, as the Quintus was ever and anon crying out to
his attendant : " Coosh, Schil" (*Couche, Gilles*), it
must apparently have been the Devil that had just
then planted the Lord of Aufhammer among the trees
and bushes in such a way, that this whole travestying
and docking of his name—for Gilles means Egidius—
must fall directly into his ear. Fixlein could neither
speak French, nor any offence to mortal : he knew not
head or tail of what *couche* signified.; a word, which,
in Paris, even the plebeian dogs are now in the habit
of saying to their *valets de chiens.* But there were
three things which Von Aufhammer never recalled ;
his error, his anger, and his word. The provokee,
therefore, determined that the plebeian provoker and
honour-stealer should never more speak to him, or—
get a doit from him.

I return. After dinner he gazed out of the little
window into the garden, and saw his path of life divi-
ding into four branches, leading towards just as many
skyward Ascensions ; towards the Ascension into the
Parsonage, and that into the Castle to Thiennette, for
this day ; and towards the third into Schadeck for the

morrow; and lastly, into every house in Hukelum as
the fourth. And now when the mother had long
enough kept cheerfully gliding about on tiptoe " not
to disturb him in studying his Latin Bible," (the *Vul-
gata*), that is, in reading the *Litteraturzeitung*, he at
last rose to his own feet; and the humble joy of the
mother ran long after the courageous son, who dared
to go forth and speak to a Senior, quite unappalled.
Yet it was not without reverence that he entered the
dwelling of his old, rather grey than bald headed teacher, who was not only Virtue itself, but also Hunger,
eating frequently, and with the appetite of Pharoah's
lean kine. A schoolman that expects to become a professor, will scarcely deign to cast an eye on a pastor; but one, who is himself looking up to a parsonage as to his working-house and breeding-house,
knows how to value such a character. The new parsonage—as if it had, like a *Casa Santa*, come flying
out of Erlang, or the Berlin Friedrichs-strasse, and
alighted in Hukelum—was for the Quintus a Temple
of the Sun, and the Senior a Priest of the Sun. To
be Parson there himself, was a thought overlaid with
virgin honey; such a thought as occurs but one other
time in History, namely, in the head of Hannibal, when
he projected stepping over the Alps, that is to say,
over the threshold of Rome.

The landlord and his guest formed an excellent *bu-
reau d'esprit*: people of office, especially of the same
office, have more to tell each other, namely, their own

history, than your idle May-chafers and Court-celes-
tials, who must speak only of other people's.—The
Senior made a soft transition from his iron-ware (in
the stable furniture), to the golden age of his Academic life, of which such people like as much to think, as
poets do of their childhood. So good as he was, he still
half joyfully recollected that he had once been less so :
but joyful remembrances of wrong actions are their
half repetition, as repentant remembrances of good ones
are their half abolishment.

Courteously and kindly did Zebedäus (who could
not even enter in his Notebook the name of a person
of quality without writing an H. for Herr before it)
listen to the Academic Saturnalia of the old gentleman, who in Wittenberg had toped as well as written,
and thirsted not more for the Hippocrene than for
Gukguk.*

Herr Jerusalem has observed, that the barbarism
which often springs up, close on the brightest efflorescence of the sciences, is a sort of strengthening mud-
bath, good for averting the over-refinement, wherewith such efflorescence always threatens us. I believe
that a man who considers how high the sciences have
mounted with our upper classes—for instance with
every Patrician's son in Nürnberg, to whom the public must present 1000 florins for studying with,—I be-

---

* A university beer.

lieve that such a man will not grudge the Son of the Muses a certain barbarous Middle-age (the Burschen or Student Life, as it is called), which may again so case-harden him that his refinement shall not go beyond the limits. The Senior, while in Wittenberg, had protected the one hundred and eighty Academic Freedoms—so many of them has Petrus Rebuffus summed up*—against prescription, and lost none except his moral one, of which truly a man, even in a convent, can seldom make much. This gave our Quintus courage to relate certain pleasant somersets of his own, which at Leipzig, under the Incubus-pressure of poverty, he had contrived to execute. Let us hear him: His landlord, who was at the same time Professor and Miser, maintained in his enclosed court a whole community of hens: Fixlein, in company with three roommates, without difficulty, mastered the rent of a cham-

---

* From Peter I will copy one or two of these privileges: the whole of which were once, at the origin of universities, in full force. For instance, a student can compel a citizen to let him his house and his horse; an injury, done even to his relations, must be made good fourfold; he is not obliged to fulfil the written commands of the Pope; the neighbourhood must indemnify him for what is stolen from him; if he and a non-student are living at variance, the latter only can be expelled from the boarding-house; a Doctor is obliged to support a poor student; if he is killed, the next ten houses are laid under interdict till the murderer is discovered; his legacies are not abridged by *falcidia*, &c. &c.

ber, or closet : in general their main equipments, like
Phœnixes, existed but in the singular number; one
bed, in which always the one pair slept before midnight, the other after midnight, like nocturnal watchmen ; one coat, in which one after the other they appeared in public, and which, like a watch-coat, was the
national uniform of the company ; and several other
ones, Unities both of Interest and Place. Nowhere
can you collect the stress-memorials and siege-medals
of Poverty more pleasantly and philosophically than at
College ; the Academic burgher exhibits to us how
many humourists and Diogeneses Germany has in it.
Our Unitarians had just one thing four times, and that
was hunger. The Quintus related, perhaps with a too
pleasurable enjoyment of the recollection, how one of
this famishing *coro* invented means of appropriating the
Professor's hens as just tribute, or subsidies. He said
(he was a Jurist), they must once for all borrow a le-
gal fiction from the Feudal code, and look on the Professor as the soccage tenant, to whom the usufruct of
the hen-yard and hen-house belonged ; but on themselves, as the feudal superiors of the same, to whom
accordingly the vassal was bound to pay his feudal
dues. And now, that the Fiction might follow Nature,
continued he—" *fictio sequitur naturam*,"—it behoved
them to lay hold of said Yule-hens, by direct personal
distraint. But into the court-yard there was no getting.
The feudalist, therefore, prepared a fishing-line ; stuck
a bread-pill on the hook, and lowered his fishing-tackle,

anglerwise, down into the court. In a few seconds the
barb stuck in a hen's throat, and the hen now com-
municating with its feudal superior, could silently, like
ships by Archimedes, be heaved aloft to the hungry
air-fishing society, where, according to circumstances,
the proper feudal name and title of possession failed not
to be awaiting her : for the updrawn fowls were now
denominated Christmas-fowls, now Forest-hens, Bai-
liff-hens, Pentecost and Summer-hens. "I begin," said
the angling lord of the manor, "with taking *Rutcher-
dues*, for so we call the triple and quintuple of the original quit rent, when the vassal, as is the case here,
has long neglected payment." The Professor, like any
other prince, observed with sorrow the decreasing
population of his hen-yard, for his subjects, like the
Hebrews, were dying by enumeration. At last he had
the happiness, while reading his lecture—he was just
come to the subject of *Forest Salt and Coin Regalities*
—to descry through the window of his auditorium a
quitrent hen suspended, like Ignatius Loyola in prayer,
or Juno in her punishment, in middle air : he followed
the incomprehensible direct ascension of the aeronautic
animal, and at last descried at the upper window the
attracting artist, and animal-magnetiser, who had drawn
his lot for dinner from the hen-yard below. Contrary
to all expectation, he terminated this fowling sport
sooner than his Lecture on Regalities.

Fixlein walked home, amid the vesperal melodies of
the steeple sounding-holes ; and by the road, courteous-

ly took off his hat before the empty windows of the
Castle : houses of quality were to him like persons of
quality, as in India the Pagoda at once represents the
temple and the god. To the mother he brought feign-
ed compliments, which she repaid with authentic ones :
for this afternoon she had been over, with her historical tongue and nature-interrogating eye, visiting the
white-muslin Thiennette. The mother was wont to
show her every spare-penny which he dropped into
her large empty purse, and so raise him in the good
graces of the Fraülein ; for women feel their hearts
much more attracted towards a son, who tenderly re-
serves for a mother some of their benefits, than we do
to a daughter anxiously caring for her father ; perhaps
from a hundred causes, and this among the rest, that
in their experience of sons and husbands they are more
used to find these persons mere six-feet thunder-
clouds, forked waterspouts, or even reposing torna-
does.

Blessed Quintus ! on whose Life this other distinction like an order of nobility does also shine, that thou
canst tell it over to thy mother ; as, for example, this
past afternoon in the parsonage. Thy joy flows into
another heart, and streams back from it redoubled, into
thy own. There is a closer approximating of hearts,
and also of sounds, than that of the *Echo ;* the highest
approximation melts Tone and Echo into *Resonance*
together.

It is historically certain that both of them supped

this evening; and that instead of the whole dinner fragments which to-morrow might themselves represent a dinner, nothing but the cake-offering or pudding was laid upon the altar of the table. The mother, who for her own child would willingly have neglected not herself only, but all other people, now made a motion that to the Quintaner, who was sporting out of doors and baiting a bird instead of himself, there should no crumb of the precious pastry be given, but only table-bread without the crust. But the Schoolman had a Christian disposition, and said that it was Sunday, and the young man liked something delicate to eat as well as he. Fixlein—the counterpart of great men and geniuses,—was inclined to treat, to gift, to gratify a serving house-mate, rather than a man who is for the first time passing through the gate, and at the next post-stage will forget both his hospitable landlord and the last postmaster. On the whole, our Quintus had a touch of honour in him, and notwithstanding his thrift and sacred regard for money, he willingly gave it away in cases of honour, and unwillingly in cases of overpowering sympathy, which too painfully filled the cavities of his heart, and emptied those of his purse. Whilst the Quintaner was exercising the *jus compascui* on the cake, and six arms were peacefully resting on Thiennette's free-table, Fixlein read to himself and the company the Flachsenfingen Address-calendar; any higher thing, except Meusel's *Gelehrtes Deutschland,*

* *Literary Germany*, a work (I believe of no great merit) which Richter often twitches in the same style.—ED-

he could not figure : the Kammerherrs and Raths of
of the Calendar went tickling over his tongue like the
raisins of the cake ; and of the more rich church-livings
he, by reading, as it were levied a tithe.

He purposely remained his own Edition in Sunday
Wove-paper ; I mean, he did not lay away his Sunday
coat, even when the Prayer-bell tolled ; for he had still
much to do.

After supper, he was just about visiting the Fraülein, when he descried her in person, like a lily dipt in
the red twilight, in the Castle-garden, whose western
limit his house constituted, the southern one being
the Chinese wall of the Castle . . . . By the way, how
I got to the knowledge of all this, what Letter-boxes
are, whether I myself was ever there, &c. &c.—the
whole of this shall, upon my life, be soon and faithfully communicated to the reader, and that too in the present Book.

Fixlein hopped forth like a Will-o'-wisp into the
garden, whose flower-perfume was mingling with his
supper-perfume. No one bowed lower to a nobleman
than he, not out of plebeian servility, nor of self-inte-
rested cringing, but because he thought " a nobleman
was a nobleman." But in this case his bow, instead
of falling forwards, fell obliquely to the right, as it
were after his hat : for he had not risked taking a
stick with him ; and hat and stick were his prop-
page and balance-wheel, in short, his bowing-gear,
without which it was out of his power to produce
any courtly bow, had you offered him the High Church

of Hamburg for so doing. Thiennette's mirthfulness
soon unfolded his crumpled soul into straight form,
and into the proper tone. He delivered her a long
neat Thanksgiving and Harvest sermon for the scaly
cake ; which appeared to her at once kind and tedious. Young women without the polish of high life
reckon tedious pedantry, merely like snuffing, one of
the necessary ingredients of a man : they reverence
us infinitely ; and as Lambert could never speak to the
King of Prussia, by reason of his sun-eyes, except in
the dark, so they, I believe, often like better—also by
reason of our sublime air—if they can catch us in the
dark too. *Him* Thiennette edified by the Imperial
History of Herr von Aufhammer and Her Ladyship his
spouse, who meant to put him, the Quintus, in her
will ; *her* he edified by his Literary History, as relating
to himself and the Subrector ; how, for instance, he was
at present vicariating in the Second Form, and ruling
over scholars as long in stature as himself. And thus
did the two in happiness, among red bean-blossoms,
red may-chafers, before the red of the twilight burning
lower and lower on the horizon, walk to and fro in the
garden ; and turn always with a smile as they approached the head of the ancient gardeneress, standing like a
window-bust through the little lattice, which opened in
the bottom of a larger one.

To me it is incomprehensible he did not fall in love.
I know his reasons, indeed : in the first place, she had
nothing ; secondly, he had nothing, and school-debts

to boot; thirdly, her genealogical tree was a boundary tree and warning-post; fourthly, his hands were tied up by another nobler thought, which, for good cause, is yet reserved from the reader. Nevertheless—Fixlein! I durst not have been in thy place! I should have looked at her, and remembered her virtues and our school-years, and then have drawn forth my too fusible heart, and presented it to her as a bill of exchange, or insinuated it as a summons. For I should have considered that she resembled a nun in two senses, in her good heart and in her good pastry; that, in spite of her intercourse with male vassals, she was no Charles Genevieve Louise Auguste Timothé Eon de Beaumont,* but a smooth, fair-haired, white-capped dove; that she sought more to please her own sex than ours; that she showed a melting heart, not previously borrowed from the Circulating Library, in tears, for which in her innocence she rather took shame than credit.— At the very first cheapening, I should, on these grounds, have been out with my heart.—Had I fully reflected, Quintus! that I knew her as myself; that her hands and mine (to wit, had I been thou) had both been guided by the same Senior to Latin penmanship; that we two, when little children, had kissed each other before the glass, to see whether the two image-children would do it likewise in the mirror; that often we had put hands of both sexes into the same muff, and there

---

* See *Schmelzle's Journey*, p. 77.—ED.

played with them in secret ; had I, lastly, considered
that we were here standing before the glass-house, now
splendent in the enamel of twilight, and that on the
cold panes of this glass-house we two (she within, I
without) had often pressed our warm cheeks together,
parted only by the thickness of the glass,—then had I
taken this poor gentle soul, pressed asunder by Fate,
and seeing, amid her thunder-clouds, no higher elevation to part them and protect her than the grave, and
had drawn her to my own soul, and warmed her on
my heart, and encompassed her about with my eyes.

In truth, the Quintus would have done so too, had
not the above-mentioned nobler thought, which I yet
disclose not, kept him back. Softened, without knowing the cause—(accordingly he gave his mother a kiss)
—and blessed without having had a literary conversation ; and dismissed with a freight of humble compliments, which he was to disload on the morrow before
the Dragoon Rittmeisterinn, he returned to his little
cottage, and looked yet a long while out of its dark
windows, at the light ones of the Castle.   And then,
when the first quarter of the moon was setting, that is,
about midnight, he again, in the cool sigh of a mild,
fanning, moist, and directly heart-addressing night-
breeze, opened the eyelids of a sight already sunk in
dreaming . . . . .

Sleep, for to-day thou hast done nought ill !   I,
whilst the drooping shut flower-bell of thy spirit sinks
on thy pillow, will look forth into the breezy night

over thy morning footpath, which, through the translu-
cent little wood, is to lead thee to Schadeck, to thy
patroness. All prosperity attend thee, thou foolish
Quintus!—

SECOND LETTER-BOX.

Frau von Aufhammer.   Childhood-Resonance.
Authorcraft.

THE early piping which the little thrush last night
adopted by the Quintaner from its nest, started for vic-
tual about two o'clock, soon drove our Quintus into his
clothes ; whose calender-press and parallel-ruler the
hands of his careful mother had been, for she would
not send him to the Rittmeisterinn " like a runagate
dog." The Shock was incarcerated, the Quintaner
taken with him, as likewise many wholesome rules
from Mother Fixlein, how to conduct himself towards
the Rittmeisterinn. But the son answered : " Mamma,
when a man has been in company, like me, with high
people, with a Fraülein Thiennette, he soon knows
whom he is speaking to, and what polished manners
and Saver di veaver (*Savoir vivre*) require."

He arrived with the Quintaner, and green fingers
(dyed with the leaves he had plucked on the path),
and with a half-nibbled rose between his teeth, in presence of the sleek lackeys of Schadeck.—If women are

flowers—though as often silk and Italian and gum-
flowers, as botanical ones—then was Frau von Aufhammer, a ripe flower, with (adipose) neck-bulb, and
tuberosity (of lard). Already, in the half of her body,
cut away from life by the apoplexy, she lay upon her
lard-pillow but as on a softer grave : nevertheless, the
portion of her that remained, was at once lively, pious,
and proud. Her heart was a flowing cornucopia to all
men, yet this not from philanthropy, but from rigid devotion : the lower classes she assisted, cherished, and
despised, regarding nothing in them, except it were
their piety. She received the bowing Quintus with
the back-bowing air of a patroness ; yet she brightened
into a look of kindliness at his disloading of the compliments from Thiennette.

She began the conversation, and long continued it
alone, and said—yet without losing the inflation of
pride from her countenance : " She should soon die ;
but the god-children of her husband she would remember in her will." Farther, she told him directly
in the face, which stood there all over-written with
the Fourth Commandment before her, that " he must
not build upon a settlement in Hukelum ; but to the
Flachsenfingen Conrectorate (to which the Burgermeister and Council had the right of nomination), she
hoped to promote him, as it was from the then Burgermeister that she bought her coffee, and from the
Town-Syndic (he drove a considerable wholesale and
retail trade in Hamburg candles) that she bought both
her wax and tallow lights."

And now by degrees he arrived at his humble petition, when she asked him sick-news of Senior Astmann, who guided himself more by Luther's Catechism, than by the Catechism of Health. She was
Astmann's patroness in a stricter than ecclesiastical
sense ; and she even confessed that she would soon follow this true shepherd of souls, when she heard, here
at Schadeck, the sound of his funeral-bell. Such strange
chemical affinities exist between our dross and our silver veins ; as, for example, here between Pride and
Love : and I could wish that we would pardon this
hypostatic union in all persons, as readily as we do it
in the fair, who, with all their faults, are nevertheless
by us,—as, according to Du Fay, iron, though mixed
with any other metal, is, by the magnet,—attracted and
held fast.

Supposing even that the Devil *had*, in some idle
minute, sown a handful or two of the seeds of Envy in
our Quintus' soul, yet they had not sprouted ; and to-
day especially they did not, when he heard the praises
of a man who had been his teacher, and who—what
he reckoned a Titulado of the Earth, not from vanity
but from piety—was a clergyman. So much, however, is, according to History, not to be denied : That
he now straightway came forth with his petition to the
noble lady, signifying that " indeed he would cheerfully
content himself for a few years in the school ; but yet
in the end he longed to be in some small quiet priestly
office." To her question, " But was he orthodox ?"

4

he answered, that " he hoped so ; he had in Leipzig, not only attended all the public lectures of Dr Bur-scher, but also had taken private instructions from se-veral sound teachers of the faith, well knowing that the Consistorium, in its examinations as to purity of doc-trine, was now more strict than formerly."

The sick lady required him to make a proof-shot, namely, to administer to her a sick-bed exhortation. By Heaven ! he administered to her one of the best. Her pride of birth now crouched before his pride of office and priesthood; for though he could not, with the Dominican monk, Alanus de Rupe, believe that a priest was greater than God, inasmuch as the latter could only make a World, but the former a God (in the mass) ; yet he could not but fall in with Hostiensis, who shows that the priestly dignity is seven thousand six hundred and forty-four times greater than the king-ly, the Sun being just so many times greater than the Moon.—But a Rittmeisterinn—*she* shrinks into abso-lute nothing before a parson.

In the servants' hall he applied to the lackeys for the last annual series of the *Hamburg Political Jour-nal ;* perceiving, that with these historical documents of the time, they were scandalously papering the but-tons of travelling raiment. In gloomy harvest even-ings, he could now sit down and read for himself what good news were transpiring in the political world—twelve months ago.

On a Triumphal Car, full-laden with laurel, and to

which Hopes alone were yoked, he drove home at
night, and by the road advised the Quintaner not to
be puffed up with any earthly honour, but silently to
thank God, as himself was now doing.

The thickset blooming grove of his four canicular
weeks, and the flying tumult of blossoms therein, are
already painted on three of the sides. I will now clutch
blindfold into his days, and bring out one of them : one
smiles and sends forth its perfumes like another.

Let us take, for instance, the Saint's day of his mother, *Clara*, the twelfth of August. In the morning,
he had perennial, fire-proof joys, that is to say, Employments. For he was writing, as I am doing.
Truly, if Xerxes proposed a prize for the invention of
a new pleasure, any man who had sat down to write
his thoughts on the prize-question, had the new pleasure already among his fingers. I know only one thing
sweeter than making a book, and that is, to project
one. Fixlein used to write little works, of the twelfth
part of an alphabet in size, which in their manuscript
state he got bound by the bookbinder in gilt boards,
and betitled with printed letters, and then inserted
them among the literary ranks of his book-board.
Every one thought they were novelties printed in writing types. He had laboured—I shall omit his less interesting performances—at a *Collection of Errors of
the Press*, in German writings : he compared *Errata*
with each other ; showed which occurred most fre-

quently ; observed that important results were to be
drawn from this, and advised the reader to draw them.

Moreover, he took his place among the German *Ma-
sorites*. He observes with great justice in his Preface : " The Jews had their *Masora* to show, which
told them how often every letter was to be found in
their Bible ; for example, the Aleph (the A) 42,377
times ; how many verses there are in which all the
consonants appear (there are 26 verses), or only eighty (there are 3) ; how many verses we have into which
42 words and 160 consonants enter (there is just one,
Jeremiah, xxi. 7) ; which is the middle letter in certain books (in the Pentateuch, it is in Leviticus, xi.
42, the noble V *), or in the whole Bible itself. But
where have we Christians any similar Masora for Luther's Bible to show ? Has it been accurately investigated which is the middle word, or the middle
letter here, which vowel appears seldomest, and how
often each vowel ? Thousands of Bible-Christians go
out of the world, without ever knowing that the German A occurs 323,015 times (therefore above 7 times
oftener than the Hebrew one) in their Bible."

I could wish that inquirers into Biblical Literature
among our Reviewers would publicly let me know, if
on a more accurate summation they find this number
incorrect.†

---

* As in the State.—[V. or Von, *de*, *of*, being the symbol of
the nobility, the middle order of the State.—ED.]

† In Erlang, my petition has been granted. The *Bible Insti-*

Much also did the Quintus *collect :* he had a fine
Almanack Collection, a *Catechism* and *Pamphlet Collection ;* also, a *Collection of Advertisements,* which
he began, is not so incomplete as you most frequently
see such things. He puts high value on his *Alphabet-
ical Lexicon of German Subscribers for Books,* where
my name also occurs among the J's.

But what he liked best to produce were Schemes of
Books. Accordingly, he sewed together a large work,
wherein he merely advised the Learned of things they
ought to introduce in Literary History, which History
he rated some ells higher than Universal or Imperial
History. In his Prolegomena to this performance, he
transiently submitted to the Literary republic that Hom-
mel had given a register of Jurists who were sons of
wh—, of others who had become Saints ; that Baillet
enumerates the Learned who *meant* to write something ;
and Ancillon those who wrote nothing at all; and the Lübeck Superintendant Götze, those who were shoemakers,
those who were drowned ; and Bernhard those whose
fortunes and history before birth were interesting. This
(he could now continue) should, as it seems, have exci-

tution of that town have found instead of the 116,301 A's, which
Fixlein at first pretended with such certainty to find in the Bi-
ble-books (which false number was accordingly given in the first
Edition of this Work, p. 81), the above-mentioned 323,015 ; which
(uncommonly singular) is precisely the sum of all the letters in
the Koran put together. See *Lüdeke's Beschr. des Türk. Reichs,*
(Lüdeke's Decription of the Turkish Empire. New edition,
1780).

ted ūs to similar muster-rolls and matriculations of other
kinds of Learned; whereof he proposed a few : for example, of the Learned, who were unlearned ; of those who
were entire rascals ; of such as wore their own hair,—of
cue-preachers, cue-psalmists, cue-annalists, and so forth ;
of the Learned who had worn black leather breeches,
of others who had worn rapiers ; of the Learned who
had died in their eleventh year,—in their twentieth—
twenty-first, &c.,—in their hundred and fiftieth, of
which he knew no instance, unless the Beggar Thomas
Parr might be adduced ; of the Learned who wrote a
more abominable hand than the other Learned (whereof we know only Rolfinken and his letters, which were
as long as his hands*) ; or of the Learned who had
clipt nothing from each other but the beard (whereof
no instance is known, save that of Philelphus and Timotheus.†)

Such bye studies did he carry on along with his official labours : but I think the State in viewing these
matters is actually mad ; it compares the man who is
great in Philosophy and Belles Lettres at the expense
of his jog-trot officialities, to *concert-clocks*, which,
though striking their hours in flute-melodies, are worse
time-keepers than your gross stupid *steeple-clocks*.

---

* *Paravicini Singularia de viris claris. Cent. I. 2.*

† *Ejusd. Cent. II.* Philelphus quarrelled with the Greek
about the quantity of a syllable : the prize or bet was the beard
of the vanquished. Timotheus lost his.

To return to St Clara's day. Fixlein, after such mental exertions, bolted out under the music-bushes, and rustling trees ; and returned not again out of warm Nature, till plate and chair were already placed at the table. In the course of the repast, something occurred which a Biographer must not omit : for his mother had, by request, been wont to map out for him, during the process of mastication, the chart of his child's-world, relating all the traits, which in any way prefigured what he had now grown to. This perspective sketch of his early Past, he committed to certain little leaves, which merit our undivided attention. For such leaves exclusively, containing scenes, acts, plays of his childhood, he used chronologically to file and arrange in separate drawers in a little child's-desk of his ; and thus to divide his Biography, as Moser did his Publicistic Materials, into separate *letter-boxes*. He had boxes or drawers for memorial-letters of his twelfth, of his thirteenth, fourteenth, &c. of his twenty-first year, and so on. Whenever he chose to conclude a day of pedagogic drudgery by an evening of peculiar rest, he simply pulled out a letter-drawer, a register-bar in his Life-hand-organ, and recollected the whole.

And here must I in reference to those reviewing Mutes, who may be for casting the noose of strangulation round my neck, most particularly beg, that, before doing so on account of my Chapters being called Letter-boxes, they would have the goodness to look whose blame it was, and to think whether I could possibly help it, seeing the Quintus had divided his Biography into such Boxes himself: they have Christian bowels.

But about his elder brother he put no saddening question to his mother : this poor boy a peculiar Fate had laid hold of, and with all his genial endowment, dashed to pieces on the ice-berg of Death. For he chanced to leap on an ice-board that had jammed itself among several others ; but these recoiled, and his shot forth with him ; melted away as it floated under his feet, and so sunk his heart of fire amid the ice and waves. It grieved his mother that he was not found, that her heart had not been harrowed by the look of the swoln corpse.—O good mother, rather thank God for it !—

After breakfast, to fortify himself with new vigour for his desk, he for some time strolled idly over the house, and, like a Police Fire-inspector, visited all the nooks of his cottage, to gather from them here and there a live ember from the ash-covered rejoicing-fire of his childhood. He mounted to the garret, to the empty bird-coops of his father, who in winter had been a birder ; and he transiently reviewed the lumber of his old playthings, which were lying in the net- ted enclosure of a large canary breeding-cage. In the minds of children, it is regular *little* forms, such as those of balls and dies, that impress and express themselves most forcibly. From this may the reader explain to himself Fixlein's delight in the red acorn- blockhouse, in the sparwork glued together out of white chips and husks of potatoe-plums, in the cheerful glass-house of a cube-shaped lantern, and other the like products of his early architecture. The following, however, I explain quite differently: he had ventured, without leave given from any lord of the manor, to build a clay house; not for cottagers, but for flies; and which, therefore, you could readily enough have put in your pocket. This fly-hospital had its glass windows, and a red coat of colouring, and very many alcoves, and three balconies: balconies, as a sort of house within a house, he had loved from of old so much, that he could scarcely have liked Jerusalem well, where (according to Lightfoot) no such thing is permitted to be built. From the glistening eyes, with which the architect had viewed his tenantry creeping about the windows or feeding out of the sugar-trough—for like the Count St Germain, they ate nothing but sugar,—from this joy an adept in the art of education might easily have prophesied his turn for household contraction; to his fancy, in those times, even gardeners'-huts were like large waste Arks and Halls, and nothing bigger than such a fly-Louvre, seemed a true, snug, citizen's-house. He now felt and handled his old high child's-stool, which had, in former days, resembled the *Sedes Exploratoria* of the Pope; he gave his child's-coach a tug and made it run; but he could not understand what balsam and holiness so much distinguished it from all other child's-coaches. He wondered that the real sports of children should not so delight him, as the

emblems of these sports, when the child that had carried them on was standing grown up to manhood in
his presence.

Before one article in the house he stood heart-melt-
ed and sad ; before a little angular clothes-press, which
was no higher than my table, and which had belonged
to his poor drowned brother. When the boy with the
key of it was swallowed by the waves, the excruciated
mother had made a vow that this toy-press of his should
never be broken up by violence. Most probably there
is nothing in it, but the poor soul's playthings. Let us
look away from this bloody urn.—   —

Bacon reckons the remembrances of childhood among
wholesome medicinal things ; naturally enough, therefore, they acted like a salutary digestive on the Quintus. He could now again betake him with new heart
to his desk, and produce something quite peculiar—
petitions for church livings. He took the Address-calendar, and for every country parish that he found in
it, got a petition in readiness ; which he then laid aside,
till such time as the present incumbent should decease.
For Hukelum alone he did not solicit.—It is a pretty
custom in Flachsenfingen that for every office which is
vacant, you are required, if you want it, to sue. As the
higher use of Prayer consists not in its fulfilment, but
in its accustoming you to pray ; so likewise petitionary
papers ought to be given in, not indeed that you may
get the office—this nothing but your money can do—
but that you may learn to write petitions. In truth, if

among the Calmucks, the turning of a calebash* stands
in place of Prayer, a slight movement of the purse, may
be as much as if you supplicated in words.

Towards evening—it was Sunday—he went out ro-
ving over the village ; he pilgrimed to his old sport-
ing-places, and to the common where he had so often
driven his snails to pasture ; visited the peasant, who,
from school-times upwards, had been wont, to the
amazement of the rest, to *thou*† him ; went, an Academic Tutor, to the Schoolmaster ; then to the Senior ; then to the Episcopal-barn or church. This last
no mortal understands, till I explain it. The case was
this : some three-and-forty years ago, a fire had destroyed the church (not the steeple), the parsonage,

---

* Their prayer-barrel, Kürüdu, is a hollowed shell, a cale-
bash, full of unrolled formulas of prayer ; they sway it from side
to side, and then it works. More philosophically viewed, since
in prayer, the feeling only is of consequence, it is much the same
whether this express itself by motion of the mouth or of the ca-
lebash.

† In German, as in some other languages, the common mode
of address is by the *third* person : plural, it indicates respect ;
singular, command : the *second* person is also used ; plural, it
generally denotes indifference ; singular, great familiarity, and
sometimes its product, contempt. *Dutzenfreund, Thouing-friend*,
is the strictest term of intimacy ; and among the wild *Burschen*
(Students) many a duel (happily, however, often ending like the
Polemo-Middinia in *one* drop of blood) has been fought, in consequence of saying *Du* (thou) and *Sie* (they) in the wrong place.
—ED.

and—what was not to be replaced—the church-records. (For this reason, it was only the smallest portion of the Hukelum people that knew exactly how old they were; and the memory of our Quintus himself vibrated between adopting the thirty-third year, and the thirty-second.) In consequence, the preaching had now to be carried on where formerly there had been thrashing; and the seed of the divine word to be turned over on the same threshing-floor with natural corn-seed. The Chanter and the Schoolboys took up the threshing-floor; the female mother-church-people stood on the one sheaves-loft, the Schadeck womankind on the other; and their husbands clustered pyramidically, like groschen and farthing-gallery men, about the barn-stairs; and far up on the straw-loft, mixed souls stood listening. A little flute was their organ, an upturned beer-cask their altar, round which they had to walk. I confess, I myself could have preached in such a place, not without humour. The Senior (at that time still a Junior), while the parsonage was building, dwelt and taught in the Castle; it was here, accordingly, that Fixlein had learned the *Irregular Verbs* with Thiennette.

These voyages of discovery completed, our Hukelum voyager could still, after evening prayers, pick leaf-insects, with Thiennette, from the roses; worms from the beds, and a Heaven of joy from every minute. Every dew-drop was coloured as with oil of cloves and oil of gladness; every star was a sparkle from the sun of happiness; and in the closed heart of the maiden,

there lay near to him, behind a little wall of separation, (as near to the Righteous man behind the thin
wall of Life,) an outstretched blooming Paradise....
I mean, she loved him a little.

He might have known it, perhaps. But to his compressed delight he gave freer vent, as he went to bed,
by early recollections on the stair. For in his childhood he had been accustomed, by way of evening-
prayer, to go over, under his coverlid, as it were, a
rosary, including fourteen Bible Proverbs, the first
verse of the Psalm, " All people that on Earth," the
Tenth Commandment, and, lastly, a long blessing. To
get the sooner done with it, he had used to begin his
devotion, not only on the stair, but before leaving that
place where Alexander studied men, and Semler stupid
books.   Moored in the haven of the down-waves, he
was already over with his evening supplication ; and
could now, without farther exertion, shut his eyes and
plump into sleep.——Thus does there lurk, in the smallest *homunculus*, the model of—the Catholic Church.

So far the Dog-days of Quintus Zebedäus Egidius
Fixlein.—I, for the second time, close a Chapter of this
Life, as Life itself is closed, with a sleep.

THIRD LETTER-BOX.

Christmas Recollections. New Occurrence.

FOR all of us the passage to the grave is, alas ! a
string of empty insipid days, as of glass pearls, only
here and there divided by an orient one of price. But
you die murmuring, unless, like the Quintus, you regard your existence as a drum : this has only one single
tone, but variety of *time* gives the sound of it cheerfulness enough. Our Quintus taught in the Fourth Class ;
vicariated in the Second ; wrote at his desk by night ;
and so lived on in the usual monotonous fashion—all
the time from the Holidays—till Christmas-eve, 1791 ;
and nothing was remarkable in his history except this
same eve, which I am now about to paint.

But I shall still have time to paint it, after, in the
first place, explaining shortly how, like birds of passage,
he had contrived to soar away over the dim cloudy
Harvest. The secret was, he set upon the *Hamburg
Political Journal*, with which the lackeys of Schadeck
had been for papering their buttons. He could now
calmly, with his back at the stove, accompany the winter campaigns of the foregoing year ; and fly after every
battle, as the ravens did after that of Pharsalia. On the
printed paper he could still, with joy and admiration,
walk round our German triumphal arches and scaffold-
ings for fireworks ; while to the people in the town,

who got only the newest newspapers, the very fragments of these our trophies, maliciously torn down by
the French, were scarcely discernible; nay, with old
plans he could drive back and discomfit the enemy,
while later readers in vain tried to resist them with
new ones.

Moreover, not only did the facility of conquering
the French prepossess him in favour of this journal;
but also the circumstance that it—cost him nothing.
His attachment to gratis reading was decided.   And
does not this throw light on the fact, that he, as Morhof advised, was wont sedulously to collect the separate leaves of waste-paper books as they came from
the grocer, and to rake among the same, as Virgil did
in Ennius ? Nay, for him the grocer was a Fortius (the
scholar), or a Frederick (the king), both which persons were in the habit of simply cutting from complete
books such leaves as contained anything.   It was also
this respect for all waste-paper that inspired him with
such esteem for the aprons of French cooks, which it
is well known consist of printed paper ; and he often
wished some German would translate these aprons :
indeed I am willing to believe that a good version of
more than one of such paper aprons might contribute to
elevate our Literature (this Muse *à belles fesses*), and
serve her in place of drivel-bib.—On many things a
man puts a *pretium affectionis*, simply because he hopes
he may have half stolen them : on this principle, combined with the former, our Quintus adopted into his

belief anything he could snap away from an open Lecture, or as a visitor in class-rooms ; opinions only for
which the Professor must be paid, he rigorously examined.—I return to the Christmas-eve.

At the very first, Egidius was glad, because out of
doors millers and bakers were at fisty-cuffs (as we
say of drifting snow in large flakes), and the ice-
flowers of the window were blossoming ; for external
frost, with a snug warm room, was what he liked. He
could now put fir wood into his stove, and Mocha
coffee into his stomach ; and shove his right foot (not
into the slipper, but) under the warm side of his Shock,
and also on the left keep swinging his pet Starling,
which was pecking at the snout of old Schil ; and then
with the right hand—with the left he was holding his
pipe—proceed, so undisturbed, so entrenched, so cloud-
capt, without the smallest breath of frost, to the highest enterprise which a Quintus can attempt,—to writing the Class-prodromus of the Flachsenfingen Gymnasium, namely, the eighth part thereof. I hold the
first printing in the history of a literary man to be
more important than the *first printing* in the history
of Letters : Fixlein could not sate himself with speci-
fying what he purposed, God willing, in the following
year, to treat of ; and accordingly, more for the sake of
printing than of use, he farther inserted three or four
pedagogic glances at the plan of operations to be followed by his schoolmaster colleagues as a body.

He lastly introduced a few dashes, by way of hook-ing his thoughts together ; and then laid aside the *Opus*, and would no longer look at it, that so, when printed, he might stand astonished at his own thoughts. And now he could take the Leipzig Fair Catalogue, which he purchased yearly, instead of the books therein, and open it without a sigh : he too was in print, as well as I am.

The happy fool, while writing, had shaken his head, rubbed his hands, hitched about on his chair, puckered his face, and sucked the end of his cue.—He could now spring up about five o'clock in the evening, to recreate himself ; and across the magic vapour of his pipe, like a new-caught bird, move up and down in his cage. On the warm smoke, the long galaxy of street-lamps was gleaming ; and red on his bed-curtains lay the fitful reflection of the blazing windows, and illuminated trees in the neighbourhood. And now he shook away the snow of Time from the wintergreen of Memory ; and beheld the fair years of his childhood, uncovered, fresh, green, and balmy, standing afar off before him. From his distance of twenty years, he looked into the quiet cottage of his parents, where his father and his brother had not yet been reaped away by the sickle of Death. He said to himself : " I will go through the whole Christmas-eve from the very dawn, as I had it of old :"

At his very rising he finds spangles on the table ; sacred spangles from the gold-leaf and silver-leaf, with

3

which the Christ-child * has been emblazoning and coat‑
ing his apples and nuts, the presents of the night.—On
the mint-balance of joy, this metallic foam pulls heavier
than the golden calves, and golden Pythagoras'-legs,
and golden Philistine-mice of wealthier capitalists.—
Then came his mother, bringing him both Christianity
and clothes : for in drawing on his trowsers, she easily
recapitulated the Ten Commandments, and, in tying
his garters, the Apostles' Creed. So soon as candle-
light was over, and day-light come, he clambers to the
arm of the settle, and then measures the nocturnal
growth of the yellow wiry grove of Christmas-Birch ;
and devotes far less attention than usual to the little
white winter-flowerage, which the seeds shaken from
the bird-cage are sending forth in the wet joints of
the window-panes.—I nowise grudge J. J. Rousseau
his *Flora Petrinsularis ;* † but let him also allow
our Quintus his *Window-flora.*—There was no such

---

* These antique Christmas festivities Richter describes with
equal *gusto* in another work (*Briefe und Zukünftige Lebenslemf*) ;
where the Christ-child (falsely reported to the young ones, to
have been seen flying through the air, with gold wings) ; the
Birch-bough fixed in a corner of the room, and by him made to
grow ; the fruit, of gilt sweatmeats, apples, nuts, which (for good
boys) it suddenly produces, &c. &c. are specified with the same
fidelity as here.—ED.

† Which he purposed to make for his Island of St Pierre in
the Bienne Lake.

thing as school all day; so he had time enough to seek
his Flescher (his brother), and commence (when could
there be finer frost for it?) the slaughtering of their
winter-meat. Some days before, the brother, at the
peril of his life and of a cudgelling, had caught their
stalled-beast—so they called the sparrow—under a window-sill in the Castle. Their slaughtering wants not
an axe (of wood), nor puddings, nor potted meat.—
About three o'clock the old Gardener, whom neigh-
bours must call the Professor of Gardening, takes his
place on his large chair, with his Cologne tobacco-
pipe; and after this no mortal shall work a stroke.
He tells nothing but lies; of the aeronautic Christ-
child, and the jingling Ruprecht with his bells. In the
dusk, our little Quintus takes an apple; divides it into
all the figures of stereometry, and spreads the fragments in two heaps on the table: then as the lighted
candle enters, he starts up in amazement at the unex-
pected present, and says to his brother : " Look what
the good Christ-child has given thee and me ; and I
saw one of his wings glittering." And for this same
glittering he himself lies in wait the whole evening.

About eight o'clock,—here he walks chiefly by the
chronicle of his letter-drawer—both of them, with necks
almost excoriated with washing, and in clean linen,
and in universal anxiety least the Holy Christ-child
find them up, are put to bed. What a magic night!—
What tumult of dreaming hopes!—The populous, motley, glittering cave of Fancy opens itself, in the length

of the night, and in the exhaustion of dreamy effort, still darker and darker, fuller and more grotesque; but the awakening gives back to the thirsty heart its hopes. All accidental tones, the cries of animals, of watchmen, are, for the timidly devout Fancy, sounds out of Heaven: singing voices of Angels in the air, church-music of the morning worship.—

Ah! it was not the mere Lubberland of sweetmeats and playthings which then, with its perspective, stormed like a river of joy against the chambers of our hearts; and which yet in the moonlight of memory, with its dusky landscapes, melts our souls in sweetness. Ah! this was it, that then for our boundless wishes there were still boundless hopes : but now reality is round us, and the wishes are all that we have left!

At last came rapid lights from the neighbourhood playing through the window on the walls, and the Christmas trumpets, and the crowing from the steeple, hurries both the boys from their bed. With their clothes in their hands, without fear for the darkness, without feeling for the morning-frost, rushing, intoxicated, shouting, they hurry down stairs into the dark room. Fancy riots in the pastry and fruit perfume of the still eclipsed treasures, and paints her air-castles by the glimmering of the Hesperides-fruit with which the Birch-tree is loaded. While their mother strikes a light, the falling sparks sportfully open and shroud the dainties on the table, and the many-coloured grove on the wall; and a single atom of that fire bears on it a hanging garden of Eden.— — —

—On a sudden all grew light; and the Quintus got
—the Conrectorship, and a table-clock.

FOURTH LETTER-BOX.

*Office-brokage. Discovery of the promised Secret,
Hans von Füchslein.*

FOR while the Quintus, in his vapoury chamber,
was thus running over the sounding-board of his early
years, the Rathsdiener, or City-officer, entered with a
lantern and the Presentation; and behind him the courier of the Frau von Aufhammer with a note and a
table-clock. The Rittmeisterinn had transformed her
payment for the Dog-days sickbed-exhortation into a
Christmas present; which consisted, *first*, of a table-
clock, with a wooden ape thereon, starting out when
the hours struck, and drumming along with every stroke;
secondly, of the Conrectorate, which she had procured
for him.

As in the public this appointment from the private
Flachsenfingen Council has not been judged of as it
deserved, I consider it my duty to offer a defence for
the body corporate; and that rather here, than in the
Reichsanzeiger, or *Imperial Indicator*.—I have already
mentioned, in the Second Letter-Box, that the Town-
Syndic drove a trade in Hamburg candles; and the then
Burgermeister in coffee-beans, which he sold as well

whole as ground. Their joint traffic, however, which they carried on exclusively, was in the eight School-offices of Flachsenfingen: the other members of the Council acting only as bale-wrappers, shopmen, and accountants in the Council wareroom. A Council-house, indeed, is like an India-house, where not only resolutions or appointments, but also shoes and cloth, are exposed to sale. Properly speaking, the Councillor derives his freedom of office-trading from that principle of the Roman law : *Cui jus est donandi, eidem et vendendi jus est,* that is to say, He who has the right of giving anything away, has also a right to dispose of it for money, if he can. Now as the Council-members have palpably the right of conferring offices gratis, the right of selling them must follow of course.

Short Extra-word on Appointment-brokers in general.

My chief anxiety is lest the Academy-product-sale-Commission* of the State carry on its office-trade too slackly. And what but the commonweal must suffer in the long run, if important posts are distributed, not according to the current cash, which is laid down for them, but according to connexions, relationships, party recommendations, and bowings and cringings ? Is it

---

* Borrowed from the " Imperial Mine-product-sale-Commission," in Vienna : in their very names these Vienna people show taste

not a contradiction, to charge titulary offices dearer
than real ones ? Should one not rather expect that the
real Hofrath would pay higher by the *alterum tantum,*
than the mere titulary Hofrath?—Money, among European nations, is now the equivalent and representative of value in all things, and consequently in understanding ; the rather as a *head* is stamped on it : to pay
down the purchase money of an office is therefore neither more nor less than to stand an *examen rigorosum,*
which is held by a good *schema examinandi.* To invert this, to pretend exhibiting your qualifications, in
place of these their surrogates, and assignates and *mon-
noie de confiance,* is simply to resemble the crazy philosophers in *Gulliver's Travels,* who, for social converse,
instead of names of things, brought the things themselves tied up in a bag ; it is, indeed, plainly as much
as trying to fall back into the barbarous times of trade
by barter, when the Romans, instead of the figured cattle
on their leather money, drove forth the beeves themselves.

From all such injudicious notions I myself am so far
removed, that often when I used to read that the King
of France was devising new offices, to stand and sell
them under the booth of his Baldaquin, I have set myself to do something of the like. This I shall now at
least calmly propose ; not vexing my heart whether Governments choose to adopt it or not. As our Sovereign
will not allow us to multiply offices purely for sale, nay,
on the contrary, is day and night (like managers of stroll-

ing companies) meditating how to give more parts to one State-actor; and thus to the Three Stage Unities to add a Fourth, that of Players; as the above French method, therefore, will not apply, could we not at least contrive to invent some Virtues harmonizing with the offices, along with which they might be sold as titles? Might we not, for instance, with the office of a Referendary, put off at the same time a titular Incorruptibility, for a fair consideration; and so that this virtue, as not belonging to the office, must be separately paid for by the candidate? Such a market-title and patent of nobility could not but be ornamental to a Referendary. We forget that in former times such high titles were appended to all posts whatsoever: the scholastic Professor then wrote himself (besides his official designation) " The Seraphic," " The Incontrovertible," " The Penetrating;" the King wrote himself, " The Great," " The Bald," " The Bold," and so also did the Rabbins. Could it be unpleasant to gentlemen in the higher stations of Justice, if the titles of Impartiality, Rapidity, &c. might be conferred on them by sale, as well as the posts themselves? Thus with the appointment of a Kammerrath, or Councillor of Revenue, the virtue of Patriotism might fitly be conjoined; and I believe, few Advocates would grudge purchasing the title of Integrity (as well as their common one of Government-advocacy), were it to be had in the market. If, however, any candidate chose to take his post without the virtues, then it would stand with himself to do so, and in the adoption of this reflex morality, Government should not constrain him.

It might be that, as according to Tristram Shandy, clothes; according to Walter Shandy and Lavater proper names exert an influence on men, appellatives would do so still more ; since, on us, as on testaceous animals, *the foam so often hardens into shell :* but such internal morality is not a thing the State can have an eye to ; for as in the fine arts, it is not this but the *representation* of it which forms her true aim.

I have found it rather difficult to devise for our different offices different verbal-virtues ; but I should think there might many such divisions of Virtue (at this moment, Love of Freedom, Public-spirit, Sincerity, and Uprightness occur to me) be hunted out ; were but some well-disposed minister of state to appoint a Virtue-board or Moral Address Department, with some half dozen secretaries, who, for a small salary, might devise various virtues for the various posts. Were I in their place, I should hold a good prism before the white ray of Virtue, and divide it completely. Pity that it were not crimes we wanted—their subdivision I mean ;—our country Judges might then be selected for this purpose. For in their tribunals, where only inferior jurisdiction, and no penalty above five florins Frankish, is admitted, they have a daily training how out of every mischief to make several small ones, none of which they ever punish to a greater amount than their five florins. This is a precious moral *Rolfinkenism,* which our Jurists

have learned from the great Sin-cutters, St Augustin
and his Sorbonne, who together have carved more sins
on Adam's Sin-apple, than ever Rolfinken did faces on
a cherrystone. How different one of our Judges from
a Papal Casuist, who, by side-scrapings, will rasp you
down the best deadly sin into a venial!—

School-offices (to come to these) are a small branch
of traffic certainly; yet still they are monarchies,—
school-monarchies, to wit,—resembling the Polish
crown, which, according to Pope's verse, is twice exposed to sale in the century; a statement, I need hardly say, arithmetically false, Newton having settled the
average duration of a reign at twenty-two years. For
the rest, whether the city Council bring the young
of the community a Hamel's *Rat*-and-Child-*catcher;* or
a Weissen's *Child's-friend,*—this to the Council can
make no difference; seeing the Schoolmaster is not a
horse, for whose secret defects the horse-dealer is to
be responsible. It is enough if Town-Syndic and
Co. cannot reproach themselves with having picked
out any fellow of genius; for a genius, as he is useless
to the State, except for recreation and ornament, would
at the very least exclude the duller, cooler head, who
properly forms the true care and profit of the State; as
your costly carat-pearl is good for show alone, but coarse
grain-pearls for medicine. On the whole, if a schoolmaster be adequate to flog his scholars, it should suffice; and I cannot but blame our Commission of In-
spectors when they go examining schools, that they do

not make the schoolmaster go through the duty of firk-
ing one or two young persons of his class in their presence, by way of trial, to see what is in him.

End of the Extra-word on Appointment-brokers in general.

Now again to our history ! The Councillor Heads
of the Firm had conferred the Conrectorate on my hero,
not only with a view to the continued consumpt of
candles and beans, but also on the strength of a quite
mad notion : they believed, the Quintus would very
soon die.

—And here I have reached a most important circumstance in this History, and one into which I have
yet let no mortal look : now, however, it no longer depends on my will whether I shall shove aside the fold-
ing-screen from it or not ; but I must positively lay it
open, nay, hang a reverberating-lamp over it.

In medical history, it is a well-known fact that in
certain families the people all die precisely at the same
age, just as in these families they are all born at the
same age (of nine months) ; nay, from Voltaire, I recollect one family, the members of which at the same
age all killed themselves. Now, in the Fixleinic line-
age, it was the custom that the male ascendants uniformly on Cantata-Sunday, in their thirty-second year,
took to bed and died : every one of my readers would
do well to insert in his copy of the *Thirty Years' War*,

Schiller having entirely omitted it, the fact, that in the course thereof, one Fixlein died of the plague, another of hunger, another of a musket-bullet; all in their thirty-second year. True Philosophy explains the matter thus : " The first two or three times, it happened purely by accident; and the other times, the people died of sheer fright : if not so, the whole fact is rather to be questioned."

But what did Fixlein make of the affair ? Little or nothing : the only thing he did was, that he took little or no pains to fall in love with Thiennette; that so no other might have cause for fear on his account. He himself, however, for five reasons, minded it so little, that he hoped to be older than Senior Astmann before he died : First, because three Gipsies, in three different places, and at three different times, had each shown him the same long vista of years in her magic mirror. Secondly, because he had a sound constitution. Thirdly, because his own brother had formed an exception, and perished before the thirties. Fourthly, on this ground : When a boy he had fallen sick of sorrow, on the very Cantata-Sunday when his father was lying in the winding-sheet, and only been saved from death by his playthings; and with this Cantata-sickness, he conceived that he had given the murderous Genius of his race the slip. Fifthly, the church-books being destroyed, and with them the certainty of his age, he could never fall into a right definite deadly fear : " It may be," said he, " that I have got whisked away over

this whoreson year, and no one the wiser." I will not
deny that last year he had fancied he was two-and-
thirty: " however," said he, " if I am not to be so till,
God willing, the next (1792), it may run away as
smoothly as the last ; am I not always in *His* keeping ? And were it unjust if the pretty years that were
broken off from the life of my brother should be added
to mine ?"—Thus, under the cold snow of the Present,
does poor man strive to warm himself, or to mould out
of it a fair snow-man.

The Councillor Oligarchy, however, built upon the
opposite opinion ; and, like a Divinity, elevated our
Quintus all at once from the Quintusship to the Conrectorate ; swearing to themselves, that he would soon
vacate it again. Properly speaking, by school-senior-
ity, this holy chair should have belonged to the Subrector Hans von Füchslein ; but he wished it not ; being minded to become Hukelum Parson ; especially, as
Astmann's Death-angel, according to sure intelligence,
was opening more and more widely the door of this
spiritual sheepfold. " If the fellow weather another
year, 'tis more than I expect," said Hans.

This Hans was such a churl, that it is pity he had
not been a Hanoverian Postboy ; that so, by the Man-
date of the Hanoverian Government, enjoining on all
its Post-officers an elegant style of manners, he might
have somewhat refined himself. To our poor Quintus,
whom no mortal disliked, and who again could hate no
mortal, he alone bore a grudge ; simply because *Fix-*

lein did not write himself *Füchslein*, and had not chosen
along with him to purchase a Patent of Nobility. The
Subrector, on this his Patent triumphal chariot, drawn
by a team of four specified ancestors, was obliged to
see the Quintus, who was related to him, clutching by
the lackey-straps behind the carriage ; and to hear him,
in the most despicable raiment, saying to the train :
" He that rides there is my cousin, and a mortal, and
I always remind him of it." The mild compliant Quintus never noticed this large wasp-poisonbag in the
Subrector, but took it for a honeybag ; nay, by his
brotherly warmness, which the nobleman regarded as
mere show, he concreted these venomous juices into
still feller consistency. The Quintus, in his simplicity,
took Füchslein's contempt for envy of his pedagogic
talents.

A Catherinenhof, an Annenhof, an Elizabethhof,
Stralenhof, and Petershof, all these Russian pleasure
palaces, a man can dispense with (if not despise), who
has a room, in which on Christmas-eve he walks about
with a Presentation in his hand. The new Conrector
now longed for nothing but—daylight : joys always
(cares never) nibbled from him, like sparrows, his sleep-
grains ; and to-night, moreover, the registrator of his
glad time, the clock-ape, drummed out every hour to
him, which, accordingly, he spent in gay dreaming,
rather than in sound snoring.

On Christmas-morn, he looked at his Class-prodromus, and thought but little of it : he scarcely knew

what to make of his last night's foolish inflation about his Quintusship : " the Quintus-post," said he to himself, " is not to be named in the same day with the Conrectorate ; I wonder how I could parade so last night before my promotion ; at present, I had more reason." To-day he eat, as on all Sundays and holydays, with the Master-Butcher Steinberger, his former Guardian. To this man, Fixlein was, what common people are *always*, but polished, philosophical, and sentimental people very *seldom* are,—*thankful :* a man thanks you the less for presents the more inclined he is to give presents of his own ; and the beneficent is rarely a grateful person. Meister Steinberger, in the character of store-master, had introduced into the wire-cage of a garret, where Fixlein, while a Student at Leipzig, was suspended, many a well-filled trough with good canary-meat, of hung-beef, of household bread, and *Sauerkraut.* Money indeed was never to be wrung from him : it is well known that he often sent the best calfskins gratis to the tanner, to be boots for our Quintus ; but the tanning-charges the Ward himself had to bear.—On Fixlein's entrance, as was at all times customary, a smaller damask table-cloth was laid upon the large coarser one ; the arm-chair ; silver implements, and a wine-soup were handed him ; mere waste, which, as the Guardian used to say, suited well enough for a Scholar ; but for a Flesher not at all. Fixlein first took his victuals, and then signified that he was made Conrector. " Ward," said Steinberger, " if you are made

that, it is well.—Seest thou, Eva, I cannot buy a tail
of thy cows now ; I must have smelt it beforehand."
He was hereby informing his daughter that the cash
set apart for the fatted cattle must now be applied to
the Conrectorate ; for he was in the habit of advancing
all instalment-dues to his ward, at an interest of four
and a half per cent. Fifty gulden he had already lent
the Quintus on his advancement to the Quintusship :
of these the interest had to be duly paid ; yet, on the
day of payment, the Quintus always got some abate-
ment ; being wont every Sunday after dinner to in-
struct his guardian's daughter in arithmetic, writing,
and geography. Steinberger with justice required of
his own grown-up daughter that she should know all
the towns, where he in his wanderings as a journey-
man had slain fat oxen ; and if she slipped, or wrote
crookedly, or subtracted wrong, he himself, as Aca-
demical Senate and Justiciary, was standing behind
her chair, ready, so to speak, with the forge-hammer
of his fist to beat out the dross from her brain, and at
a few strokes hammer it into right ductility. The soft
Quintus, for his part, had never struck her. On this
account she had perhaps, with a few glances, appointed him executor and·assignee of her heart. The old
Flescher—simply because his wife was dead—had
constantly been in the habit of searching with mine-
lamps and pokers into all the corners of Eva's heart ;
and had in consequence long ago observed—what the
Quintus never did—that she had a mind for the said

Quintus. Young women conceal their sorrows more easily than their joys : to-day at the mention of this Conrectorate, Eva had become unusually *red*.

When she went after breakfast to bring in coffee, which the Ward had to drink down to the grounds : " I beat Eva to death if she but look at him," said he. Then addressing Fixlein : " Hear you, Ward, did you never cast an eye on my Eva ? She can suffer you, and if you want her, you get her; but *we* have done with one another : for a learned man needs quite another sort of thing."

" Herr Regiments-Quartermaster," said Fixlein (for this post Steinberger filled in the provincial Militia), " such a match were far too rich, at any rate, for a Schoolman." The Quartermaster nodded fifty times ; and then said to Eva as she returned,—at the same time taking down from the shelf a wooden crook, on which he used to rack out and suspend his slain calves : " Stop !—Hark, dost' wish the present Herr Conrector here for thy husband ?"

" Ah, good Heaven !" said Eva.

" Mayst wish him or not," continued the Flescher , " with this crook, thy father knocks thy brains out, if thou but think of a learned man. Now make his coffee." And so by the dissevering stroke of this wooden crook was a love easily smitten asunder, which in a higher rank, by such cutting through it with the sword, would only have foamed and hissed the keenlier.

Fixlein might now, at any hour he liked, lay hold of

fifty florins Frankish, and clutch the pedagogic sceptre, and become coadjutor of the Rector, that is, Conrector. We may assert, that it is with debts, as with
proportions in Architecture ; of which Wolf has shown
that those are the best, which can be expressed in the
smallest numbers. Nevertheless, the Quartermaster
cheerfully took learned men under his arm : for the
notion that his debtor would decease in his thirty-second year, and that so Death, as creditor in the first
rank, must be paid his Debt of Nature, before the other
creditors could come forward with their debts—this
notion he named stuff and old-wifery ; he was neither
Superstitious nor Fanatical, and he walked by firm
principles of action, such as the common man much
oftener has than your vapouring man of letters, or your
empty dainty man of rank.

As it is but a few clear Ladydays, warm Mayday-
nights, at the most a few odorous Rose-weeks, which
I am digging from this Fixlienic Life, embedded in the
dross of week-day cares ; and as if they were so many
veins of silver, am separating, stamping, smelting, and
burnishing for the reader,—I must now travel on with
the stream of his history to Cantata-Sunday, 1792, before
I can gather a few handfulls of this gold-dust, to carry
in and wash in my biographical gold-hut. That Sunday, on the contrary, is very metalliferous : do but consider that Fixlein is yet uncertain (the ashes of the
Church-books not being legible) whether it is con-

ducting him into his thirty-second or his thirty-third year.

From Christmas till then he did nothing, but simply became Conrector. The new chair of office was a Sun-altar, on which, from his Quintus-ashes, a young Phœnix combined itself together. Great changes—in offices, marriages, travels—make us younger; we always date our history from the last revolution, as the French have done from theirs. A colonel, who first set foot on the ladder of seniority as corporal, is five times younger than a king, who in his whole life has never been aught else except a—crown-prince.

FIFTH LETTER-BOX.

*Cantata-Sunday.   Two Testaments.   Pontac ;
Blood ; Love.*

THE Spring months clothe the earth in new variegated hues ; but man they usually dress in black. Just when our icy regions are becoming fruitful, and the flower-waves of the meadows are rolling together over our quarter of the globe, we on all hands meet with men in sables, the beginning of whose Spring is full of tears. But, on the other hand, this very upblooming of the renovated earth is itself the best balm for sorrow over those who lie under it ; and graves are better hid by blossoms than by snow.

In April, which is no less deadly than it is fickle, old

Senior Astmann, our Conrector's teacher, was overta-
ken by death. His departure it was meant to hide from
the Rittmeisterinn ; but the unusual ringing of funereal
peals carried his swan-song to her heart ; and gradually
set the curfew-bell of her life into similar movement.
Age and sufferings had already marked out the first
incisions for Death, so that he required but little effort
to cut her down ; for it is with men as with trees, they
are notched long before felling, that their life-sap may
exude. The second stroke of apoplexy was soon followed by the last : it is strange that Death, like criminal courts, cites the apoplectic thrice.

Men are apt to postpone their *last* will as long as
their *better* one : the Rittmeisterinn would perhaps have
let all her hours, till the speechless and deaf one, roll
away without testament, had not Thiennette, during
the last night, before from sick-nurse she became corpse-
watcher, reminded the patient of the poor Conrector,
and of his meagre hunger-bitten existence, and of the
scanty aliment and board-wages which Fortune had
thrown him, and of his empty Future, where, like a
drooping yellow plant in the parched deal-box of the
school-room between scholars and creditors, he must
languish to the end. Her own poverty offered her a
model of his ; and her inward tears were the fluid tints
with which she coloured her picture. As the Rittmeisterinn's testament related solely to domestics and
dependents, and as she began with the male ones, Fixlein stood at the top ; and Death, who must have been

a special friend of the Conrector's, did not lift his scythe
and give the last stroke till his protegee had been with
audible voice declared testamentary heir ; then he cut
all away, life, testament, and hopes.

When the Conrector, in a wash-bill from his mother,
received these two Death's-posts and Job's-posts in his
class, the first thing he did was to dismiss his class-
boys, and break into tears before reaching home.
Though the mother had informed him that he had been
remembered in the will (I could wish, however, that
the Notary had blabbed how much it was), yet almost
with every O which he masoretically excerpted from his
German Bible, and entered in his Masoretic Work, great
drops fell down on his pen, and made his black ink
pale.   His sorrow was not the gorgeous sorrow of the
Poet, who veils the gaping wounds of the departed in
the winding-sheet, and breaks the cry of anguish in soft
tones of plaintiveness ; nor the sorrow of the Philosopher, who, through one open grave, must look into the
whole catacomb-Necropolis of the Past, and before whom
the spectre of a friend expands into the spectral Shadow
of this whole Earth : but it was the woe of a child, of a
mother, whom this thought itself, without subsidiary
reflections, bitterly cuts asunder : " So I shall never more
see thee ; so must thou moulder away, and I shall never
see thee, thou good soul, never, never any more !"—
And even because he neither felt the philosophical nor
the poetical sadness, every trifle could make a division,
a break in his mourning ; and, like a woman, he was

that very evening capable of sketching some plans for the future employment of his legacy.

Four weeks after, to wit, on the 5th of May, the testament was unsealed; but not till the 6th (Cantata-Sunday) did he go down to Hukelum. His mother met his salutations with tears; which she shed, over the corpse for grief, over the testament for joy.—To the now Conrector Egidius Zebedäus was left: *In the first place*, a large sumptuous bed, with a mirror-tester, in which the giant Goliath might have rolled at his ease, and to which I and my fair readers will by and by approach nearer, to examine it; *secondly*, there was devised to him, as unpaid Easter-godchild-money, for every year that he had lived, one ducat; *thirdly*, all the admittance and instalment dues, which his elevation to the Quintate and Conrectorate had cost him, were to be made good to the utmost penny. " And dost thou know, then," proceeded the mother, " what the poor Fräulein has got? Ah Heaven! Nothing! Not one brass farthing!" For Death had stiffened the hand, which was just stretching itself out to reach the poor Thienette a little rain-screen against the foul weather of life. The mother related this perverse trick of Fortune with true condolence; which in women dissipates envy, and comes easier to them than congratulation, a feeling belonging rather to men. In many female hearts sympathy and envy are such near door-neighbours that they could be virtuous nowhere except in Hell, where men have such frightful times of it; and vicious nowhere except in Heaven, where people have more happiness than they know what to do with.

The Conrector was now enjoying on Earth that Heaven to which his benefactress had ascended. First of all, he started off—without so much as putting up his handkerchief, in which lay his emotion—up stairs to see the legacy-bed unshrouded ; for he had a *female* predilection for furniture. I know not whether the reader ever looked at or mounted any of these ancient chivalric beds, into which, by means of a little stair without balustrades, you can easily ascend ; and in which you, properly speaking, sleep always at least one story above ground. Nanzianzen informs us (*Orat. XVI.*) that the Jews, in old times, had high beds with cock-ladders of this sort ; but simply because of vermin. The legacy bed-Ark was quite as large as one of these ; and a flea would have measured it not in Diameters of the Earth, but in Distances of Sirius. When Fixlein beheld this colossal dormitory, with the curtains drawn asunder, and its canopy of looking-glass, he could have longed to be in it ; and had it been in his power to cut from the opaque hemisphere of Night, at that time in America, a small section, he would have established himself there along with it, just to swim about, for one half hour, with his thin lath figure, in this sea of down. The mother, by longer chains of reasoning and chains of calculation than the bed was, had not succeeded in persuading him to have the broad mirror on the top cut in pieces, though his large dressing-table had nothing to see itself in but a mere shaving-glass : he let the mirror lie where it was for this reason : " Should I ever, God willing, get married," said he, " I shall then, towards morning, be able to look at my sleeping wife, without sitting up in bed."

As to the second article of the testament, the god-child Easter-pence, his mother had, last night, arranged it perfectly. The Lawyer took her evidence on the years of the heir ; and these she had stated at exactly the teeth-number, two-and-thirty. She would willingly have lied, and passed off her son, like an Inscription, for older than he was : but against this *venia ætatis*, she saw too well, the authorities would have taken exception, " that it was falsehood and cozenage ; had the son been two-and-thirty, he must have been dead some time ago, as it could not but be presumed that he then was."

And just as she was recounting this, a servant from Schadeck called ; and delivered to the Conrector, in return for a discharge and ratification of the birth-certificate given out by his mother, a gold bar of two-and-thirty ducat age-counters, like a helm-bar for the voyage of his life : Herr von Aufhammer was too proud to engage in any pettifogging discussion over a plebeian birth certificate.

And thus, by a proud open-handedness, was one of the best lawsuits thrown to the dogs : seeing this gold bar might, in the wire-mill of the judgment-bench, have been drawn out into the finest threads. From such a tangled lock, which was not to be unravelled—for, in the first place, there was no document to prove Fixlein's age; in the second place, so long as he lived, the necessary conclusion was, that he was not yet thirty-two *—from such a lock, might not only silk and hanging-cords, but whole drag-nets have been spun and twisted. Clients in general would have less reason to complain of their causes, if these lasted longer : Philosophers contend for thousands of years over philosophical questions ; and it seems an unaccountable thing, therefore, that Advocates should attempt to end their juristical questions in a space of eighty, or even sometimes of sixty years. But the professors of Law are not to blame for this : on the other hand, as Lessing asserts of Truth, that not the *finding* but the *seeking* of it profits men, and that he himself would willingly make over his claim to all truths in return for the sweet labour of investigation, so is the professor of Law not profited by the finding and deciding, but by the investigation of a juridical truth—which is called pleading and practising—and he would willingly consent to approximate to Truth for ever, like an hyperbola to its

* As, by the evidence at present before us, we can found on no other presumption, than that he must die in his thirty-second year ; it would follow, that, in case he died two-and-thirty years after the death of the testatrix, no farthing could be claimed by him ; since, according to our fiction, at the making of the testament he was not even one year old.

asymptote, without ever meeting it, seeing he can subsist as an honourable man with wife and child, let such
approximation be as tedious as it likes.

The Schadeck servant had, besides the gold legacy,
a farther commission from the Lawyer, whereby the
testamentary heir was directed to sum up the mint-dues
which he had been obliged to pay while lying under
the coining-press of his superiors, as Quintus and Conrector ; the which, properly documented and authen-
ticated, were forthwith to be made good to him.

Our Conrector, who now rated himself among the
great capitalists of the world, held his short gold-roll
like a sceptre in his hand ; like a basket-net lifted from
the sea of the Future, which was now to run on, and
bring him all manner of fed-fishes, well-washed, sound,
and in good season.

I cannot relate all things at once ; else I should ere
now have told the reader, who must long have been
waiting for it, that to the monied Conrector his two-
and-thirty godchild-pennies but too much prefigured
the two-and-thirty years of his age ; besides which, to-
day the Cantata-Sunday, this Bartholomew-night and
Second of September of his family, came in as a farther aggravation. The mother, who should have known
the age of her child, said she had forgotten it ; but
durst wager he was thirty-two a year ago ; only the
Lawyer was a man you could not speak to. " I
could swear it myself,". said the capitalist ; " I recollect how stupid I felt on Cantata-Sunday last year.

Fixlein beheld Death, not as the poet does, in the up-towering, asunder-driving concave-mirror of Imagination; but as the child, as the savage, as the peasant, as the woman does, in the plane octavo-mirror on the board of a Prayer-book; and Death looked to him like an old white-headed man, sunk down into slumber in some latticed pew.—

And yet he thought oftener of him than last year: for joy readily melts us into softness; and the lackered Wheel of Fortune is a cistern-wheel that empties its water in our eyes .... But the friendly Genius of this terrestrial, or rather aquatic Ball—for, in the physical and in the moral world, there are more tear-seas than firm land—has provided for the poor water-insects that float about in it, for us namely, a quite special elixir against spasms in the soul : I declare this same Genius must have studied the whole pathology of man with care ; for to the poor devil who is no Stoic, and can pay no Soul-doctor, that for the fissures of his cranium and his breast might prepare costly prescriptions of simples, he has stowed up cask-wise in all cellarages a precious wound-water, which the patient has only to take and pour over his slashes and bone-breakages—gin-twist, I mean, or beer, or a touch of wine .... By Heaven ! it is either stupid ingratitude towards this medicinal Genius on the one hand, or theological confusion of permitted tippling with prohibited drunkenness on the other, if men do not thank God that they have something at hand, which, in the nervous vertigos of life, will instantly supply the place of Philosophy, Christianity, Judaism, Paganism, and *Time ;*—liquor, as I said.

The Conrector had long before sunset given the village post three groschens of post-money, and commissioned—for he had a whole cabinet of ducats in his pocket, which all day he was surveying in the dark with his hand—three thalers' worth of Pontac from the town. " I must have a Cantata merry-making," said he ; " if it be my last day, let it be my gayest too !" I could wish he had given a larger order ; but he kept the bit of moderation between his teeth, at all times ; even in a threatened sham-death-night, and in the midst of jubilee. The question is, Whether he would not have restricted himself to a single bottle, if he had not wished to treat his mother and the Fräulein. Had he lived in the tenth century, when the Day of Judgment was thought to be at hand, or in other centuries, when new Noah's Deluges were expected, and when, accordingly, like sailors in a shipwreck, people bouzed up all,—he would not have spent one kreuzer more on that account. His joy was, that with his legacy he could now satisfy his head-creditor Steinberger, and leave the world an honest man : just people, who make much of money, pay their debts the most punctually.

The purple Pontac arrived at a time when Fixlein could compare the red-chalk-drawings and red-letter-titles of joy, which it would bring out on the cheeks of its drinker and drinkeresses,—with the Evening-carnation of the last clouds about the Sun . . . .

I declare, among all the spectators of this History, no one can be thinking more about poor Thiennette than I ; nevertheless, it is not permitted me to bring her out from her tiring-room to my historical scene, before the time. Poor girl ! The Conrector cannot wish more warmly than his Biographer, that, in the Temple of Nature as in that of Jerusalem, there were a special door—besides that of Death—standing open, through which only the afflicted entered, that a Priest might give them solace. But Thiennette's heart-sickness over all her vanished prospects, over her entombed benefactress, over a whole life enwrapped in the pall, had hitherto, in a grief which the stony Rittmeister rather made to bleed than alleviated, swept all away from her, occupations excepted ; had fettered all her steps which led not to some task, and granted to her eyes nothing to dry them or gladden them, save down-falling eyelids full of dreams and sleep.

All sorrow raises us above the civic Ceremonial-law, and makes the Prosaist a Psalmist : in sorrow alone have women courage to front opinion. Thiennette walked out only in the evening, and then only in the garden.

The Conrector could scarcely wait for the appearance of his fair friend, to offer his thanks,—and to-night also—his Pontac. Three Pontac decanters and three wine-glasses were placed outside on the project-

ing window-sill of his cottage ; and every time he returned from the dusky covered-way amid the flower-
forests, he drank a little from his glass,—and the mother sipped now and then from within through the
opened window.

I have already said, his Life-laboratory lay in the
south-west corner of the garden or park, over against
the Castle-Escurial, which stretched back into the village. In the north-west corner bloomed an acacia
grove, like the floral crown of the garden. Fixlein
turned his steps in that direction also ; to see if, perhaps, he might not cast a happy glance through the
wide-latticed grove over the intervening meads to Thiennette. He recoiled a little before two stone steps
leading down into a pond before this grove, which were
sprinkled with fresh blood. On the flags, also, there
was blood hanging. Man shudders at this oil of our
life's lamp where he finds it shed : to him it is the red
death-signature of the Destroying Angel. Fixlein hurried apprehensively into the grove ; and found here his
paler benefactress leaning on the flower-bushes ; her
hands with their knitting-ware sunk into her bosom,
her eyes lying under their lids as if in the bandage of
slumber ; her left arm in the real bandage of blood-
letting ; and with cheeks to which the twilight was
lending as much red, as late woundings—this day's
included—had taken from them. Fixlein, after his
first terror—not at this flower's-sleep, but at his own
abrupt entrance—began to unrol the spiral butterfly's-

sucker of his vision, and to lay it on the motionless leaves of this same sleeping flower. At bottom, I may assert, that this was the first time he had ever looked at her : he was now among the thirties ; and he still continued to believe, that, in a young lady, he must look at the clothes only, not the person, and wait on her with his ears, not with his eyes.

I impute it to the elevating influences of the Pontac, that the Conrector plucked up courage to—turn, to come back, and employ the resuscitating means of coughing, sneezing, trampling, and calling to his Shock, in stronger and stronger doses on the fair sleeper. To take her by the hand, and, with some medical apology, gently pull her out of sleep, this was an audacity of which the Conrector, so long as he could stand for Pontac, and had any grain of judgment left, could never dream.

However, he did awake her, by those other means.

Wearied, heavy-laden Thiennette ! how slowly does thy eye open ! The warmest balsam of this earth, soft sleep has shifted aside, and the night-air of memory is again blowing on thy naked wounds !—And yet was the smiling friend of thy youth the fairest object which thy eye could light on, when it sank from the hanging garden of Dreams into this lower one round thee.

She herself was little conscious,—and the Conrector not at all,—that she was bending her flower-leaves imperceptibly towards a terrestrial body, namely, to- wards Fixlein : she resembled an Italian flower, that contains cunningly concealed within it a newyear's gift, which the receiver knows not at first how to extract. But now the golden chain of her late kind deed, attracted her as well towards him, as him towards her.—She at once 'gave her eye and her voice a mask of joy ; for she did not put her tears, as Catholics do those of Christ, in relic-vials, upon altars to be worshipped. He could very suitably preface his invitation to the Pontac festival, with a long acknowledgment of thanks for the kind intervention which had opened to him the sources for procuring it. She rose slowly, and walked with him to the banquet of wine ; but he was not so discreet, as at first to attempt leading her, or rather not so courageous ; he could more easily have offered a young lady his hand (that is, with marriage ring) than offered her his arm. One only time in his life had he escorted a female, a Lombard Countess from the theatre ; a thing truly not to be believed, were not this the secret of it, that he was obliged ; for the lady, a foreigner, parted in the press from all her people, in a bad night, had laid hold of him as a sable Abbé by the arm, and requested him to take her to her inn. He, however, knew the fashions of society, and attended her no farther than the porch of his Quintus-mansion, and there directed her with his finger to her inn, which, with thirty blazing windows, was looking down from another street.

These things he cannot help. But to-night he had scarcely, with his fair faint companion, reached the bank of the pond, into which some superstitious dread

of water-sprites had lately poured the pure blood of
her left arm,—when, in his terror lest she fell in, with
the rest of her blood, over the brink, he quite valiantly
laid hold of the sick arm. Thus will much Pontac and a
little courage at all times put a Conrector in case to
lay hold of a Fräulein. I aver, that, at the banquet-
board of the wine, at the window-sill, he continued in
the same conducting position. What a soft group in
the penumbra of the Earth, while Night, with its dusky
waters, was falling deeper and deeper, and the silver-
light of the Moon was already glancing back from the
copper ball of the steeple! I call the group soft, because it consists of a maiden that in two senses has
been bleeding; of a mother again with tears giving her
thanks for the happiness of her child; and of a pious,
modest man, pouring wine, and drinking health to both,
and who traces in his veins a burning lava-stream, which
is boiling through his heart, and threatening piece by
piece to melt it and bear it away.—A candle stood
without among the three bottles, like Reason among
the Passions; on this account the Conrector looked
without intermission at the window-panes, for on them
(the darkness of the room served as mirror-foil) was
painted, among other faces which Fixlein liked, the
face he liked best of all, and which he dared to look at
only in reflexion, the face of Thiennette.

Every minute was a Federation-festival, and every
second a Preparation-Sabbath for it. The Moon was
gleaming from the evening dew, and the Pontac from

their eyes, and the bean-stalks were casting a shorter grating of shadow.—The quicksilver-drops of stars were hanging more and more continuous in the sable of night.—The warm vapour of the wine set our two friends (like steam-engines) again in motion.

Nothing makes the heart fuller and bolder than walking to and fro in the night. Fixlein now led the Fräulein in his arm without scruple. By reason of her lancet-wound, Thiennette could only put her hand, in a clasping position, in his arm ; and he, to save her the trouble of holding fast, held fast himself, and pressed her fingers as well as might be with his arm to his heart. It would betray a total want of polished manners to censure his. At the same time, trifles are the provender of Love ; the fingers are electric dischargers of a fire sparkling along every fibre ; sighs are the guiding tones of two approximating hearts ; and the worst and most effectual thing of all in such a case is some misfortune ; for the fire of Love, like that of Naphtha, likes to swim on water. Two teardrops, one in another's, one in your own eyes, compose, as with two convex lenses, a microscope which enlarges everything, and changes all sorrows into charms. Good sex ! I too consider every sister in misfortune as fair ; and, perhaps, thou wouldst deserve the name of the Fair, even because thou art the Suffering sex !

And if Professor Hunczogsky in Vienna modelled all the wounds of the human frame in wax, to teach his pupils how to cure them, I also, thou good sex, am representing in little figures the cuts and scars of thy spirit, though only to keep away rude hands from inflicting new ones. . . . .

Thiennette felt not the loss of the inheritance, but of her that should have left it; and this more deeply for one little trait, which she had already told his mother, as she now told him: In the last two nights of the Rittmeisterinn, when the feverish watching was holding up to Thiennette's imagination, nothing but the winding-sheet ánd the mourning-coaches of her protectress; while she was sitting at the foot of the bed, looking on those fixed eyes, unconsciously quick drops often trickled over her cheeks, while in thought she prefigured the heavy, cumbrous dressing of her benefactress for the coffin. Once after midnight, the dying lady pointed with her finger to her own lips. Thiennette understood her not; but rose and bent over her face. The Enfeebled tried to lift her head, but could not,—and only rounded her lips. At last, a thought glanced through Thiennette, that the Departing, whose dead arms could now press no beloved heart to her own, wished that she herself should embrace her. O then, that instant, keen and tearful she pressed her warm lips on the colder,—and she was silent like her that was to speak no more,—and she embraced alone and was not embraced. About four o'clock, the finger waved again;—she sank down on the stiffened lips— but this had been no signal, for the lips of her friend under the long kiss had grown stiff and cold. . . . .

How deeply now, before the infinite Eternity's-countenance of Night, did the cutting of this thought pass through Fixlein's warm soul: "O thou forsaken one beside me! No happy accident, no twilight hast thou, like that now glimmering in the heavens, to point to the prospect of a sunny day: without parents art thou, without brother, without friend; here alone on a dis-blossomed, emptied corner of the Earth; and thou, left Harvest-flower, must wave lonely and frozen over the withered stubble of the Past." That was the meaning of his thoughts, whose internal words were: "Poor young lady! Not so much as a half-cousin left; no nobleman will seek her, and she grows old so forgotten, and she is so good from the very heart—Me she has made happy—Ah, had I the presentation to the parish of Hukelum in my pocket, I should make a trial." ... Their mutual lives, which a straitcutting bond of Destiny was binding so closely together, now rose before him overhung with sable,—and he forthwith conducted his friend (for a bashful man may in an hour and a half be transformed into the boldest, and then continues so) back to the last flask, that all these upsprouting thistles and passion-flowers of sorrow might therewith be swept away. I remark, in passing, that this was stupid: the torn vine is full of water-veins as well as grapes; and a soft oppressed heart the beverage of joy can melt only into tears.

If any man disagree with me, I shall desire him to look at the Conrector, who demonstrates my experi-

mental maxim like a very syllogism.—One might arrive at some philosophic views, if one traced out the
causes, why liquors—that is to say, in the long run,
more plentiful secretion of the nervous spirits—make
men at once pious, soft, and poetical. The Poet, like
Apollo his father, is *for ever a youth;* and is, what
other men are only once, namely in love,—or only after
Pontac, namely intoxicated,—all his life long. Fixlein,
who had been no poet in the morning, now became one
at night : wine made him pious and soft ; the Harmonica-bells in man, which sound to the tones of a higher
world, must, like the glass Harmonica-bells, if they are
to act, be kept *moist.*

He was now standing with her again beside the wavering pond, in which the second blue hemisphere of
heaven, with dancing stars and amid quivering trees,
was playing ; over the green hills ran the white crooked footpaths dimly along ; on the one mountain was
the twilight sinking together, on the other was the mist
of night rising up ; and over all these vapours of life,
hung motionless and flaming the thousand-armed lustre
of the starry heaven, and every arm held in it a burning galaxy . . . .

It now struck eleven . . . Amid such scenes, an unknown hand stretches itself out in man, and writes in
foreign language on his heart, a dread *Mene Mene
Tekel Upharsin.* " Perhaps by twelve I am dead,"
thought our friend, in whose soul the Cantata-Sunday,
with all its black funeral piles, was mounting up.

The whole future Crucifixion-path of his friend lay prickly and bethorned before him ; and he saw every bloody trace from which she lifted her foot,—she who had made his own way soft with flowers and leaves. He could no longer restrain himself ; trembling in his whole frame, and with a trembling voice, he solemnly said to her : " If the Lord this night call me away, let the half of my fortune be yours ; for it is your good- ness I must thank that I am free of debts, as few Teachers are."

Thiennette, unacquainted with our sex, naturally mistook this speech for a proposal of marriage ; and the fingers of her wounded arm, to-night for the first time, pressed suddenly against the arm in which they lay ; the only living mortal's arm, by which Joy, Love, and the Earth, were still united with her bosom. The Conrector, rapturously terrified at the first pressure of a female hand, bent over his right to take hold of her left ; and Thiennette observing his unsuccessful move- ment, lifted her fingers, and laid her whole wounded arm in his, and her whole left hand in his right. Two lovers dwell in the Whispering-gallery,* where the faintest breath bodies itself forth into a sound. The good Conrector received and returned this blissful love- pressure, wherewith our poor powerless soul, stammer- ing, hemmed in, longing, distracted, seeks for a warmer

---

* In St Paul's Church at London, where the slightest whisper sounds over, across a space of 143 feet.

language, which exists not : he was overpowered ; he had not the courage to look at her ; but he looked into the gleam of the twilight, and said (and here for un-speakable love the tears were running warm over his cheeks) : " Ah, I will give you all ; fortune, life, and all that I have, my heart and my hand."

She was about to answer, but casting a side glance, she cried, with a shriek : " Ah, Heaven !" He started round ; and perceived the white muslin sleeve all dyed with blood ; for in putting her arm into his, she had pushed away the bandage from the open vein. With the speed of lightning, he hurried her into the acacia grove ; the blood was already running from the mus-lin ; he grew paler than she, for every drop of it was coming from his heart. The blue-white arm was bared ; the bandage was put on ; he tore a piece of gold from his pocket ; clapped it, as one does with open arteries, on the spouting fountain, and bolted with this golden bar, and with the bandage over it, the door out of which her afflicted life was hurrying.—

When it was over, she looked up to him ; pale, lan-guid, but her eyes were two glistening fountains of an unspeakable love, full of sorrow, and full of gratitude. —The exhausting loss of blood was spreading her soul asunder in sighs. Thiennette was dissolved into inex-pressible softness ; and the heart, lacerated by so many years, by so many arrows, was plunging with all its wounds in warm streams of tears, to be healed ; as chapped flutes close together by lying in water, and get

back their tones.—Before such a magic form, before
such a pure heavenly love, her sympathising friend was
melted between the flames of joy and grief; and sank,
with stifled voice, and bent down by love and rapture,
on the pale angelic face, the lips of which he timidly
pressed, but did not kiss, till all-powerful Love bound
its girdles round them, and drew the two closer and
closer together, and their two souls, like two tears,
melted into one. O now, when it struck twelve, the
hour of death, did not the lover fancy that her lips
were drawing his soul away, and all the fibres and all
the nerves of his life closed spasmodically round the
last heart in this world, round the last rapture of existence .... Yes, happy man, thou didst express thy love ;
for in thy love thou thoughtest to die....

However, he did not die. After midnight, there
floated a balmy morning air through the shaken flowers,
and the whole spring was breathing. The blissful lover,
setting bounds even to his sea of joy, reminded his delicate beloved, who was now his bride, of the dangers
from night-cold ; and himself of the longer night-
cold of Death, which was now for long years passed
over.—Innocent and blessed, they rose from the grove
of their betrothment, from its dusk broken by white
acacia flowers, and straggling moonbeams. And without, they felt as if a whole wide Past had sunk away
in a convulsion of the world ; all was new, light, and
young. The sky stood full of glittering dewdrops from
the everlasting Morning ; and the stars quivered joy-

fully asunder, and sank, resolved into beams, down into the hearts of men.—The Moon, with her fountain of light, had overspread and kindled all the garden ; and was hanging above in a starless Blue, as if she had consumed the nearest stars ; and she seemed like a smaller wandering Spring, like a Christ's-face smiling in love of man.—

Under this light, they looked at one another for the first time, after the first words of love ; and the sky gleamed magically down on the disordered features with which the first rapture of love was still standing written on their faces . . . .

Dream, ye beloved, as ye wake, happy as in Paradise, innocent as in Paradise !

SIXTH LETTER-BOX.

Office-impost.   One of the most important of Petitions.

THE finest thing was his awakening in his European Settlement in the giant Schadeck bed !—With the inflammatory, tickling, eating fever of love in his breast ; with the triumphant feeling, that he had now got the introductory program of love put happily by ; and with the sweet resurrection from his living prophetic burial ; and with the joy that now, among his thirties, he could, for the first time, cherish hopes of a longer life (and

did not longer mean at least till seventy?) than he could
ten years ago;—with all this stirring life-balsam, in
which the living fire-wheel of his heart was rapidly re-
volving, he lay here, and laughed at his glancing portrait in the bed-canopy ; but he could not do it long,
he was obliged to move. For a less happy man, it
would have been gratifying to have measured—as pil-
grims measure with the length of their pilgrimage—not
so much by steps as by body-lengths, like Earth-dia-
meters, the superficial content of the bed. But Fixlein, for his own part, had to launch from his bed into
warm billowy Life, he had now his dear good Earth
again to look after, and a Conrectorship thereon, and
a bride to boot. Besides all this, his mother down
stairs now admitted that he had last night actually
glided through beneath the scythe of Death, like sup-
ple grass, and that yesterday she had not told him
merely out of fear of his fear. Still a cold shudder
went over him—especially as he was sober now—when
he looked round at the high Tarpeian Rock, four hours'
distance behind him, on the battlements of which he
had last night walked hand in hand with Death.

The only thing that grieved him was, that it was
Monday, and that he must back to the Gymnasium.
Such a freightage of joys he had never taken with him
on his road to town. After four, he issued from his
house, satisfied with coffee (which he drank in Hukelum merely for his mother's sake, who, for two days
after, would still have portions of this woman's-wine to

draw from the lees of the pot-sediment) into the *cool-ing* dawning May-morning (for joy needs coolness, sorrow sun) ; his Betrothed comes—not indeed to meet him, but still—into his hearing, by her distant morning hymn ; he makes but one momentary turn into the blissful haven of the blooming acacia-grove, which still, like the covenant sealed in it, has no thorns ; he dips his warm hand in the cold-bath of the dewy leaves ; he wades with pleasure through the beautifying-water of the dew, which, as it imparts colour to faces, eats it away from boots, (" but with thirty ducats, a Conrec-tor may make shift to keep two pairs of boots on the hook").—And now the Moon, as it were the hanging seal of his last night's happiness, dips down into the West, like an emptied bucket of light, and in the East the other overrunning bucket, the Sun, mounts up, and the gushes of light flow broader and broader.—

The city stood in the celestial flames of Morning. Here his divining-rod (his gold-roll, which, excepting one sixteenth of an inch broken off from it, he carried along with him) began to quiver over all the spots where booty and silver-veins of enjoyment were con-cealed ; and our rod-diviner easily discovered that the city and the future were a true entire Potosi of de-lights.

In his Conrectorate closet, he fell upon his knees, and thanked God—not so much for his heritage and bride as—for his life : for he had gone away on Sun-day morning with doubts whether he should ever come back; and it was purely out of love to the reader, and fear lest he might fret himself too much with apprehension, that I cunningly imputed Fixlein's journey more to his desire of knowing what was in the will, than of making his own will in presence of his mother. Every recovery is a bringing back and palingenesia of our youth: one loves the Earth and those that are on it with a new love.—The Conrector could have found in his heart to take all his class by the locks, and press them to his breast; but he only did so to his adjutant, the Quartaner, who, in the first Letter-box, was still sitting in the rank of a Quintaner...

His first expedition, after school hours, was to the house of Meister Steinberger, where, without speaking a word, he counted down fifty florins cash, in ducats, on the table: " At last I repay you," said Fixlein, " the moiety of my debt, and give you many thanks."

" Ey, Herr Conrector," said the Quartermaster, and continued calmly stuffing puddings as before, " in my bond it is said, *payable at three months' mutual notice.* How could a man like me go on, else?—However, I will change you the gold-pieces." Thereupon he advised him that it might be more judicious to take back a florin or two, and buy himself a better hat, and whole shoes: " if you like," added he, " to get a calfskin and half a dozen hareskins dressed, they are lying up stairs."—I should think, for my own part, that to the reader it must be as little a matter of indifference as it was to the Butcher, whether the hero of such a History appear before him with an old tattered potlid of a hat, and a pump-sucker and leg-harness pair of boots, or in suitable apparel.—In short, before St John's day, the man was dressed with taste and pomp.

But now came two most peculiarly important papers—at bottom only one, the Petition for the Hukelum parsonship—to be elaborated; in regard to which I feel as if I myself must assist......It were a simple turn, if now at least the assembled public did not pay attention.

In the first place, the Conrector searched out and sorted all the Consistorial and Councillor quittances, or rather the toll-bills of the road-money, which he had been obliged to pay, before the toll-gates at the Quintusship and Conrectorship had been thrown open : for the executor of the Schadeck testament had to reimburse him the whole, as his discharge would express it, " to penny and farthing." Another would have summed up this post-excise much more readily ; by merely looking what he—owed ; as these debt-bills and those toll-bills, like parallel passages, elucidate and confirm each other. But in Fixlein's case, there was a small circumstance of peculiarity at work ; which I cannot explain till after what follows.

It grieved him a little that for his two offices he had been obliged to pay and to borrow no larger a sum than 135 florins, 41 kreutzers, and one half-penny.

The legacy, it is true, was to pass directly from the hands of the testamentary executor into those of the Regiments-Quartermaster ; but yet he could have liked well had he—for man is a fool from the very foundation of him—had more to pay, and therefore to inherit. The whole Conrectorate he had, by a slight deposit of 90 florins, plucked, as it were, from the Wheel of Fortune ; and so small a sum must surprise my reader : but what will he say, when I tell him that there are countries where the entry-money into schoolrooms is even more moderate? In Scherau, a Conrector is charged only 88 florins, and perhaps he may have an income triple of this sum. Not to speak of Saxony (what, in truth, was to be expected from the cradle of the Reformation, in Religion and Polite Literature), where a schoolmaster and a parson have *nothing* to pay,— even in Bayreuth, for example, in Hof, the progress of improvement has been such that a Quartus—a Quartus, do I say,—a Tertius—a Tertius, do I say,—a Conrector, at entrance on his post, is not required to pay down more than :

Fl. rhen.	Kr. rhen.	
30	49	For taking the oaths at the Consistorium.
4	0	To the Syndic for the Presentation.
2	0	To the then Burgermeister.
45	$7\frac{1}{2}$	For the Government-sanction.

Total 81 fl. $56\frac{1}{2}$ kr.

If the printing-charges of a Rector do stand a little higher in some points, yet, on the other hand, a Tertius, Quartus, &c., come cheaper from the press than even a Conrector. Now, it is clear, that in this case a schoolmaster can subsist; since, in the course of the very first year, he gets an overplus beyond this *dock-money* of his office. A schoolmaster must, like his scholars, have been advanced from class to class, before these his loans to Government, together with the interest for delay of payment, can jointly amount to so much as his yearly income in the highest class. Another thing in his favour is, that our institutions do not—as those of Athens did—prohibit people from entering on office, while in debt; but every man, with his debt-knapsack on his shoulders, mounts up, step after step, without obstruction. The Pope, in large benefices, appropriates the income of the first year under the title of *Annates*, or First Fruits; and accordingly he, in all cases, bestows any large benefice on the possessor of a smaller one, thereby to augment both his own revenues, and those of others; but it shows, in my opinion, a bright distinction between Popery and Lutheranism, that the Consistoriums of the latter abstract from their school-ministers and church-ministers not perhaps above two-thirds of their first yearly income; though they too, like the Pope, must naturally have an eye to vacancies.

It may be that I shall here come in collision with the Elector of Mentz, when I confess, that in Schmau-

sen's *Corp. jur. pub. Germ.,* I have turned up the
Mentz-Imperial-Court-Chancery-tax-ordinance of the
6th January 1659 ; and there investigated how much
this same Imperial-Court-Chancery demands, as con-
trasted with a Consistorium. For example, any man
that wishes to be baked or sodden into a *Poet Lau-
reate,* has 50 florins tax-dues, and 20 florins Chancery-
dues, to pay down ; whereas, for 20 florins more, he
might have been made a Conrector, who is a poet of
this species, as it were by the bye and *ex officio.*—The
institution of a Gymnasium is permitted for 1000 florins ; an extraordinary sum, with which the whole body
of the teachers in the instituted Gymnasium might
with us clear off the entrymonies of their schoolrooms.
Again, a Freiherr, who, at any rate, often enough grows
old without knowing how, must purchase the *venia
ætatis* with 200 hard florins ; while with the half sum
he might have become a schoolmaster, and here *age*
would have come of its own accord.—And a thousand
such things !—They prove, however, that matters can
be at no bad pass in our Governments and Circles,
where promotions are sold dearer to Folly than to Di-
ligence, and where it costs more to institute a school
than to serve in one.

The remarks I made on this subject to a Prince, as
well as the remarks a Town-Syndic made on it to myself, are too remarkable to be omitted for mere dread
of digressiveness.

The Syndic—a man of enlarged views, and of fiery

patriotism, the warmth of which was the more beneficent that he collected all the beams of it into one focus, and directed them to himself and his family—gave
me (I had perhaps been comparing the School-bench
and the School-stair to the *bench* and the *ladder*, on
which people are laid when about to be tortured) the
best reply : " If a schoolmaster consume nothing but
30 reichsthalers ;* if he annually purchase manufactured goods, according as Political Economists have
calculated for each individual, namely, to the amount
of 5 reichsthalers ; and no more hundredweights of vic-
tual than these assume, namely 10 ; in short, if he live
like a substantial wood-cutter,—then the Devil must
be in it, if he cannot yearly lay by so much net profit,
as shall, in the long run, pay the interest of his entry-
debts."

The Syndic must have failed to convince me at that
time, since I afterwards told the Flachsenfingen Prince:†
" Illustrious Sir, you know not, but I do—not a play-

---

* So much, according to Political Economists, a man yearly
requires in Germany.

† This singular tone of my address to a Prince can only be
excused by the equally singular relation, wherein the Biographer
stands to the Flachsenfingen Sovereign, and which I would willingly unfold here, were it not that, in my Book, which, under
the title of *Dog-post-days*, I mean to give to the world at Easter-
fair 1795, I hoped to expound the matter to universal satisfaction.

er in your Theatre would act the Schoolmaster in En-
gel's *Prodigal Son,* three nights running, for such a
sum as every real Schoolmaster has to take for acting
it all the days of the year.—In Prussia, Invalids are
made Schoolmasters; with us, Schoolmasters are made
Invalids."....

But to our story! Fixlein wrote out the inventory
of his Crown-debts; but with quite a different purpose
than the reader will guess, who has still the Schadeck
testament in his head. In one word, he wanted to be
Parson of Hukelum. To be a clergyman, and in the
place where his cradle stood, and all the little gardens
of his childhood, his mother also, and the grove of betrothment,—this was an open gate into a New Jerusalem, supposing even that the living had been nothing
but a meagre penitentiary. The main point was, he
might marry, if he were appointed. For, in the capacity of lank Conrector, supported only by the strength-
ening-girth of his waistcoat, and with emoluments
whereby scarcely the purchase-money of a—purse was
to be come at; in this way he was more like collecting
wick and tallow for his burial torch than for his bridal
one.

For the Schoolmaster class are, in well-ordered
states, as little permitted to marry as the Soldiery.
In *Conringius de Antiquitatibus Academicis,* where
in every leaf it is proved that all cloisters were ori-
ginally schools, I hit upon the reason. Our schools

are now cloisters, and consequently we endeavour to
maintain in our teachers at least an imitation of the
Three Monastic Vows. The vow of Obedience might
perhaps be sufficiently enforced by School-Inspectors ;
but the second vow, that of Celibacy, would be more
hard of attainment, were it not that, by one of the
best political arrangements, the third vow, I mean a
beautiful equality in Poverty, is so admirably attended
to, that no man who has made it needs any farther
testimonium paupertatis ;—and now *let* this man, if he
likes, lay hold of a matrimonial half, when of the two
halves each has a whole stomach, and nothing for it
but half-coins and half-beer !....

I know well, millions of my readers would themselves compose this Petition for the Conrector, and
ride with it to Schadeck to His Lordship, that so the
poor rogue might get the sheepfold, with the annexed
wedding-mansion : for they see clearly enough, that
directly thereafter one of the best Letter-Boxes would
be written that ever came from such a repository.

Fixlein's Petition was particularly good and striking :
it submitted to the Rittmeister four grounds of preference : 1. " He was a native of the parish : his parents and ancestors had already done Hukelum service ;
therefore he prayed," &c.

2. " The here documented official debts of 135
florins, 41 kreutzers, and one halfpenny, the cancelling
of which a never-to-be-forgotten testament secured
him, he himself could clear, in case he obtained the

living, and so hereby give up his claim to the legacy,"
&c.

Voluntary Note by me. It is plain he means to
bribe his Godfather, whom the lady's testament has put
into a fume. But, gentle reader, blame not without
mercy a poor, oppressed, heavy-laden school-man and
school-horse for an indelicate insinuation, which truly
was never mine. Consider, Fixlein knew that the
Rittmeister was a cormorant towards the poor, as he
was a squanderer towards the rich. It may be, too, the
Conrector might once or twice have heard, in the Law
Courts, of patrons, by whom not indeed the church
and churchyard—though these things are articles of
commerce in England—so much as the true management of them had been sold, or rather farmed to farm-
ing-candidates. I know from Lange,* that the Church
must support its patron, when he has nothing to live
upon : and might not a nobleman, before he actually
began begging, be justified in taking a little advance,
a fore-payment of his alimentary monies, from the hands
of his pulpit-farmer ?—

3. " He had lately betrothed himself with Fräulein
von Thiennette, and given her a piece of gold, as mar-
riage-pledge ; and could therefore wed the said Fräulein, were he once provided for," &c.

Voluntary Note by me. I hold this ground to be the

---

* His *Clerical Law*, p. 551.

strongest in the whole Petition. In the eyes of Herr
von Aufhammer, Thiennette's genealogical tree was
long since stubbed, disleaved, worm-eaten, and full of
millepedes: she was his Œconoma, his Castle-Stew-
ardess, and Legatess *a Latere* for his domestics; and
with her pretensions for an alms-coffer, was threatening in the end to become a burden to him. His indignant wish that she had been provided for with Fixlein's
legacy might now be fulfilled. In a word, if Fixlein
become Parson, he will have the third ground to thank
for it; not at all the mad fourth.....

4. " He had learned with sorrow, that the name of
his Shock, which he had purchased from an Emigrant
at Leipzig, meant Egidius in German; and that the
dog had drawn upon him the displeasure of His Lordship. Far be it from him so to designate the Shock in
future; but he would take it as a special grace, if for
the dog, which he at present called without any name,
His Lordship would be pleased to appoint one himself."

My Voluntary Note. The dog then, it seems, to
which the nobleman has hithertoo been godfather, is to
receive its name a *second* time from him !—But how
can the famishing gardener's son, whose career never
mounted higher than from the school-bench to the
school-chair, and who never spoke with polished ladies, except singing, namely in the church, how can he
be expected, in fingering such a string, to educe from
it any finer tone than the pedantic one ? And yet the

source of it lies deeper: not the contracted *situation*, but the contracted *eye*, not a favourite science, but a narrow plebeian soul, makes us pedantic, a soul that cannot *measure* and *separate* the *concentric* circles of human knowledge and activity, that confounds the focus of universal human life, by reason of the focal distance, with every two or three converging rays; and that cannot see all, and tolerate all——In short, the true Pedant is the Intolerant.

The Conrector wrote out his Petition splendidly in five propitious evenings; employed a peculiar ink for the purpose; worked not indeed so long over it as the stupid Manucius over a Latin letter, namely, some months, if Scioppius' word is to be taken; still less so long as another scholar at a Latin epistle, who—truly we have nothing but Morhof's word for it—hatched it during four whole months; inserting his variations, adjectives, feet, with the authorities for his phrases, accurately marked between the lines. Fixlein possessed a more thorough-going genius, and had completely mastered the whole enterprise in sixteen days. While sealing, he thought, as we all do, how this cover was the seed-husk of a great entire Future, the rind of many sweet or bitter fruits, the swathing of his whole after life.

Heaven bless his cover; but I let you throw me from the Tower of Babel, if he get the parsonage: can't you see, then, that Aufhammer's hands are tied?

In spite of all his other faults, or even because of them, he will stand like iron by his word, which he has given so long ago to the Subrector. It were another matter had he been resident at Court; for there, where old German manners still are, no promise is kept; for as, according to Möser, the Ancient Germans kept only such promises as they made in the *forenoon* (in the afternoon they were all dead-drunk),—so the Court Germans likewise keep no afternoon promise; fore-noon ones they would keep if they made any, which, however, cannot possibly happen, as at those hours they are—sleeping.

SEVENTH LETTER-BOX.

Sermon. School-Exhibition. Splendid Mistake.

THE Conrector received his 135 florins, 43 kreut-zers, one halfpenny Frankish; but no answer: the dog remained without name, his master without parsonage. Meanwhile the summer passed away; and the Dra-goon Rittmeister had yet drawn out no pike from the Candidate *breeding-pond*, and thrown him into the *feed-ing-pond* of the Hukelum parsonage. It gratified him to be behung with prayers like a Spanish guardian Saint; and he postponed (though determined to prefer the Sub-rector) granting any one petition, till he had seven-and-thirty dyers', buttonmakers', tinsmiths' sons, whose

petitions he could at the same time refuse. Grudge
not him of Aufhammer this outlengthening of his elec-
torial power ! He knows the privileges of rank ; feels
that a nobleman is like Timoleon, who gained his
greatest victories on his birth-day, and had nothing
more to do than name some squiress, countess, or the
like, as his mother. A man, however, who has been
exalted to the Peerage, while still a fœtus, may with
more propriety be likened to the *spinner,* which, contrariwise to all other insects, passes from the chrysalis
state, and becomes a perfect insect in its mother's
womb.—

But to proceed ! Fixlein was at present not without
cash. It will be the same as if I made a present of it
to the reader, when I reveal to him, that of the legacy,
which was clearing off old scores, he had still 35 florins left to himself, as *allodium* and pocket-money,
wherewith he might purchase whatsoever seemed good
to him. And how came he by so large a sum, by so
considerable a competence ? Simply by this means :
Every time he changed a piece of gold, and especially
at every payment he received, it had been his custom
to throw in, blindly at random, two, three, or four
small coins, among the papers of his trunk. His purpose was to astonish himself one day, when he summed
up and took possession of this sleeping capital. And,
by Heaven ! he reached it too, when on mounting
the throne of his Conrectorate, he drew out these funds
from among his papers, and applied them to the coro-

nation charges. For the present, he sowed them in
again among his waste letters. Foolish Fixlein! I
mean, had he not luckily exposed his legacy to jeo-
pardy, having offered it as bounty-money, and luckpenny to the patron, this false clutch of his at the
knocker of the Hukelum church door, would certainly
have vexed him; but now if he had missed the knocker, he had the luckpenny again, and could be merry.

I now advance a little way in his History, and hit,
in the rock of his Life, upon so fine a vein of silver, I
mean upon so fine a day, that I must (I believe) content myself even in regard to the twenty-third of Trinity-term, when he preached a vacation sermon in his
dear native village, with a brief transitory notice.

In itself the sermon was good and glorious ; and the
day a rich day of pleasure ; but I should really need
to have more hours at my disposal, than I can steal
from May, in which I am at present living and writing ; and more strength than wandering through this
fine weather has left me for landscape pictures of the
same, before I could attempt, with any well-founded
hope, to draw out a mathematical estimate of the
length and thickness, and the vibrations and accordant
relations to each other, of the various strings, which
combined together to form for his heart a Music of the
Spheres, on this day of Trinity-term, though such a
thing would please myself as much as another. . . . . .
Do not ask me ! In my opinion, when a man preaches
on Sunday before all the peasants, who had carried

him in their arms when a gardener's boy; farther, before his mother, who is leading off her tears through
the conduit of her satin muff; farther, before His Lordship, whom he can positively command to be blessed;
and finally, before his muslin bride, who is already
blessed, and changing almost into stone, to find that
the same lips can both kiss and preach: in my opinion,
I say, when a man effects all this, he has some right to
require of any Biographer who would paint his situation, that he—hold his jaw; and of the reader who
would sympathize with it, that he open his, and preach
himself.— —

But what I must *ex officio* depict, is the day to
which this Sunday was but the prelude, the vigil, and
the whet; I mean the prelude, the vigil and the whet
to the *Martini Actus*, or *Martinmas Exhibition*, of
his school.   On Sunday was the sermon, on Wednesday the Actus, on Tuesday the Rehearsal.   This Tuesday shall now be delineated to the universe.

I count upon it that I shall not be read by mere
people of the world alone, to whom a School-Actus
cannot truly appear much better, or more interesting,
than some Investiture of a Bishop, or the *opera seria*
of a Frankfort Coronation; but that I likewise have
people before me, who have been at schools, and who
know how the school-drama of an Actus, and the
stage-manager, and the playbill (the Program) thereof
are to be estimated, still without over-rating their importance.

Before proceeding to the Rehearsal of the *Martini Actus*, I impose upon myself, as dramaturgist of the play, the duty, if not of extracting, at least of recording the Conrector's Letter of Invitation. In this composition he said many things; and (what an author likes so well) made proposals rather than reproaches; interrogatively reminding the public, Whether in regard to the well-known head-breakages of Priscian on the part of the Magnates in Pest and Poland, our school-houses were not the best quarantine and lazar-houses to protect us against infectious *barbarisms?* Moreover, he defended in schools what could be defended (and nothing in the world is sweeter or easier than a defence); and said, Schoolmasters, who not quite justifiably, like certain Courts, spoke nothing, and let nothing be spoken to them but Latin, might plead the Romans in excuse, whose subjects, and whose kings, at least in their epistles and public transactions, were obliged to make use of the Latin tongue. He wondered why only our Greek, and not also our Latin Grammars, were composed in Latin, and put the pregnant question : Whether the Romans, when they taught their little children the Latin tongue, did it in any other than in this same ? Thereupon he went over to the Actus, and said what follows, in his own words :

" I am minded to prove, in a subsequent Invitation, that everything which can be said or known about the great founder of the Reformation, the subject of our present Martini Prolusions, has been long ago exhausted, as well by Seckendorf as others. In fact, with regard to Luther's personalities, his table-talk, incomes, journeys, clothes, and so forth, there can now nothing new be brought forward, if at the same time it is to be true. Nevertheless, the field of the Reformation history is, to speak in a figure, by no means wholly cultivated; and it does appear to me as if the inquirer even of the present day might in vain look about for correct intelligence respecting the children, grandchildren, and children's children, down to our own times, of this great Reformer; all of whom, however, appertain, in a more remote degree, to the Reformation history, as he himself in a nearer. Thou shalt not perhaps be threshing, said I to myself, altogether empty straw, if, according to thy small ability, thou bring forward and cultivate this neglected branch of History. And so have I ventured, with the last male descendant of Luther, namely, with the Advocate Martin Gottlob Luther, who practised in Dresden, and deceased there in 1759, to make a beginning of a more special Reformation history. My feeble attempt, in regard to this Reformationary Advocate, will be sufficiently rewarded, should it excite to better works on the subject: however, the little which I have succeeded in digging up and collecting with regard to him, I here submissively, obediently, and humbly request all friends and patrons of the Flachsenfingen Gymnasium to listen to, on the 14th of November, from the mouths of six well-conditioned perorators. In the first place, shall

" *Gottlieb Spiesglass,* a Flachsenfinger, endeavour to show, in a Latin oration, that Martin Gottlob Luther was certainly descended of the Luther family.   After him strives

" *Friedrich Christian Krabbler,* from Hukelum, in German prose, to appreciate the influence which Martin Gottlob Luther exercised on the then existing Reformation ; whereupon, after him, will

" *Daniel Lorenz Stenzinger* deliver, in Latin verse, an account of Martin Gottlob Luther's lawsuits ; embracing the probable merits of Advocates generally, in regard to the Reformation.   Which then will give opportunity to

" *Nikol Tobias Pfizman* to come forward in French, and recount the most important circumstances of Martin Gottlob Luther's school-years, university-life, and riper age.   And now, when

" *Andreas Eintarm* shall have endeavoured, in German verse, to apologise for the possible failings of this representative of the great Luther, will

" *Justus Strobel,* in Latin verse according to ability, sing his uprightness and integrity in the Advocate profession ; whereafter I myself shall mount the cathedra, and most humbly thank all the patrons of the Flachsenfingen School, and then farther bring forward those portions in the life of this remarkable man, of which we yet know absolutely nothing, they being spared *Deo volente* for the speakers of the next *Martini Actus.*"

The day before the Actus offered as it were the proof-shot and sample-sheet of the Wednesday. Persons who on account of dress could not be present at the great school-festival, especially ladies, made their appearance on Tuesday, during the six proof-orations. No one can be readier than I to subordinate the proof-Actus to the Wednesday-Actus; and I do anything but need being stimulated suitably to estimate the solemn feast of a School: but on the other hand I am equally convinced that no one, who did not go to the real Actus of Wednesday, could possibly figure anything more splendid than the proof-day preceding; because he could have no object wherewith to compare the pomp in which the Primate of the festival drove in with his triumphal chariot and six—to call the six brethren-speakers coach-horses—next morning in presence of ladies and Councillor gentlemen. Smile away, Fixlein, at this astonishment over thy today's *Ovation*, which is leading on tomorrow's *Triumph* : on thy dissolving countenance quivers happy Self, feeding on these incense-fumes ; but a vanity like thine, and that only, which enjoys without comparing or despising, can one tolerate, will one foster. But what flowed over all his heart, like a melting sunbeam over wax, was his mother, who after much persuasion had ventured in her Sunday's clothes humbly to place herself quite low down, beside the door of the Prima class-room. It were difficult to say who is happier, the mother, beholding how he whom she has borne under her heart can direct such

noble young gentlemen, and hearing how he along with
them can talk of these really high things and understand them too ;—or the son, who, like some of the heroes of Antiquity, has the felicity of triumphing in the
lifetime of his mother. I have never in my writings or
doings cast a stone upon the late Burchardt Grossmann,
who under the initial letters of the stanzas in his song
" *Brich an, du liebe Morgenröthe,*" inserted the letters
of his own name ; and still less have I ever censured
any poor herbwoman for smoothing out her winding-
sheet, while still living, and making herself one-twelfth
of a dozen of grave-shifts. Nor do I regard the man
as wise—though indeed as very clever and pedantic—
who can fret his gall-bladder full because every one of
us leaf-miners views the leaf whereon he is mining as
a park-garden, as a fifth Quarter of the World (so near
and rich is it) ; the leaf-pores as so many Valleys of
Tempe, the leaf-skeleton as a Liberty-tree, a Bread-tree,
and Life-tree, and the dewdrops as the Ocean. We poor
day-moths, evening-moths, and night-moths, fall uni-
versally into the same error, only on different leaves ;
and whosoever (as I do) laughs at the important airs
with which the schoolmaster issues his programs, the
dramaturgist his playbills, the classical variation-alms-
gatherer his alphabetic letters,—does it, if he is wise
(as is the case here), with the consciousness of his own
similar folly ; and laughs in regard to his neighbour, at
nothing but mankind and himself.

The mother was not to be detained : she must off,

this very night, to Hukelum, to give the Fräulein
Thiennette at least some tidings of this glorious business.——

And now the World will bet a hundred to one, that
I forthwith take biographical wax, and emboss such a
wax-figure cabinet of the Actus itself as shall be single
of its kind.

But on Wednesday morning, while the hope-intoxi-
cated Conrector was just about putting on his fine
raiment, something knocked. —— ——

It was the well-known servant of the Rittmeister,
carrying the Hukelum Presentation for the Subrector
*Füchs*lein in his pocket. To the last-named gentleman he had been sent with this call to the parsonage :
but he had distinguished ill betwixt *Sub* and *Con-*
rector ; and had besides his own good reasons for di-
recting his steps to the latter ; for he thought : " Who
can it be that gets it, but the parson that preached last
Sunday, and that comes from the village, and is engaged to our Fräulein Thiennette, and to whom I brought
a clock and a roll of ducats already." That His Lordship could pass over his own godson, never entered the
man's head.

Fixlein read the address of the Appointment : " To
the Reverend the Parson *Fixlein* of Hukelum." He
naturally enough made the same mistake as the lackey ;
and broke up the Presentation as his own : and finding moreover in the body of the paper no special mention of persons, but only of an *Schul-unterbefehlsha-*

ber or School-undergovernor (instead of Subrector), he could not but persist in his error. Before I properly explain why the Rittmeister's Lawyer, the framer of the Presentation, had so designated a Subrector—we two, the reader and myself, will keep an eye for a moment on Fixlein's joyful saltations—on his gratefully-streaming eyes—on his full hands so laden with bounty—on the present of two ducats, which he drops into the hands of the mitre-bearer, as willingly as he will soon drop his own pedagogic office. Could he tell what to think (of the Rittmeister), or to write (to the same), or to table (for the lackey)? Did he not ask tidings of the noble health of his benefactor over and over, though the servant answered him with all distinctness at the very first? And was not this same man, who belonged to the nose-upturning, shoulder-shrugging, shoulder-knotted, toad-eating species of men, at last so moved by the joy which he had imparted, that he determined on the spot, to bestow his presence on the new clergyman's School-Actus, though no person of quality whatever was to be there? Fixlein, in the first place, sealed his letter of thanks; and courteously invited this messenger of good news to visit him frequently in the Parsonage; and to call this evening in passing at his mother's, and give her a lecture for not staying last night, when she might have seen the Presentation from His Lordship arrive to-day.

The lackey being gone, Fixlein for joy began to grow sceptical—and timorous (wherefore, to prevent filching,

2

he stowed his Presentation securely in his coffer, under
keeping of two padlocks) ; and devout and softened,
since he thanked God without scruple for all good that
happened to him, and never wrote this Eternal Name
but in pulpit characters, and with coloured ink ; as the
Jewish copyists never wrote it except ornamental letters and when newly washed ;*—and deaf also did the
parson grow, so that he scarcely heard the soft wooing-
hour of the Actus—for a still softer one beside Thiennette, with its rose-bushes and rose-honey, would not
leave his thoughts. He who of old, when Fortune made
a wry face at him, was wont, like children in their sport
at one another, to laugh at her so long till she herself
was obliged to begin smiling—he was now flying as on
a huge seesaw higher and higher, quicker and quicker
aloft.

But before the Actus, let us examine the Shadeck
Lawyer. *Fixlein* instead of *Füchslein*† he had written
from uncertainty about the spelling of the name; the more
naturally as in transcribing the Rittmeisterinn's will
the former had occurred so often. *Von*, this triumphal
arch, he durst not set up before Füchslein's new name,
because Aufhammer forbade it, considering Hans Füchslein as a mushroom who had no right to *vons* and titles

---

* Eichhorn's *Einleit ins A. T.* (Introduction to the Old Testament), vol. II.
† Both have the same sound. *Füchslein* means Foxling, Fox-
whelp.—ED.

of nobility, for all his patents. In fine, the Presenta-
tion-writer was possessed with Campe's* whim of Ger-
manising everything, minding little though when Ger-
manised it should cease to be intelligible ;—as if a word
needed any better act of naturalisation than that which
universal intelligibility imparts to it. In itself it is the
same—the rather as all languages, like all men, are
cognate, intermarried and intermixed—whether a word
was invented by a savage or a foreigner ; whether
it grew up like moss amid the German forests, or like
street-grass, in the pavement of the Roman Forum.
The Lawyer, on the other hand, contended that it was
different; and accordingly he hid not from any of his
clients that *Tagefarth* (Day-turn) meant *Term*, and
that *Appealing* was *Berufen* (Becalling). On this principle, he dressed the word *Subrector* in the new livery
of *School-undergovernor*. And this version farther con-
verted the Schoolmaster into Parson : to such a degree
does our *civic* fortune—not our *personal* well-being,
which supports itself on our own internal soil and re-

---

* Campe, a German philologist, who, along with several others
of that class, has really proposed, as represented in the Text, to
substitute for all Greek or Latin derivatives corresponding German terms of the like import. *Geography*, which may be *Erdbe-
schreibung* (Earth-description), was thenceforth to be nothing
else ; a *Geometer* became an *Earthmeasurer*, &c. &c. *School-
undergovernor*, instead of *Subrector*, is by no means the happiest
example of the system, and seems due rather to the Schadeck
Lawyer than to Campe, whom our Author has elsewhere more
than once eulogized for his project in similar style.—ED.

sources—grow merely on the *drift-mould* of accidents,
connexions, acquaintances, and Heaven or the Devil
knows what !—

By the bye, from a Lawyer, at the same time a
Country Judge, I should certainly have looked for
more sense ; I should (I may be mistaken) have presumed he knew that the *Acts*, or Reports, which in
former times (see Hoffmann's *German, or un-German
Law-practice*) were written in Latin, as before the
times of Joseph the Hungarian,—are now, if we may
say so without offence, perhaps written fully more in
the German dialect than in the Latin ; and in support
of this opinion, I can point to whole lines of German
language, to be found in these Imperial-Court-Confes-
sions. However, I will not believe that the Jurist is
endeavouring, because Imhofer declares the Roman
tongue to be the mother tongue in the other world,
to disengage himself from a language, by means of
which, like the Roman *Eagle,* or later, like the Roman *Fish-heron* (Pope), he has clutched such abun-
dant booty in his talons.— —

Toll, toll your bell for the Actus ; stream in, in to
the ceremony : who cares for it ? Neither I nor the
Ex-Conrector. The six pigmy Ciceros will in vain set
forth before us in sumptuous dress their thoughts and
bodies. The draught-wind of Chance has blown away
from the Actus its powder-nimbus of glory ; and the
Conrector that was has discovered how small a matter
a cathedra is, and how great a one a pulpit : " I should

not have thought," thought he now, " when I became
Conrector, that there could be anything grander, I
mean a Parson." Man, behind his everlasting blind,
which he only colours differently, and makes no thin-
ner, carries his pride with him from one step to another ;
and, on the higher step, blames only the pride of the
lower.

The best of the Actus was, that the Regiments-
Quartermaster, and Master Butcher, Steinberg, attended there, embaled in a long woollen shag. During
the solemnity, the Subrector Hans von Füchslein cast
several gratified and inquiring glances on the Shadeck
servant, who did not once look at him : Hans would
have staked his head, that after the Actus, the fellow
would wait upon him. When at last the sextuple cock-
erel-brood had on their dunghill done crowing, that is
to say, had perorated, the scholastic cocker, over whom
a higher banner was now waving, himself came upon the
stage ; and delivered to the School-Inspectorships, to
the Subrectorship, to the Guardianship, and the Lack-
eyship, his most grateful thanks for their attendance ;
shortly announcing to them at the same time, " that
Providence had now called him from his post to another ; and committed to him, unworthy as he was, the
cure of souls in the Hukelum parish, as well as in the
Schadeck chapel of ease."

This little address, to appearance, well nigh blew
up the then Subrector Hans von Füchslein from his
chair ; and his face looked of a mingled colour, like red

bole, green chalk, tinsel-yellow, and *vomissement de la reine.*

The tall Quartermaster erected himself considerably in his shag, and hummed loud enough in happy forgetfulness : " The Dickens !—Parson ?"——

The Subrector dashed by like a comet before the lackey ; ordered him to call and take a letter for his master ; strode home, and prepared for his patron, who at Schadeck was waiting for a long thanksgiving psalm, a short satirical epistle, as nervous as haste would permit, and mingled a few nicknames and verbal injuries along with it.

The courier handed in, to his master, Fixlein's song of gratitude, and Füchslein's invectives, with the same hand. The Dragoon Rittmeister, incensed at the ill-mannered churl, and bound to his word, which Fixlein had publicly announced in his Actus, forthwith wrote back to the new Parson an acceptance and ratification ; and Fixlein is and remains, to the joy of us all, incontestible ordained parson of Hukelum.

His disappointed rival has still this consolation, that he holds a seat in the wasp-nest of the *Neue Allgemeine Deutsche Bibliothek.** Should the Parson ever chrysalise himself into an author, the watch-wasp may then buzz out, and dart its sting into the chrysalis, and

---

* *New Universal German Library*, a reviewing periodical ; in those days conducted by Nicolai, a sworn enemy to what has since been called the New School. (See § Tieck in vol. II.)—ED.

put its own brood in the room of the murdered butterfly. As the Subrector everywhere went about, and threatened in plain terms that he would review his colleague, let not the public be surprised that Fixlein's *Errata,* and his Masoretic *Exercitationes,* are to this hour withheld from it.

In spring, the widowed church receives her new husband; and how it will be, when Fixlein, under a canopy of flower-trees, takes the *Sponsa Christi* in one hand, and his own *Sponsa* in the other—this, without an Eighth Letter-Box, which, in the present case, may be a true jewel-box and rainbow-key,* can no mortal figure, except the *Sponsus* himself.

EIGHTH LETTER-BOX.

Instalment in the Parsonage.

ON the 15th of April 1793, the reader may observe, far down in the hollow, three baggage-waggons groaning along. These baggage-waggons are transporting the house-gear of the new Parson to Hukelum : the proprietor himself, with a little escort of his parishioners, is marching at their side, that of his china sets and

---

* Superstition declares, that on the spot where the rainbow rises, a golden key is left.

household furniture, there may be nothing broken in the eighteenth century, as the whole came down to him unbroken from the seventeenth. Fixlein hears the School-bell ringing behind him ; but this chime now sings to him, like a curfew, the songs of future rest : he is now escaped from the Death-valley of the Gym- nasium, and admitted into the abodes of the Blessed. Here dwells no envy, no colleague, no Subrector ; here in the heavenly country, no man works in the *New Universal German Library;* here, in the heavenly Hukelumic Jerusalem, they do nothing but sing praises in the church ; and here the Perfected requires no more increase of knowledge . . . Here too one need not sor- row that Sunday and Saint's day so often fall together into one.

Truth to tell, the Parson goes too far : but it was his way from of old never to paint out the whole and half shadows of a situation, till he was got into a new one ; the beauties of which he could then enhance by contrast with the former. For it requires little reflec- tion to discover that the torments of a schoolmaster are nothing so extraordinary ; but, on the contrary, as in the Gymnasium, he mounts from one degree to another, not very dissimilar to the common torments of Hell, which, in spite of their eternity, grow weaker from century to century. Moreover, since, according to the saying of a Frenchman, *deux afflictions mises ensemble peuvent devenir une consolation,* a man gets afflictions enow in a school to console him ; seeing out of eight combined afflictions—I reckon only one for every teacher—certainly more comfort is to be extracted than out of two. The only pity is, that school-people will never act towards each other as court-people do : none but polished men and polished glasses will readily cohere. In addition to all this, in schools—and in offices generally— one is always recompensed : for, as in the second life, a greater virtue is the recompense of an earthly one, so, in the Schoolmaster's case, his merits are always rewarded by more opportunities for new merits ; and often enough he is not dismissed from his post at all.—

Eight Gymnasiasts are trotting about in the Parsonage, setting up, nailing to, hauling in. I think, as a scholar of Plutarch, I am right to introduce such seeming *minutiæ*. A man whom grown-up people love, children love still more. The whole school had smiled on the smiling Fixlein, and liked him in their hearts, because he did not thunder, but sport with them ; because he said *Sie* (They), to the Secundaners, and the Subrector said *Ihr* (Ye) ; because his uprearing forefinger was his only sceptre and baculus ; because in the Secunda he had interchanged Latin epistles with his scholars ; and in the Quinta, had taught not with Napier's Rods (or rods of a sharper description), but with sticks of barley-sugar.

To-day his churchyard appeared to him so solemn and festive, that he wondered (though it was Monday) why his parishioners were not in their holiday, but merely in their weekday drapery. Under the door

of the Parsonage stood a weeping woman ; for she w s
too happy, and he was her—son.   Yet the mother, in
the height of her emotion, contrives quite readily to
call upon the carriers, while disloading, not to twist
off the four corner globes from the old Frankish chest
of drawers. Her son now appeared to her as venerable, as if he had sat for one of the copperplates in her
pictured Bible ; and that simply, because he had cast
off his pedagogue hair-cue, as the ripening tadpole does
its tail ; and was now standing in a clerical perriwig before her : he was now a Comet, soaring away from the
profane Earth, and had accordingly changed from a
stella caudata into a *stella crinita.*

His bride also had, on former days, given sedulous
assistance in this new improved edition of his house,
and laboured faithfully among the other furnishers and
furbishers. But to-day she kept aloof ; for she was too
good to forget the maiden in the bride. Love, like
men, dies oftener of excess than of hunger ; it lives on
love, but it resembles those Alpine flowers, which
freed themselves by *suction* from the wet clouds, and
die if you *besprinkle* them.—

At length the Parson is settled, and of course he
must—for I know my fair readers, who are bent on it
as if they were bridemaids—without delay get married.
But he may not : before Ascension-day there can nothing be done, and till then are full four weeks and a
half. The matter was this : He wished in the first
place to have the murder-Sunday, the Cantata, behind

him ; not indeed because he doubted of his earthly
continuance, but because he would not (even for the
bride's sake) that the slightest apprehension should
mingle with these weeks of glory.

The main reason was, He did not wish to marry till
he were betrothed ; which latter ceremony was appointed, with the Introduction Sermon, to take place
next Sunday. It is the Cantata-Sunday. Let not the
reader afflict himself with fears. Indeed, I should not
have molested an enlightened century with this Sunday-
Wauwau at all, were it not that I delineate with such
extreme fidelity. Fixlein himself—especially as the
Quartermaster asked him if he was a baby—at last
grew so sensible, that he saw the folly of it ; nay, he
went so far, that he committed a greater folly. For as
dreaming that you die signifies, according to the exe-
getic *rule of false*, nothing else than long life and wel-
fare, so did Fixlein easily infer that his death-imagina-
tion was just such a lucky dream ; the rather as it was
precisely on this Cantata-Sunday that Fortune had
turned up her cornucopia over him, and at once show-
ered down out of it a bride, a presentation, and a roll
of ducats. Thus can Superstition imp its wings, let
Chance favour it or not.

A Secretary of State, a Peace-treaty writer, a Notary, any such incarcerated Slave of the Desk, feels
excellently well how far he is beneath a Parson composing his inaugural sermon. The latter (do but look
at my Fixlein) lays himself heartily over the paper—

injects the venous system of his sermon-preparation
with coloured ink—has a Text-Concordance on the
right side, and a Song-Concordance on the left; is
there digging out a marrowy sentence, here clipping
off a song-blossom with both to garnish his homiletic
pastry;—sketches out the finest plan of operations,
not, like a man of the world, to subdue the heart of
one woman, but the hearts of all women that hear him,
and of their husbands to boot;—draws every peasant
passing by his window into some niche of his discourse, to co-operate with the result;—and, finally,
scoops out the butter of the smooth soft hymn-book,
and therewith exquisitely fattens the black broth of
his sermon, which is to feed five thousand men.— —

At last, in the evening, as the red sun is dazzling
him at the desk, he can rise with heart free from guilt;
and, amid twittering sparrows and finches, over the
cherry-trees encircling the parsonage, look toward the
west, till there is nothing more in the sky but a faint
gleam among the clouds. And then when Fixlein,
amid the tolling of the evening prayer-bell, *slowly* de-
scends the stair to his cooking mother, there must be
some miracle in the case, if for him whatever has been
done or baked, or served up in the lower regions, is
not right and good .... A bound, after supper, into
the Castle; a look into a pure loving eye; a word without falseness to a bride without falseness; and then
under the coverlid, a soft-breathing breast, in which
there is nothing but Paradise, a sermon, and evening

prayer . . . . I swear, with this I will satisfy a My-
thic God, who has left his Heaven, and is seeking a
new one among us here below !

Can a mortal, can a Me in the wet clay of Earth,
which Death will soon dry into dust, ask more in one
week, than Fixlein is gathering into his heart ? I see
not how : At least I should suppose, if such a dust-
framed being, after such a twenty-thousand prize from
the Lottery of Chance, could require aught more, it
would at most be the twenty-one-thousand prize,
namely, the inaugural discourse itself.

And this prize our Zebedäus actually drew on Sunday:
he preached—he preached with unction,——he did it
before the crowding, rustling, press of people ; before his
Guardian, and before the Lord of Aufhammer, the godfather of the priest and the dog ;—a flock with whom in
childhood he had driven out the Castle herds about the
pasture, he was now, himself a spiritual sheep-smearer,
leading out to pasture ;—he was standing to the an-
cles among Candidates and Schoolmasters, for to-day
(what none of them could) at the altar, with the nail
of his finger, he might scratch a large cross in the air,
baptisms and marriages not once mentioned I
believe, I should feel less scrupulous than I do to che-
quer this sunshiny esplanade with that thin shadow
of the grave, which the preacher threw over it, when,
in the application, with wet heavy eyes, he looked
round over the mute attentive church, as if in some
corner of it he would seek the mouldering teacher of

his youth and of this congregation, who without, under the white tombstone, the wrong-side of life, had laid away the garment of his pious spirit.   And when he, himself hurried on by the internal stream, inexpressibly softened by the farther recollections of his own fear of death on this day, of his life now overspread with flowers and benefits, of his entombed benefactress resting here in her narrow bed—when he now—before the dissolving countenance of her friend, his Thiennette,—overpowered, motionless, and weeping, looked down from the pulpit to the door of the Schadeck vault, and said : " Thanks, thou pious soul, for the good thou hast done to this flock and to their new teacher ; and, in the fulness of time, may the dust of thy god-fearing and man-loving breast gather itself, transfigured as gold-dust, round thy reawakened heavenly heart,"—was there an eye in the audience dry ? Her husband sobbed aloud, and Thiennette, her beloved, bowed her head, sinking down with inconsolable remembrances, over the front of the seat, like kindred mourners in a funeral train.

No fairer forenoon could prepare the way for an afternoon in which a man was to betroth himself for ever, and to unite the exchanged rings with the Ring of Eternity.   Except the bridal pair, there was none present but an ancient pair ; the mother and the long Guardian. The bridegroom wrote out the marriage-contract or marriage-charter with his own hand ; hereby making over to his bride, from this day, his whole

moveable property (not, as you may suppose, his
pocket-library, but his whole library; whereas, in the
Middle Ages, the daughter of a noble was glad to get
one or two books for marriage-portion);—in return for
which, she liberally enough contributed—a whole nup-
tial coach or car, laden as follows : with nine pounds
of feathers, not feathers for the cap such as we carry,
but of the lighter sort such as carry us;—with a
sumptuous dozen of godchild-plates and godchild-
spoons (gifts from Schadeck), together with a fish-
knife ;—of silk, not only stockings (though even King
Henry II. of France could dress no more than his legs
in silk), but whole gowns ;—with jewels and other
furnishings of smaller value. Good Thiennette ! in
the chariot of thy spirit lies the true dowry ; namely,
thy noble, soft, modest heart, the morning-gift of Nature !

The Parson,—who, not from mistrust but from "the
uncertainty of life," could have wished for a notary's
seal on everything ; to whom no security but a hypo-
thecary one appeared sufficient, and who, in the depo-
siting of every barleycorn, required quittances and con-
tracts,—had now, when the marriage-charter was completed, a lighter heart; and through the whole evening the good man ceased not to thank his bride for
what she had given him. To me, however, a marriage-
contract were a thing as painful and repulsive,—I confess it candidly, though you should in consequence
upbraid me with my great youth,—as if I had to take

my love-letter to a Notáry Impérial, and make him
docket and contersign it before it could be sent. Heavens ! to see the light flower of Love, whose perfume
acts not on the balance, so laid like tulip-bulbs on the
hay-beam of Law ; two hearts on the cold councillor
and flesh beam of relatives and Advocates, who are
heaping on the scales nothing but houses, fields, and
tin—this, to the interested party, may be as delightful
as, to the intoxicated suckling and nursling of the
Muses and Philosophy, it is to carry the evening and
morning sacrifices he has offered up to his goddess into
the book-shop, and there to change his devotions into
money, and sell them by weight and measure.—   —
    From Cantata-Sunday to Ascension, that is, to mar-
riage day, are one and a half weeks—or one and a half
blissful eternities. If it is pleasant that nights or winter separate the days and seasons of joy to a comforta-
ble distance ; if, for example, it is pleasant that birth-
day, Saint's-day, betrothment, marriage, and baptismal
day, do not all occur on the same day (for with very
few do those festivities, like Holiday and Apostle's
day, commerge),—then is it still more pleasant to
make the interval, the flower-border, between betrothment and marriage, of an extraordinary breadth. Before the marriage-day are the true honey-weeks ; then
come the wax-weeks ; then the honey-vinegar-weeks.
    In the Ninth Letter-Box, our Parson celebrates his
wedding ; and here, in the Eighth, I shall just briefly
skim over his way and manner of existence till then :

an existence, as might have been expected, celestial
enough. To few is it allotted, as it was to him, to
have at once such wings and such flowers (to fly over)
before his nuptials ; to few is it allotted, I imagine, to
purchase flour and poultry on the same day, as Fixlein did ;—to stuff the wedding-turkey with hangman-
meals;—to go every night into the stall, and see whether
the wedding-pig, which his Guardian has given him by
way of marriage-present, is still standing and eating ;—
to spy out for his future wife the flax-magazines and
clothes-press-niches in the house;—to lay in new wood-
stores in the prospect of winter ;— to obtain from the
Consistorium directly, and for little smart-money,
their Bull of Dispensation, their remission of the three-
fold proclamation of banns ;—to live not in a city,
where you must send to every fool (because you are
one yourself), and disclose to him that you are going
to be married ; but in a little angular hamlet, where
you have no one to tell aught, but simply the Schoolmaster that he is to ring a little later, and put a knee-
cushion before the altar. — —

O ! if the Ritter Michaelis maintains that Paradise
was little, because otherwise the people would not
have found each other,—a hamlet and its joys are little
and narrow, so that some shadow of Eden may still
linger on our Ball. — —

I have not even hinted that, the day before the wedding, the Regiments-Quartermaster came uncalled, and
killed the pig, and made puddings gratis, such as were
never eaten at any Court.

And besides, dear Fixlein, on this soft rich oil of joy there was also floating gratis a vernal sun,—and red twilights,—and flower-garlands,—and a bursting half world of buds ! . . . .

How didst thou behave thee in these hot whirlpools of pleasure ?—Thou movedst thy Fishtail (Reason), and therewith describedst for thyself a rectilineal course through the billows.   For even half as much would have hurried another Parson from his study ; but the very crowning felicity of ours was, that he stood as if rooted to the boundary-hill of Moderation, and from thence looked down on what thousands flout away.   Sitting opposite the Castle-windows, he was still in a condition to reckon up that *Amen* occurs in the Bible one hundred and thirty times.   Nay, to his old learned laboratory he now appended a new chemical stove : he purposed writing to Nürnberg and Bayreuth, and there offering his pen to the Brothers Senft, not only for composing practical *Receipts* at the end of their *Almanacks*, but also for separate *Essays* in front under the copperplate title of each Month, because he had a thought of making some reformatory cuts at the common people's mental habitudes ... And now, when in the capacity of Parson he had less to do, and could add to the holy resting-day of the congregation six literary creating-days, he determined (even in these Carnival weeks) to strike his plough into the hitherto quite fallow History of Hukelum, and soon to follow the plough with his drill. . . . .

Thus roll his minutes, on golden wheels-of-fortune, over the twelve days, which form the glancing star-paved road to the third heaven of the thirteenth, that is, to the

NINTH LETTER-BOX,

Or to the Marriage.

RISE, fair Ascension and Marriage day, and gladden readers also ! Adorn thyself with the fairest jewel, with the bride, whose soul is as pure and glittering as its vesture ; like pearl and pearl-muscle, the one as the other, lustrous and ornamental ! And so over the espalier, whose fruit-hedge has hitherto divided our darling from his Eden, every reader now presses after him !—

On the 9th of May 1793, about three in the morning, there came a sharp peal of trumpets, like a light-beam, through the dim-red May-dawn : two twisted horns, with a straight trumpet between them, like a note of admiration between interrogation-points, were clanging from a house in which only a parishioner (not the Parson) dwelt and blew : for this parishioner had last night been celebrating the same ceremony which the pastor had this day before him. The joyful tallyho raised our Parson from his broad bed (and the Shock from beneath it, who some weeks ago had been exiled from the white sleek coverlid), and this so early, that in the pourtraying tester, where on every former morning he had observed his ruddy visage, and his white bedclothes, all was at present dim and crayonned.

I confess, the new-painted room, and a gleam of dawn on the wall, made it so light, that he could see his knee-buckles glancing on the chair. He then softly awakened his mother (the other guests were to lie for hours in the sheets), and she had the city cook-maid to awaken, who, like several other articles of wedding-furniture, had been borrowed for a day or two from Flachsenfingen. At two doors he knocked in vain, and without answer; for all were already down at the hearth, cooking, blowing, and arranging.

How softly does the Spring day gradually fold back its nun-veil, and the Earth grow bright, as if it were the morning of a Resurrection!—The quicksilver-pillar of the barometer, the guiding Fire-pillar of the weather-prophet, rests firmly on Fixlein's Ark of the Covenant. The Sun raises himself, pure and cool, into the morning-blue, instead of into the morning-red. Swallows, instead of clouds, shoot skimming through the melodious air ... O, the good Genius of Fair Weather, who deserves many temples and festivals (because without him no festival could be held), lifted an æthe-rial azure Day, as it were, from the well-clear atmosphere of the Moon, and sent it down, on blue butter-fly-wings—as if it were a *blue* Monday—glittering below the Sun, in the zigzag of joyful quivering descent, upon the narrow spot of Earth, which our heated fancies are now viewing .... And on this balmy vernal spot, stand amid flowers, over which the trees are shaking blossoms instead of leaves, a bride and a bridegroom. .... Happy Fixlein! how shall I paint thee without deepening the sighs of longing in the fairest souls?——

But soft! we will not drink the magic cup of Fancy to the bottom, at six in the morning; but keep sober till towards night!

At the sound of the morning prayer-bell, the bridegroom, for the din of preparation was disturbing his quiet orison, went out into the churchyard, which (as in many other places) together with the church, lay round his mansion like a court. Here on the moist green, over whose closed flowers the churchyard wall was still spreading broad shadows, did his spirit cool itself from the warm dreams of Earth: here, where the white flat grave-stone of his Teacher lay before him like the fallen-in door on the Janus'-temple of Life, or like the windward side of the narrow house, turned towards the tempests of the world: here, where the little shrunk metallic door on the grated cross of his father uttered to him the inscriptions of death, and the year when his parent departed, and all the admonitions and mementos, graven on the lead;—there, I say, his mood grew softer and more solemn; and he now lifted up by heart his morning prayer, which usually he read; and entreated God to bless him in his office, and to spare his mother's life, and to look with favour and acceptance on the purpose of to-day.—Then over the graves, he walked into his fenceless little angular flower-garden; and here, composed and confident in the divine keeping, he pressed the stalks of his tulips deeper into the mellow earth.

But on returning to the house, he was met on all hands by the bell-ringing and the Janizary-music of wedding-gladness;—the marriage guests had all thrown off their nightcaps, and were drinking diligently;—there was a clattering, a cooking, a frizzling;—tea-services, coffee-services, and warm beer-services, were advancing in succession; and plates full of bride-cakes were going round like potter's frames or cistern-wheels.—The School-master, with three young lads, was heard rehearsing from his own house an *Arioso*, with which, so soon as they were perfect, he purposed to surprise his clerical superior.—But now rushed all the arms of the foaming joy-streams into one, when the sky-queen besprinkled with blossoms, the bride, descended upon Earth in her timid joy, full of quivering humble love;—when the bells began;—when the procession-column set forth with the whole village round and before it;—when the organ, the congregation, the officiating priest, and the sparrows on the trees of the church-window, struck louder and louder their rolling peals on the drum of the jubilee-festival.... The heart of the singing bride-groom was like to leap from its place for joy, " that on his bridal-day, it was all so respectable and grand."

—Not till the marriage benediction could he pray a little.

Still worse and louder grew the business during dinner, when pastry-work and marchpane-devices were brought forward,—when glasses, and slain fishes (laid under the napkins to frighten the guests) went round;—and when the guests rose, and themselves went round, and at length danced round : for they had instrumental music from the city there.

One minute handed over to the other the sugar-bowl and bottle-case of joy : the guests heard and saw less and less, and the villagers began to see and hear more and more, and towards night they penetrated like a wedge into the open door,—nay, two youths ventured even in the middle of the parsonage-court, to mount a plank over a beam, and commence seesawing.—Out of doors, the gleaming vapour of the departed Sun was encircling the Earth, the evening-star was glittering over parsonage and churchyard ; no one heeded it.

However, about nine o'clock,—when the marriage-guests had well nigh forgotten the marriage-pair, and were drinking or dancing along for their own behoof ; when poor mortals, in this sunshine of Fate, like fishes in the sunshine of the sky, were leaping up from their wet cold element ; and when the bridegroom under the star of happiness and love, casting like a comet its long train of radiance over all his heaven, had in secret pressed to his joy-filled breast his bride and his mother,—then did he lock a slice of wedding-bread privily into a press, in the old superstitious belief, that this residue secured continuance of bread for the whole marriage. As he returned, with greater love for the sole partner of his life, she herself met him with his mother, to deliver him in private the bridal-nightgown and bridal-shirt, as is the ancient usage. Many a countenance grows pale in violent emotions, even of joy : Thiennette's wax-face was bleaching still whiter under the sunbeams of Happiness. O never fall, thou lily of Heaven, and may four springs instead of four seasons open and shut thy flower-bells to the sun !—All the arms of his soul as he floated on the sea of joy were quivering to clasp the soft warm heart of his beloved, to encircle it gently and fast, and draw it to his own . . . .

He led her from the crowded dancing-room into the cool evening. Why does the evening, does the night put warmer love in our hearts ? Is it the nightly pressure of helplessness ; or is it the exalting separation from the turmoil of life ; that veiling of the world, in which for the soul nothing more remains but souls ;— is it therefore, that the letters in which the loved name stands written on our spirit appear, like phosphorus-writing, by night *in fire*, while by day in their *cloudy* traces they but smoke ?

He walked with his bride into the Castle-garden : she hastened quickly through the Castle, and past its servants'-hall, where the fair flowers of her young life had been crushed broad and dry, under a long dreary pressure; and her soul expanded, and breathed in the free open garden, on whose flowery soil destiny had cast forth the first seeds of the blossoms which to-day were gladdening her existence. Still Eden! Green flower-chequered *chiaroscuro!*—The moon is sleeping under ground like a dead one; but beyond the garden the sun's red evening-clouds have fallen down like rose-leaves; and the evening-star, the brideman of the sun, hovers, like a glancing butterfly, above the rosy red, and, modest as a bride, deprives no single starlet of its light.

The wandering pair arrived at the old gardener's hut; now standing locked and dumb, with dark windows in the light garden, like a fragment of the Past surviving in the Present. Bared twigs of trees were folding, with clammy half-formed leaves, over the thick intertwisted tangles of the bushes.—The Spring was standing, like a conqueror, with Winter at his feet.—In the blue pond, now bloodless, a dusky evening-sky lay hollowed out, and the gushing waters were moistening the flower-beds.—The silver sparks of stars were rising on the altar of the East, and falling down extinguished in the red sea of the West.

The wind whirred, like a night-bird, louder through the trees; and gave tones to the acacia-grove, and the tones called to the pair who had first become happy within it: " Enter, new mortal pair, and think of what is past, and of my withering and your own; and be holy as Eternity, and weep not only for joy, but for

5

gratitude also !"—And the wet-eyed bridegroom led his wet-eyed bride under the blossoms, and laid his soul, like a flower, on her heart, and said : " Best Thiennette, I am unspeakably happy, and would say much, and cannot—Ah, thou Dearest, we will live like angels, like children together ! Surely I will do all that is good to thee ; two years ago I had nothing, no nothing ; ah, it is through thee, best love, that I am happy. I call thee Thou, now, thou dear good soul !" She drew him closer to her, and said, though without kissing him : " Call me Thou always, Dearest !"

And as they stept forth again from the sacred grove into the magic-dusky garden, he took off his hat ; first, that he might internally thank God, and secondly, because he wished to look into this fairest evening sky.

They reached the blazing, rustling, marriage-house, but their softened hearts sought stillness ; and a foreign touch, as in the blossoming vine, would have disturbed the flower-nuptials of their souls. They turned rather, and winded up into the churchyard to preserve their mood. Majestic on the groves and mountains stood the Night before man's heart, and made it also great. Over the *white* steeple-obelisk the sky rested *bluer*, and *darker ;* and behind it, wavered the withered summit of the May-pole with faded flag. The son noticed his father's grave, on which the wind was opening and shutting, with harsh noise, the little door of the metal cross, to let the year of his death be read on the brass plate within. An overpowering sadness seized his heart with violent streams of tears, and drove him to the sunk hillock, and he led his bride to the grave, and said: " Here sleeps he, my good father ; in his thirty-second year, he was carried hither to his long rest. O thou good, dear father, couldst thou to-day but see the happiness of thy son, like my mother ! But thy eyes are empty, and thy breast is full of ashes, and thou seest us not."—He was silent. The bride wept aloud ; she saw the mouldering coffins of her parents open, and the two dead arise and look round for their daughter, who had stayed so long behind them, forsaken on the Earth. She fell upon his heart, and faltered : " O beloved, I have neither father nor mother, do not forsake me !"

O thou who hast still a father and a mother, thank God for it, on the day when thy soul is full of joyful tears, and needs a bosom wherein to shed them. . . .

And with this embracing at a father's grave, let this day of joy be holily concluded.—

TENTH LETTER-BOX.

St Thomas'-day and Birth-day.

An Author is a sort of bee-keeper for his reader-swarm ; in whose behalf he separates the Flora kept for their use into different seasons, and here accelerates, and there retards, the blossoming of many a flower, that so in all chapters there be blooming.

The goddess of Love and the angel of Peace conducted our married pair on tracks running over full meadows, through the Spring ; and on footpaths hidden by high cornfields, through the Summer ; and Autumn, as they advanced towards Winter, spread her marbled leaves under their feet. And thus they arrived before the low dark gate of Winter, full of life, full of love, trustful, contented, sound and ruddy.

On St Thomas' day was Thiennette's birthday as well as Winter's. About a quarter past nine, just when the singing ceases in the church, we shall take a peep through the window into the interior of the parsonage. There is nothing here but the old mother, who has all day (the son having restricted her to rest, and not work) been gliding about, and brushing, and burnishing, and scouring, and wiping : every carved chair-leg, and every brass nail of the waxcloth-covered table, she has polished into brightness ;—everything hangs, as with all married people who have no children, in its right place, brushes, fly-flaps, and almanacks ;—the chairs are stationed by the room-police in their ancient corners ;— a flax-rock, encircled with a diadem, or scarf of azure ribband, is lying in the Schadeckbed, because, though it is a half holiday, some spinning may go on ;—the narrow slips of paper, whereon heads of sermons are so be arranged, lie white beside the sermons themelves, that is, beside the octavo paper-book which holds them, for the Parson and his work-table, by reason of the cold, have migrated from the study to the sitting-room ;—his large furred doublet is hanging beside his clean bridegroom-nightgown : there is nothing wanting in the room but He and She. For he had preached her with him to-night into the empty Apostle's-day church, that so her mother, without witnesses —except the two or three thousand readers who are peeping with me through the window—might arrange the provender-baking, and whole commissariat department of the birthday-festival, and spread out her best table-gear and victual-stores without obstruction.

The soul-curer reckoned it no sin to admonish, and exhort, and encourage, and threaten his parishioners, till he felt pretty certain that the soup must be smoking on the plates. Then he led his birthday helpmate home, and suddenly placed her before the altar of meat-offering, before a sweet title-page of bread-tart, on which her name stood baked, in true *monastic characters*, in tooth-letters of almonds. In the background of time and of the room, I yet conceal two—bottles of Pontac. How quickly, under the sunshine of joy, do thy cheeks grow ripe, Thiennette, when thy husband solemnly says : " This is thy birthday ; and may the Lord bless thee and watch over thee, and cause his countenance to shine on thee, and send thee, to the joy of our mother and thy husband especially, a happy, glad *recovery*. Amen !"—And when Thiennette perceived that it was the old mistress who had cooked and

served up all this herself, she fell upon her neck, as if
it had been not her husband's mother, but her own.

Emotion conquers the appetite. But Fixlein's stomach was as strong as his heart ; and with him no species of movement could subdue the peristaltic. Drink
is the friction-oil of the tongue, as eating is its drag.
Yet, not till he had eaten and spoken much, did the
pastor fill the glasses. Then indeed he drew the cork-
sluice from the bottle, and set forth its streams. The
sickly mother, of a being still hid beneath her heart,
turned her eyes, in embarrassed emotion, on the old
woman only ; and could scarcely chide him for sending to the city wine-merchant on her account. He took
a glass in each hand, for each of the two whom he loved,
and handed them to his mother and his wife, and said :
" To thy long, long life, Thienette !—And your health
and happiness, Mamma !—And a glad arrival to our
little one, if God so bless us !"—" My son," said the
gardeneress, " it is to thy long life that we must drink ;
for it is by thee we are supported. God grant thee
length of days !" added she, with stifled voice, and her
eyes betrayed her tears.

I nowhere find a livelier emblem of the female sex in
all its boundless levity, than in the case where a woman
is carrying the angel of Death beneath her heart, and yet
in these nine months full of mortal tokens thinks of nothing more important, than of who shall be the gossips,
and what shall be cooked at the christening. But thou,
Thiennette, hadst nobler thoughts, though these too

along with them. The still hidden darling of thy heart was resting before thy eyes like a little angel sculptured on a grave-stone, and pointing with its small finger to the hour when thou shouldst die ; and every morning and every evening, thou thoughtest of death, with a certainty, of which I yet knew not the reasons ; and to thee it was as if the Earth were a dark mineral cave where man's blood like stalactitic water drops down, and in dropping raises shapes which gleam so transiently, and so quickly fade away ! And that was the cause why tears were continually trickling from thy soft eyes, and betraying all thy anxious thoughts about thy child : but thou repaidst these sad effusions of thy heart by the embrace in which, with new-awakened love, thou fellest on thy husband's neck, and saidst : " Be as it may, God's will be done, so thou and my child are left alive !—But I know well that thou, Dearest, lovest me as I do thee" . . . . Lay thy hand, good mother, full of blessings, on the two ; and thou kind Fate, never lift thine away from them !—

It is with emotion and good wishes that I witness the kiss of two fair friends, or the embracing of two virtuous lovers ; and from the fire of their altar sparks fly over to me : but what is this to our sympathetic exaltation, when we see two mortals, bending under the same burden, bound to the same duties, animated by the same care for the same little darlings—fall on one another's overflowing hearts, in some fair hour ? And if these, moreover, are two mortals who already

wear the mourning-weeds of life, I mean old age
whose hair and cheeks are now grown colourless, and
eyes grown dim, and whose faces a thousand thorns
have marred into images of Sorrow ;—when these two
clasp each other with such wearied aged arms, and so
near to the precipice of the grave, and when they say
or think : " All in us is dead, but not our love—O we
have lived and suffered long together, and now we will
hold out our hands to Death together also, and let him
carry us away together,"—does not all within us cry :
O Love, thy spark is superior to Time ; it burns neither in joy nor in the cheek of roses ; it dies not, neither under a thousand tears, nor under the snow of old
age, nor under the ashes of thy—beloved.   It never
dies : and Thou, All-good ! if there were no eternal
love, there were no love at all. . . . .

To the Parson it was easier than it is to me to pave
for himself a transition from the heart to the digestive
faculty. He now submitted to Thiennette (whose voice
at once grew cheerful, while her eyes time after time
began to sparkle) his purpose to take advantage of the
frosty weather, and have the winter meat slaughtered
and salted : " the pig can scarcely rise," said he ; and
forthwith he fixed the determination of the women,
farther the butcher, and the day, and all *et ceteras ;*
appointing everything with a degree of punctuality,
such as the war-college (when it applies the cupping-
glass, the battle-sword, to the overfull system of mankind) exhibits on the previous day, in its arrangements,

before it drives a province into the baiting-ring and slaughter-house.

This settled, he began to talk and feel quite joyously about the course of winter, which had commenced to-day at two-and-twenty minutes past eight in the morning : " for," said he, " newyear is close at hand ; and we shall not need so much candle tomorrow-night as to-night." His mother, it is true, came athwart him with the weapons of her five senses : but he fronted her with his Astronomical Tables, and proved that the lengthening of the day was no less undeniable than imperceptible. In the last place, like most official and married persons, heeding little whether his women took him or not, he informed them in juristico-theological phrase : " That he would put off no longer, but write this very afternoon to the venerable Consistorium, in whose hands lay the *jus circa sacra*, for a new Ball to the church-steeple ; and the rather, as he hoped before newyear's-day to raise a bountiful subscription from the parish for this purpose.—If God spare us till spring," added he with peculiar cheerfulness, " and thou wert happily recovered, I might so arrange the whole that the Ball should be set up at thy first church-going, dame !"

Thereupon he shifted his chair from the dinner and dessert table to the work-table ; and spent the half of his afternoon over the petition for the steeple-ball. As there still remained a little space till dusk, he clapped his tackle to his new learned *Opus*, of which I

must now afford a little glimpse. Out of doors among
the snow, there stood near Hukelum an old Robber-
Castle, which Fixlein, every day in Autumn, had ho-
vered round like a *revenant*, with a view to gauge it,
ichnographically to delineate it, to put every window-
bar and every bridle-hook of it correctly on paper. He
believed he was not expecting too much, if thereby—
and by some drawings of the not so much vertical as
horizontal walls—he hoped to impart to his " *Archi-
tectural Correspondence of two Friends concerning the
Hukelum Robber-Castle*" that last polish and *labor limæ*
which contents Reviewers. For towards the critical
Starchamber of the Reviewers he entertained not
that contempt which some authors actually feel—or
only affect, as for instance, I. From this mouldered
Robber-*Louvre*, there grew for him more flowers of joy,
than ever in all probability had grown from it of old for
its owners.—To my knowledge, it is an anecdote not
hitherto made public, that for all this no man but *Büsch-
ing* has to answer. Fixlein had not long ago, among
the rubbish of the church letter-room, stumbled on a
paper wherein the Geographer had been requesting special information about the statistics of the village. Büs-
ching, it is true, had picked up nothing—accordingly,
indeed, Hukelum, in his *Geography*, is still omitted
altogether;—but this pestilential letter had infected
Fixlein with the spring-fever of Ambition, so that his
palpitating heart was no longer to be stilled or held in
check, except by the assafœtida-emulsion of a review.

It is with authorcraft as with love : both of them for
decades long one may equally desire and forbear : but
is the first spark once thrown into the powder-maga-
zine, it burns to the end of the chapter.

Simply because winter had commenced by the Almanack, the fire must be larger than usual ; for warm
rooms, like large furs and bearskin-caps, were things
which he loved more than you would figure. The dusk,
this fair *chiaroscuro* of the day, this coloured fore-
ground of the night, he lengthened out as far as possible, that he might study Christmas discourses therein : and yet could his wife, without scruple, just as he
was pacing up and down the room, with the sowing-
sheet full of divine word-seeds hung round his shoul-
der,—hold up to him a spoonful of alegar, that he might
try the same in his palate, and decide whether she
should yet draw it off.   Nay, did he not in all cases,
though fonder of roe-fishes himself, order a milter to be
drawn from the herring-barrel, because his good-wife
liked it better ?—

Here light was brought in ; and as Winter was just
now commencing his glass-painting on the windows,
his ice flower-pieces, and his snow-foliage, our Parson
felt that it was time to read something cold, which he
pleasantly named his cold collation; namely, the description of some unutterably frosty land.   On the present
occasion, it was the winter history of the four Russian
sailors on Nova Zembla.   I, for my share, do often in
summer, when the sultry zephyr is inflating the flower-
bells, append certain charts and sketches of Italy, or

the East, as additional landscapes to those among which I am sitting. And yet to-night he farther took up the *Weekly Chronicle* of Flachsenfingen; and amid the bombshells, pestilences, famines, comets with long tails, and the roaring of all the Hell-floods of another Thirty Years War, he could still listen with the one ear towards the kitchen, where the sallad for his roast-duck was just a-cutting.

Good-night, old Fixlein! I am tired. May kind Heaven send thee with the young year 1794, when the Earth shall again carry her people, like precious night-moths, on leaves and flowers, the new steeple-ball, and a thick handsome—boy to boot!

ELEVENTH LETTER-BOX.

Spring; *Investiture*; *and Childbirth.*

I HAVE just risen from a singular dream; but the foregoing Box makes it natural. I dreamed that all was verdant, all full of odours; and I was looking up at a steeple-ball glittering in the sun, from my station in the window of a little white garden-house, my eye-lids full of flower-pollen, my shoulders full of thin cherry blossoms, and my ears full of humming from the neighbouring bee-hives. Then, methought, advancing slowly through the beds, came the Hukelum Parson, and stept into the garden-house, and solemnly said

to me : " Honoured Sir, my wife has just brought me
a little boy; and I make bold to solicit *your Honour*
to do the holy office for the same, when it shall be received into the bosom of the church."

I naturally started up, and there was—Parson Fixlein standing bodily at my bedside, and requesting me
to be godfather : for Thiennette had given him a son
last night about one o'clock. The confinement had
been as light and happy as could be conceived ; for this
reason, that the father had, some months before, been
careful to provide one of those *Klappersteins*, as we
call them, which are found in the airy of the eagle,
and therewith to alleviate the travail : for this stone
performs, in its way, all the service which the bonnet
of that old Minorite monk in Naples, of whom Gorani
informs us, could accomplish for people in such circumstances, who put it on. . . . . .

—I might vex the reader still longer; but I willingly give up, and show him how the matter stood.

Such a May as the present (of 1794), Nature has
not, in the memory of man—begun : for this is but the
fifteenth of it.   People of reflection have for centuries
been vexed once every year, that our German singers
should indite May-songs, since several other months
deserve such a poetical night-music much better ; and
I myself have often gone so far as to adopt the idiom
of our market-women, and instead of May butter, to
say June butter, as also June, March, April songs.—
But thou, kind May of this year, thou deservest to

thyself all the songs which were ever made on thy
rude namesakes!—By Heaven! when I now issue
from the wavering chequered acacia-grove of the Castle-
garden, in which I am writing this Chapter, and come
forth into the broad living day, and look up to the
warming Heaven, and over its Earth budding out beneath it,—the Spring rises before me like a vast full
cloud, with a splendour of blue and green.   I see the
Sun standing amid roses in the western sky, into which
he has thrown his ray-brush, wherewith he has to-day
been painting the Earth ;—and when I look round a
little in our picture-exhibition, his enamelling is still
hot on the mountains ; on the moist chalk of the moist
Earth, the flowers full of sap-colours are laid out to
dry, and the forget-me-not with miniature colours ;
under the varnish of the streams, the skyey Painter
has pencilled his own eye ; and the clouds, like a de-
coration-painter, he has touched off with wild outlines
and single tints ; and so he stands at the border of the
Earth, and looks back upon his stately Spring, whose
robe-folds are valleys, whose breast-boquet is gardens,
and whose blush is a vernal evening, and who, when
she arises, shall be—Summer.

But to proceed! Every spring—and especially in
such a spring—I imitate on foot our birds of passage ;
and travel off the hypochondriacal sediment of winter :
but I do not think I should have seen even the steeple-
ball of Hukelum, which is to be set up one of these
days, to say nothing of the Parson's family, had not I

happened to be visiting the Flachsenfingen Superintendent and Consistorialrath.   From him I got acquainted with Fixlein's history—every Candidatus must
deliver an account of his life to the Consistorium—and
with his still madder petition for a steeple-ball.   I observed, with pleasure, how gaily the cob was diving and
swashing about in his duck-pool and milk-bath of life ;
and forthwith determined on a journey to his shore.   It
is singular, that is to say, manlike, that when we have
for years kept prizing and describing some original person or original book, yet the moment we see such, they
anger us : we would have them fit us and delight us
in all points, as if any originality could do this but our
own.

It was Saturday the third of May, when I, with the
Superintendent, the *Senior Capituli*, and some tem-
poral Raths, mounted and rolled off, and in two carriages were driven to the Parson's door.   The matter
was, he was not yet—*invested*, and to-morrow this was
to be done.   I little thought, while we whirled by the
white espalier of the Castle-garden, that there I was to
write another book.

I still see the Parson, in his peruke-minever and
head-case, come springing to the coach-door and lead
us out ; so smiling—so courteous—so vain of the disloaded freight, and so attentive to it.   He looked as if
in the journey of life he had never once put on the
travelling-gauze of Sorrow : Thiennette again seemed
never to have thrown hers back.   How neat was

everything in the house, how dainty, decorated, and polished ! And yet so quiet, without the cursed alarm-ringing of servants' bells, and without the bass-drum tumult of stair-pedaling. Whilst the gentlemen, my road-companions, were sitting in state in the upper room, I flitted, as my way is, like a smell over the whole house, and my path led me through the sitting-room over the kitchen, and at last into the churchyard beside the house. Good Saturday ! I will paint thy hours as I may, with the black asphaltos of ink, on the tablets of other souls ! In the sitting-room, I lifted from the desk a volume gilt on the back and edges, and bearing this title : " *Holy Sayings, by Fixlein. First Collection.*" And as I looked to see where it had been printed, the Holy Collection turned out to be in writing. I handled the quills, and dipped into the negro-black of the ink, and I found that all was right and good : with your fluttering gentlemen of letters, who hold only a department of the foreign, and none of the home affairs, nothing (except some other things about them) can be worse than their ink and pens. I also found a little copperplate, to which I shall in due time return.

In the kitchen, a place not more essential for the writing of an English novel, than for the acting of a German one, I could plant myself beside Thiennette, and help her to blow the fire, and look at once into her face and her burning coals. Though she was in wedlock, a state in which white roses on the cheeks are changed

for red ones, and young women are similar to a simi-
litude given in my Note;*—and although the blazing
wood threw a false rouge over her, I guessed how pale
she must have been; and my sympathy in her paleness
rose still higher at the thought of the burden which
Fate had now not so much taken from her, as laid in
her arms and nearer to her heart. In truth, a man must
never have reflected on the Creation-moment, when the
Universe first rose from the bosom of an Eternity, if
he does not view with philosophic reverence a woman,
whose thread of life a secret all-wondrous Hand is
spinning to a second thread, and who veils within her
the transition from Nothingness to Existence, from
Eternity to Time;—but still less can a man have any
heart of flesh, if his soul, in presence of a woman, who,
to an unknown unseen being, is sacrificing more than
we will sacrifice when it is seen and known, namely,
her nights, her joys, often her life, does not bow lower,
and with deeper emotion, than in presence of a whole
nun-orchestra on their Sahara-desert;—and worse than
either is the man for whom his own mother has not
made all other mothers venerable.

" It is little serviceable to thee, poor Thiennette,"
thought I, " that now, when thy bitter cup of sickness
is made to run over, thou must have loud festivities

---

* To the Spring, namely, which begins with snow-drops, and
and with roses and pinks.—

come crowding round thee." I meant the Investiture
and the Ball-raising. My rank, the diploma of which
the reader will find stitched in with the *Dog-post-
days*, and which had formerly been hers, brought about
my ears a host of repelling, embarrassed, wavering
titles of address from her; which people, to whom they
have once belonged, are at all times apt to parade before superiors or inferiors, and which it now cost me
no little trouble to disperse. Through the whole Saturday and Sunday, I could never get into the right
track either with her or him, till the other guests were
gone. As for the mother, she acted, like obscure ideas,
powerfully and constantly, but out of view : this arose
in part from her idolatrous fear of us ; and partly also
from a slight shade of care (probably springing from the
state of her daughter), which had spread over her like
a little cloud.

I cruised about, so long as the moon-crescent glim-
mered in the sky, over the churchyard ; and softened
my fantasies, which are at any rate too prone to paint
with the brown of crumbling mummies, not only by
the red of twilight, but also by reflecting how easily
our eyes and our hearts can become reconciled even
to the ruins of Death ; a reflection which the Schoolmaster, whistling as he arranged the charnel-house for
the morrow, and the Parson's maid singing, as she
reaped away the grass from the graves, readily enough
suggested to me. And why should not this habituation
to all forms of Fate in the other world, also, be a gift

266   LIFE OF QUINTUS FIXLEIN.

reserved for us in our nature by the bounty of our
great Preserver ?—I perused the grave-stones ; and I
think even now that Superstition* is right in connect-
ing with the reading of such things a loss of *memory ;*
at all events, one does *forget* a thousand things belonging to this world. . . . .

The Investiture on Sunday (whose Gospel, of the
good shepherd, suited well with the ceremony) I must
despatch in few words ; because nothing truly sublime
.can bear to be treated of in many.   However, I shall
impart the most memorable circumstances, when I say
that there was—drinking (in the Parsonage),—music-
making (in the Choir),—reading (of the Presentation
by the Senior, and of the Ratification-rescript by the
lay Rath),—and preaching, by the Consistorialrath,
who took the soul-curer by the hand, and presented,
made over, and guaranteed him to the congregation,
and them to him.   Fixlein felt that he was departing
as a high-priest from the church, which he had entered
as a country parson ; and all day he had not once the
heart to ban.   When a man is treated with solemnity,
he looks upon himself as a higher nature, and goes
through his solemn feasts devoutly.

This indenturing, this monastic profession, our Head-
Rabbis and Lodge-masters (our Superintendents) have

---

* This Christian superstition is not only a Rabbinical, but also
a Roman one. *Cicero de Senectute.*

usually a taste for putting off till once the pastor has been some years ministering among the people, to whom they hereby present him; as the early Christians frequently postponed their consecration and investiture to Christianity, their baptism namely, till the day when they died: nay, I do not even think, this clerical Investiture would lose much of its usefulness, if it and the declaring-vacant of the office were reserved for the same day; the rather, as this usefulness consists entirely in two items; what the Superintendent and his Raths can eat, and what they can pocket.

Not till towards evening did the Parson and I get acquainted. The Investiture officials, and elevation pully-men, had, throughout the whole evening, been very violently—breathing. I mean thus: as these gentlemen could not but be aware, by the most ancient theories and the latest experiments, that air was nothing else than a sort of rarefied and exploded water, it became easy for them to infer that, conversely, water was nothing else than a denser sort of air. Winedrinking, therefore, is nothing else but the breathing of an air pressed together into proper spissitude, and sprinkled over with a few perfumes. Now, in our days, by clerical persons too much (fluid) breath can never be inhaled through the mouth; seeing the dignity of their station excludes them from that breathing through the *smaller* pores, which Abernethy so highly recommends under the name of *air-bath :* and can the Gullet in their case be aught else than door-neighbour

to the Windpipe, the *consonant* and fellow-shoot of the
Windpipe ?—I am running astray : I meant to signify,
that I this evening had adopted the same opinion ; only
that I used this air or æther, not like the rest for loud
laughter, but for the more quiet contemplation of life in
general. I even shot forth at my gossip certain speeches,
which betrayed devoutness : these he at first took for
jests, being aware that I was from Court, and of quality. But the concave mirror of the wine-mist at length
suspended the images of my soul, enlarged and em-
bodied like spiritual shapes, in the air before me.—Life
shaded itself off to my eyes like a hasty summer night,
which we little fire-flies shoot across with transient
gleam ;—I said to him that man must turn himself like
the leaves of the great mallow, at the different day-
seasons of his life, now to the rising sun, now to the
setting, now to the night, towards the Earth and its
graves ;—I said, the omnipotence of Goodness was
driving us and the centuries of the world towards the
gates of the City of God, as, according to Euler, the
resistance of the *Æther* leads the circling Earth towards the Sun, &c. &c.

On the strength of these entremets, he considered
me the first theologian of his age ; and had he been
obliged to go to war, would previously have taken my
advice on the matter, as belligerent powers were wont
of old from the theologians of the Reformation. I hide
not from myself, however, that what preachers call
vanity of the world, is something altogether different

from what philosophy so calls. When I, moreover, signified to him that I was not ashamed to be an Author ; but had a turn for working up this and the other biography ; and that I had got a sight of his *Life* in the hands of the Superintendent ; and might be in case to prepare a printed one therefrom, if so were he would assist me with here and there a tint of flesh-colour,— then was my silk, which, alas ! not only isolates one from electric fire, but also from a kindlier sort of it, the only grate which rose between his arms and me ; for, like the most part of poor country parsons, it was not in his power to forget the rank of any man, or to vivify his own on a higher one. He said : " He would acknowledge it with veneration, if I should mention him in print ; but he was much afraid his life was too common and too poor for a biography." Nevertheless, he opened me the drawer of his Letter-boxes ; and said, perhaps, he had hereby been paving the way for me.

The main point, however, was, he hoped that his *Errata,* his *Exercitationes,* and his *Letters on the Robber-Castle,* if I should previously send forth a Life of the Author, might be better received ; and that it would be much the same as if I accompanied them with a Preface.

In short, when on Monday the other dignitaries with their nimbus of splendour had dissipated, I alone, like a precipitate, abode with him ; and am still abiding, that is, from the fifth of May (the Public should take the Almanack of 1794, and keep it open beside them)

to the fifteenth : to-day is Thursday, to-morrow is the
sixteenth and Friday, when comes the Spinat-Kirmes,
or Spinage-Wake, as they call it, and the uplifting of
the steeple-ball, which I just purposed to await before
I went.   Now, however, I do not go so soon; for on
Sunday I have to assist at the baptismal ceremony, as
baptismal agent for my little future godson. Whoever
pays attention to me, and keeps the Almanack open,
may readily guess why the christening is put off till
Sunday : for it is that memorable Cantata-Sunday,
which once, for its mad narcotic hemlock-virtues, was
of importance in our History ; but is now so only for
the fair betrothment, which after two years we mean
to celebrate with a baptism.

   Truly it is not in my power—for want of colours
and presses—to paint or print upon my paper the soft
balmy flower-garland of a fortnight which has here
wound itself about my sickly life ; but with a single
day, I shall attempt it.   Man, I know well, cannot
prognosticate either his joys or his sorrows, still less
repeat them, either in living or writing.

   The black hour of coffee has gold in its mouth for
us and honey : here, in the morning coolness, we are
all gathered ; we maintain popular conversation that so
the parsoness and the gardeneress may be able to take
share in it. The morning service in the church, where
often the whole people* are sitting and singing, divides

---

* For according to the Jurists, fifteen persons make a people.

us. While the bell is sounding, I march with my
writing-gear into the singing Castle-garden; and seat
myself in the fresh acacia-grove, at the dewy two-leg-
ged table. Fixlein's Letter-boxes I keep by me in my
pocket; and I have only to look and abstract from his
what can be of use in my own.—Strange enough! so
easily do we forget a thing in describing it, I really
did not recollect for a moment that I am now sitting
at the very grove-table, of which I speak, and writing
all this.—

My gossip in the meantime is also labouring for the
world. His study is a sort of sacristy, and his print-
ing-press a pulpit, wherefrom he preaches to all men;
for an Author is the Town-chaplain of the Universe.
A man, who is making a Book, will scarcely hang himself; all rich Lords'-sons, therefore, should labour for
the press; for, in that case, when you awake too early
in bed, you have always a *plan*, an aim, and therefore
a cause before you why you should get out of it. Better off too is the author who collects rather than in-
vents;—for the latter with its eating fire calcines the
heart: I praise the Antiquary, the Heraldist, Note-
maker, Compiler; I esteem the *Title-perch* (a fish called
Perca-Diagramma, because of the letters on its scales),
and the *Printer* (a chafer, called *Scarabæus Typogra-
phus*, which eats letters in the bark of fir),—neither of
them needs any greater or fairer arena in the world,
than a piece of rag-paper, or any other laying-appara-
tus than a pointed pencil, wherewith to lay his four-

and-twenty letter-eggs.—In regard to the *catalogue raisonné*, which my gossip is now drawing up of German *Errata*, I have several times suggested to him, " that it were good if he extended his researches in one respect, and revised the rule, by which it has been computed, that *e. g.* for a hundredweight of pica black-letter, four hundred and fifty semicolons, three hundred periods, &c. are required ; and to recount, and see whether in Political writings and Dedications, the fifty notes of admiration for a hundredweight of pica black-letter were not far too small an allowance, and if so, what the real quantity was ?"

Several days he wrote nothing ; but wrapped himself in the slough of his parson's-cloak ; and so in his canonicals, beside the Schoolmaster, put the few A-b-c shooters, which were not, like forest-shooters, absent on forlough by reason of the spring,—through their platoon firing in the Hornbook. He never did more than his duty, but also never less. It brought a soft benignant warmth over his heart, to think that he, who had once ducked under a School-inspectorship, was now one himself.

About ten o'clock, we meet from our different museums, and examine the village, especially the Biographical furniture and holy places, which I chance that morning to have had under my pen or pantagraph ; because I look at them with more interest *after* my description than *before* it.

3

Next comes dinner.—

After the concluding grace, which is too long, we both of us set to entering the charitable subsidies, and religious donations, which our parishioners have remitted to the sinking or rather rising fund of the church-box for the purchase of the new steeple-globe, into two ledgers: the one of these, with the names of the subscribers, or (in case they have subscribed for their children) with their children's names also, is to be inurned in a leaden capsule, and preserved in the steeple-ball; the other will remain below among the parish Registers.   You cannot fancy what contributions the ambition of getting into the Ball brings us in ; I declare, several peasants who had given and well once already, contributed again when they had baptisms : must not little Hans be in the Ball too ?

After this book-keeping by double entry, my gossip took to engraving on copper.   He had been so happy as to elicit the discovery, that from a certain stroke resembling an inverted Latin S, the capital letters of our German Chancery-hand, beautiful and interwisted as you see them stand in Law-deeds and Letters-of-nobility, may every one of them be composed and spun out.

" Before you can count sixty," said he to me, " I take my fundamental-stroke and make you any letter out of it."

I merely inverted this fundamental-stroke, that is, gave him a German S, and counted sixty till he had

it done.   This line of beauty, when once it has been
twisted and flourished into all the capitals, he purposes
by copperplates which he is himself engraving, to make
more common for the use of Chanceries; and I may
take upon me to give the Russian, the Prussian, and
a few other smaller Courts, hopes of proof impressions
from his hand: to under-secretaries they are indispensable.

Now comes evening; and it is time for us both, here
forking about with our fruit-hooks on the literary Tree
of Knowledge, at the risk of our necks, to clamber
down again into the meadow-flowers and pasturages
of rural joy.   We wait, however, till the busy Thiennette, whom we are now to receive into our commu-
nion, has no more walks to take but the one between
us.   Then slowly we stept along (the sick lady was
weak) through the office-houses; that is to say, through
stalls and their population, and past a horrid lake of
ducks, and past a little milk-pond of carps, to both of
which colonies, I and the rest, like princes, gave bread,
seeing we had it in view on the Sunday after the
christening, to—take them for bread ourselves.

The sky is still growing kindlier and redder, the
swallows and the blossom-trees louder, the house-sha-
dows broader, and men more happy.   The clustering
blossoms of the acacia-grove hang down over our cold
collation; and the ham is not stuck (which always
vexes me) with flowers, but beshaded with them from
a distance. . . . .

And now the deeper evening and the nightingale conspire to soften me; and I soften in my turn the mild beings round me; especially the pale Thiennette, to whom, or to whose heart, after the apoplectic crushings of a downpressed youth, the most violent pulses of joy are heavier than the movements of pensive sadness. And thus beautifully runs our pure transparent life along, under the blooming curtains of May; and in our modest pleasures, we look with timidity neither behind us nor before; as people who are lifting treasure gaze not round at the road they came, or the road they are going.

So pass our days. To-day, however, it was different: by this time, usually, the evening meal is over; and the Shock has got the osseous-preparation of our supper between his jaws; but to-night I am still sitting here alone in the garden, writing the Eleventh Letter-Box, and peeping out every instant over the meadows, to see if my gossip is not coming.

For he is gone to town, to bring a whole magazine of spiceries: his coat-pockets are wide. Nay, it is certain enough that oftentimes he brings home with him, simply in his coat-pocket, considerable flesh-tithes from his Guardian, at whose house he alights; though truly intercourse with the polished world and city, and the refinement of manners thence arising—for he calls on the bookseller, on school-colleagues, and several respectable shopkeepers—does, much more than flesh-fetching, form the object of these journeys to the city.

This morning he appointed me regent head of the house and delivered me the *fasces* and *curule chair*. I sat the whole day beside the young pale mother; and could not but think, simply because the husband had left me there as his representative, that I liked the fair soul better. She had to take dark colours, and paint out for me the winter landscape and ice region of her sorrow-wasted youth; but often, contrary to my intention, by some simple elegiac word, I made her still eye wet; for the too full heart, which had been crushed with other than sentimental woes, overflowed at the smallest pressure. A hundred times in the recital I was on the point of saying: " O yes, it was with winter that your life began, and the course of it has resembled winter !"— Windless, cloudless day ! Three more words about thee, the world will still not take amiss from me !

I advanced nearer and nearer to the heart-central-fire of the women; and at last they mildly broke forth in censure of the Parson; the best wives will complain of their husbands to a stranger, without in the smallest liking them the less on that account. The mother and the wife, during dinner, accused him of buying lots at every book-auction; and, in truth, in such places, he does strive and bid not so much for good or for bad books—or old ones—or new ones—or such as he likes to read—or any sort of favourite books—but simply for books. The mother blamed especially his squandering so much on copperplates : yet some hours after, when the Schultheis, or Mayor, who wrote a beautiful hand, came in to subscribe for the steeple-ball, she pointed out to him how finely her son could engrave, and said that it was well worth while to spend a groschem or two on such capitals as these.

They then handed me—for when once women are in the way of a full open-hearted effusion, they like (only you must not turn the stop-cock of inquiry) to pour out the whole—a ring-case, in which he kept a Chamberlain's key that he had found, and asked me if I knew who had lost it. Who could know such a thing, when there are almost more Chamberlains than picklocks among us?—

At last I took heart, and asked after the little toy-press of the drowned son, which hitherto I had sought for in vain over all the house. Fixlein himself had in-quired for it, with as little success. Thiennette gave the old mother a persuading look full of love; and the latter led me up stairs to an outstretched hoop-petti-coat, covering the poor press as with a dome. On the way thither, the mother told me, she kept it hid from her son, because the recollection of his brother would pain him. When this deposit-chest of Time (the lock had fallen off) was laid open to me, and I had looked into the little charnel-house, with its wrecks of a child-like sportful Past, I, without saying a word, determi-ned, some time ere I went away, to unpack these play-things of the lost boy, before his surviving brother: Can there be aught finer than to look at these ash-buried, deep-sunk Herculanean ruins of childhood, now dug up and in the open air?

Thiennette sent twice to ask me whether he was come. He and she, precisely because they do not give their love the weakening expression of phrases, but the strengthening one of actions, have a boundless feeling of it towards one another. Some wedded pairs eat each other's lips and hearts and love away by kisses; as in Rome, the statues of Christ (by Angelo) have lost their feet by the same process of kissing, and got leaden ones instead; in other couples, again, you may see, by mere inspection, the number of their conflagrations and eruptions, as in Vesuvius you can discover his, of which there are now forty-three : but in these two beings, rose the Greek fire of a moderate and everlasting love, and gave warmth without casting forth sparks, and flamed straight up without crackling. The evening-red is flowing back more magically from the windows of the gardener's cottage into my grove ; and I feel as if I must say to Destiny : " Hast thou a sharp sorrow, then throw it rather into my breast, and strike not with it three good souls, who are too happy not to bleed by it, and too sequestered in their little dim village not to shrink back at the thunderbolt which hurries a stricken spirit from its earthly dwelling."— —

Thou good Fixlein ! Here comes he hurrying over the parsonage-green. What languishing looks full of love already rest in the eye of thy Thiennette !—What news wilt thou bring us to-night from the town !—How will the ascending steeple-ball refresh thy soul to-morrow !—

TWELFTH LETTER-BOX.

Steeple-ball-Ascension.　The Toy-press.

How, on this sixteenth of May, the old steeple-ball was twisted off from the Hukelum steeple, and a new one put on in its stead, will I now describe to my best ability; but in that simple historical style of the Ancients, which, for great events, is perhaps the most suitable.

At a very early hour, a coach arrived containing Messrs Court-Guilder Zeddel and Locksmith Wächser, and the new Peter's-cupola of the steeple. Towards eight o'clock the community, consisting of subscribers to the Globe, was visibly collecting. A little later came the Lord Dragoon Rittmeister von Aufhammer, as Patron of the church and steeple, attended by Mr Church-Inspector Streichert. Hereupon my Reverend Cousin Fixlein and I repaired, with the other persons whom I have already named, into the Church, and there celebrated before innumerable hearers, a weekday prayer-service. Directly afterwards, my Reverend Friend made his appearance above in the pulpit, and endeavoured to deliver a speech which might correspond to the solemn transaction;—and immediately thereafter, he read aloud the names of the patrons and charitable souls, by whose donations the Ball had been put together; and showed to the congregation the leaden box in which they were specially recorded; observing, that the book from which he had recited them was to be reposited in the Parish Register-office. Next he held it necessary to thank them and God, that he, above his deserts, had been chosen as the instrument and undertaker of such a work. The whole he concluded with a short prayer for Mr Stechmann the Slater (who was already hanging on the outside on the steeple, and loosening the old shaft); and entreated that he might not break his neck, or any of his members. A short hymn was then sung, which the most of those assembled without the church-doors sang along with us, looking up at the same time to the steeple.

All of us now proceeded out likewise; and the discarded ball, as it were the amputated cock's-comb of the church, was lowered down and untied. Church-Inspector Streichert drew a leaden case from the crumbling ball, which my Reverend Friend put into his pocket, purposing to read it at his convenience; I, however, said to some peasants : " See, thus will your names also be preserved in the new Ball, and when after long years it shall be taken down, the box lies within it, and the then parson becomes acquainted with you all."—And now was the new steeple-globe, with the leaden cup in which lay the names of the bystanders, at length full-laden, so to speak, and saturated, and fixed to the pulley-rope ;—and so did this the whilom cupping-glass of the community ascend aloft. . . . .

By Heaven! the unadorned style is here a thing
beyond my power : for when the Ball moved, swung,
mounted, there rose a drumming in the centre of the
steeple ; and the Schoolmaster, who, till now, had looked down through a sounding-hole directed towards the
congregation, now stept out with a trumpet at a side
sounding-hole, which the mounting Ball was not to
cross.—But when the whole Church rung and pealed,
the nearer the capital approached its crown,—and
when the Slater clutched it and turned it round, and
happily incorporated the spike of it, and delivered
down, between Heaven and Earth, and leaning on the
Ball, a Topstone-speech to this and all of us,—and
when my gossip's eyes, in his rapture at being Parson
on this great day, were running over, and the tears
trickling down his priestly garment ;—I believe, I was
the only man—as his mother was the only woman—
whose souls a common grief laid hold of to press them
even to bleeding ; for I and the mother had yesternight, as I shall tell more largely afterwards, discovered in the little chest of the drowned boy, from a me-
morial in his father's hand, that, on the day after the
morrow, on Cantata-Sunday and his baptismal-Sun-
day, he would be—two-and-thirty years of age. " Oh!"
thought I, while I looked at the blue heaven, the green
graves, the glittering ball, the weeping priest, " so, at
all times, stands poor man with bandaged eyes before
thy sharp sword, incomprehensible Destiny ! And when
thou drawest it and brandishest it aloft, he listens

with pleasure to the whizzing of the stroke before it falls !"—

Last night I was aware of it ; but to the reader, whom I was preparing for it afar off, I would tell nothing of the mournful news, that, in the press of the dead brother, I had found an old Bible which the boys had used at school, with a white blank leaf in it, on which the father had written down the dates of his children's birth. And even this it was that raised in thee, thou poor mother, the shade of sorrow which of late we have been attributing to smaller causes ; and thy heart was still standing amid the rain, which seemed to us already past over and changed into a rainbow !—Out of love to him, she had yearly told one falsehood, and concealed his age. By extreme good luck, he had not been present when the press was opened. I still purpose, after this fatal Sunday, to surprise him with the party-coloured reliques of his childhood, and so of these old Christmas-presents to make him new ones. In the meanwhile, if I and his mother can but follow him incessantly, like fishhook-floats, and foot-clogs, through to-morrow and next day, that no murderous accident lift aside the curtain from his birth-certificate,—all may yet be well. For now, in truth, to his eyes, this birth-day, in the metamorphotic mirror of his superstitious imagination, and behind the magnifying magic vapour of his present joys, would burn forth like a red death-warrant. . . . But besides all this, the leaf of the Bible is now sitting higher than any of us, namely, in the new steeple-ball, into which I this morning prudently introduced it. Properly speaking there is indeed no danger.

THIRTEENTH LETTER-BOX.

Christening.

TO-DAY is that stupid Cantata-Sunday; but nothing now remains of it save an hour.—By Heaven! in right spirits were we all to-day. I believe, I have drunk as faithfully as another.—In truth, one should be moderate in all things, in writing, in drinking, in rejoicing; and as we lay straws into the honey for our bees that they may not drown in their sugar, so ought one at all times to lay a few firm Principles, and twigs from the tree of Knowledge, into the Syrup of life, instead of those same bee-straws, that so one may cling thereto, and not drown like a rat. But now I do purpose in earnest to—write (and also live) with steadfastness; and therefore, that I may record the christening ceremony with greater coolness,—to besprinkle my fire with the night-air, and to roam out for an hour into the blossom-and-wave-embroidered night, where a lukewarm breath of air, intoxicated with soft odours, is sinking down from the blossom-peaks to the low-bent flowers, and roaming over the meadows, and at last launching on a wave, and with it sailing down the moonshiny brook. O, without, under the stars, under the tones of the nightingale, which seem to reverberate, not from the echo, but from the far-off down-glancing worlds; beside that moon, which the gushing brook in its flickering watery band is carrying away, and which creeps under the little shadows of the bank as under clouds—O, amid such forms and tones, the heart of man grows serious; and as of old an evening bell was rung to direct the wanderer through the deep forests to his nightly home, so in our Night are such voices within us and about us, which call to us in our strayings, and make us calmer, and teach us to moderate our own joys, and to conceive those of others.

*   *   *

I return, peaceful and cool enough, to my narrative. All yesternight I left not the worthy Parson half an hour from my sight, to guard him from poisoning the well of his life. Full of paternal joy, and with the skeleton of the sermon (he was committing it to memory) in his hand, he set before me all that he had; and pointed out to me the fruit-baskets of pleasures which Cantata-Sunday always plucked and filled for him. He recounted to me, as I did not go away, his baptisms, his accidents of office; told me of his relatives; and removed my uncertainty with regard to the public revenues—of his parish, to the number of his communicants and expected catechumens. At this point, however, I am afraid that many a reader will in vain endeavour to transport himself into my situation, and still be unable to discover why I said to Fixlein: "Worthy gossip, better no man could wish himself." I lied not, for so it is......But look in the Note.*

At last rose the Sunday, the present ; and on this holy day, simply because my little godson was for going over to Christianity, there was a vast racket made : every time a conversion happens, especially of nations, there is an uproaring and a shooting ; I refer to the two Thirty Years Wars, to the more recent one, and to the earlier, which Charlemagne so long carried on with the heathen Saxons : thus, in the *Palais Royal*, the Sun, at his transit over the meridian, fires off a cannon.† But this morning the little Unchristian, my godson, was precisely the person least attended to ; for, in thinking of the conversion, they had no time left to think of the convert. Therefore I strolled about with him myself half the forenoon ; and, in our walk, hastily conferred on him a private-bap-

---

* A long philosophical elucidation is indispensably requisite : which will be found in this Book, under the title : *Natural Magic of the Imagination.* [A part of the *Jus de Tablette* appended to this Biography, unconnected with it, and not given here.—ED.]

† This pigmy piece of ordinance, with its cunningly devised burning-glass, is still to be seen on the south side of the Paris Vanity-Fair ; and in fine weather, to be heard, on all sides thereof, proclaiming the *conversion* (so it seems to Richter) of the Day from Forenoon to Afternoon.—ED.

tism; having named him *Jean Paul* before the priest
did so. At midday, we sent the beef away as it had
come; the Sun of happiness having desiccated all our
gastric juices. We now began to look about us for
pomp; I for scientific decorations of my hair, my godson for his christening-shirt, and his mother for her
dress-cap. Yet before the child's-rattle of the christen-
ing-bell had been jingled, I and the midwife, in front
of the mother's bed, instituted Physiognomical Travels* on the countenance of the small Unchristian,
and returned with the discovery, that some features
had been embossed by the pattern of the mother, and
many firm portions resembled me; a double similarity,
in which my readers can take little interest. *Jean Paul*
looks very sensible for his years, or rather for his minutes, for it is the small one I am speaking of.—   —

But now I would ask, what German writer durst
take it upon him to spread out and paint a large his-
toric sheet, representing the whole of us as we went
to church? Would he not require to draw the father,
with swelling canonicals, moving forward slowly, devoutly, and full of emotion? Would he not have to
sketch the godfather, minded this day to lend out his
names, which he derived from two Apostles (John and
Paul), as Julius Cæsar lent out his names to two things
still living even now (to a month, and a throne)?—And

---

* See § *Musäus*, in vol. I. of this Collection.—ED.

must he not put the godson on his sheet, with whom even the Emperor Joseph (in his need of nurse-milk) might become a foster-brother, in his old days, if he were still in them ?—

In my chamber, I have a hundred times determined to smile at solemnities, in the midst of which I afterwards, while assisting at them, involuntarily wore a petrified countenance, full of dignity and seriousness. For, as the Schoolmaster, just before the baptism, began to sound the organ—an honour never paid to any other child in Hukelum,—and when I saw the wooden christening-angel, like an alighted Genius, with his painted timber arm spread out under the baptismal ewer, and I myself came to stand close by him, under his gilt wing, I protest the blood went slow and solemn, warm and close, through my pulsing head, and my lungs full of sighs ; and, to the silent darling lying in my arms, whese unripe eyes Nature yet held closed from the full perspective of the Earth, I wished, with more sadness than I do to myself, for his Future also as soft a sleep as to-day ; and as good an angel as to-day, but a more living one, to guide him into a more living religion, and, with invisible hand, conduct him unlost through the forest of Life, through its falling trees, and Wild Hunters,* and all its storms and pe-

---

* The Wild Hunter, *Wilde Jäger*, is a popular spectre of Germany.—Ed.

rils..... Will the world not excuse me, if when, by a side-glance, I saw on the paternal countenance prayers for the son, and tears of joy trickling down into the prayer ; and when I noticed on the countenance of the grandmother far darker and fast-hidden drops, which she could not restrain, while I, in answer to the ancient question, engaged to provide for the child if its parents died,—am I not to be excused if I then cast my eyes deep down on my little godson, merely to hide their running over ?—For I remembered that his father might perhaps this very day grow pale and cold before a suddenly arising mask of Death ; I thought how the poor little one had only changed his bent posture in the womb with a freer one, to bend and cramp himself ere long more harshly in the strait arena of life ; I thought of his inevitable follies, and errors, and sins ; of these soiled steps to the Grecian Temple of our Perfection ; I thought that one day his own fire of genius might reduce himself to ashes, as a man that is electrified can kill himself with his own lightning..... All the theological wishes, which, on the godson-billet printed over with them, I placed in his young bosom, were glowing written in mine..... But the white feathered-pink of my joy had then, as it always has, a bloody point within it,—I again, as it always is, went to nest, like a woodpecker, in a scull..... And as I am doing so even now, let the describing of the baptism be over for today, and proceed again tomorrow.....

FOURTEENTH LETTER-BOX.

OH, so is it ever ! So does Fate set fire to the theatre of our little plays, and our bright-painted curtain of Futurity ! So does the Serpent of Eternity wind round us and our joys, and crush, like the royal-snake, what it does not poison ! Thou good Fixlein !—Ah ! last night, I little thought that thou, mild soul, while I was writing beside thee, wert already journeying into the poisonous Earth-shadow of Death.

Last night, late as it was, he opened the lead box found in the old steeple-ball ; a catalogue of those who had subscribed to the last repairing of the church was there ; and he began to read it now ; my presence and his occupations having prevented him before. O, how shall I tell that the record of his birth-year, which I had hidden in the new Ball, was waiting for him in the old one ? that in the register of contributions he found his father's name, with the appendage, " given for his new-born son Egidius " ?—

This stroke sunk deep into his bosom, even to the rending of it asunder : in this warm hour, full of paternal joy, after such fair days, after such fair employments, after dread of death so often survived, here, in the bright smooth sea, which is rocking and bearing him along, starts snorting, from the bottomless abyss, the sea-monster Death ; and the monster's throat yawns wide, and the silent sea rushes into it in whirlpools, and hurries him along with it.

But the patient man, quietly and slowly, and with a heart silent, though deadly cold, laid the leaves together;—looked softly and firmly over the churchyard, where, in the moonshine, the grave of his father was to be distinguished;—gazed timidly up to the sky, full of stars, which a white overarching laureltree half screened from his sight;—and though he longed to be in bed, to settle there and sleep it off, yet he paused at the window to pray for his wife and child, in case this night were his last.

At this moment the steeple-clock struck twelve; but from the breaking of a pin, the weights kept rolling down, and the clock-hammer struck without stopping—and he heard with horror the chains and wheels rattling along; and he felt as if Death were hurling forth in a heap all the longer hours which he might yet have had to live—and now to his eyes, the churchyard began to quiver and heave, the moonlight flickered on the church-windows, and in the church there were lights flitting to and fro, and in the charnel-house there was a motion and a tumult.

His heart fainted within him, and he threw himself into bed, and closed his eyes that he might not see;— but Imagination in the gloom now blew aloft the dust of the dead, and whirled it into giant shapes, and chased these hollow fever-born masks alternately into lightning and shadow. Then at last from transparent

thoughts grew coloured visions, and he dreamed this
dream : He was standing at the window looking out
into the church-yard ; and Death, in size as a scorpion,
was creeping over it, and seeking for his bones. Death
found some arm-bones and thigh-bones on the graves,
and said : " They are my bones ;" and he took a spine
and the bone-legs, and stood with them, and the two
arm-bones and clutched with them, and found on the
grave of Fixlein's father a scull, and put it on.   Then
he lifted a scythe beside the little flower-garden, and
cried: " Fixlein, where art thou? My finger is an icicle
and no finger, and I will tap on thy heart with it." The
Skeleton, thus piled together, now looked for him who
was standing at the window, and powerless to stir
from it; and carried in the one hand, instead of a sand-
glass, the everstriking steeple-clock, and held out the
finger of ice, like a dagger, far into the air. . . . .
    Then he saw his victim above at the window, and rai-
sed himself as high as the laureltree to stab straight into
his bosom with the finger,—and stalked towards him.
But as he came nearer, his pale bones grew redder, and
vapours floated woolly round his haggard form. Flowers
started up from the ground ; and he stood transfigured
and without the clamm of the grave, hovering above
them, and the balm-breath from the flower-cups wafted
him gently on ;—and as he came nearer, the scythe and
cloak were gone, and in his boney breast he had a heart,
and on his boney head red lips ;—and nearer still, there
gathered on him soft, transparent, rosebalm-dipt flesh,

like the splendour of an Angel flying hither from the
starry blue ;—and close at hand, he was an Angel with
shut snow-white eyelids.....

The heart of my friend, quivering like a Harmonica-
bell, now melted in bliss in his clear bosom;—and when
the Angel opened its eyes, his were pressed together
by the weight of celestial rapture, and his dream fled
away. — —

But not his life : he opened his hot eyes, and—his
good wife had hold of his feverish hand, and was standing in room of the Angel.

The fever abated towards morning : but the certainty
of dying still throbbed in every artery of the hapless
man.   He called for his fair little infant into his sick-
bed, and pressed it silently, though it began to cry, too
hard against his paternal heavy-laden breast.   Then towards noon his soul became cool, and the sultry thunder-clouds within it drew back.   And here he described
to us the previous (as it were, arsenical) fantasies of his
usually quiet head.   But it is even those tense nerves,
which have not quivered at the touch of a poetic hand
striking them to melody of sorrow, that start and fly
asunder more easily under the fierce hand of Fate, when
with sweeping stroke it smites into discord the firmset
strings.

But towards night his ideas again began rushing in
a torch-dance, like fire-pillars round his soul : every
artery became a burning-rod, and the heart drove flaming naphtha-brooks into the brain.   All within his soul

grew bloody : the blood of his drowned brother united
itself with the blood which had once flowed from Thiennette's arm, into a bloody rain ;—he still thought he
was in the garden in the night of betrothment, he still
kept calling for bandages to staunch blood, and was for
hiding his head in the ball of the steeple. Nothing
afflicts one more than to see a reasonable moderate
man, who has been so even in his passions, raving in
the poetic madness of fever.   And yet if nothing save
this mouldering corruption can soothe the hot brain ;
and if, while the reek and thick vapour of a boiling
nervous-spirit, and the hissing water-spouts of the veins
are encircling and eclipsing the stifled soul, a higher
Finger presses through the cloud, and suddenly lifts
the poor bewildered spirit from amid the smoke to a
sun—is it more just to complain, than to reflect that
Fate is like the oculist, who, when about to open to a
blind eye the world of light, first bandages and darkens
the other eye that sees ?

  But the sorrow does affect me, which I read on
Thiennette's pale lips, though do not hear. It is not the
distortion of an excruciating agony, nor the burning of
a dried-up eye, nor the loud lamenting or violent movement of a tortured frame that I see in her ; but what I
am forced to see in her, and what too keenly cuts the
sympathising heart, is a pale, still, unmoved, undistort-
ed face, a pale bloodless head, which Sorrow is as it
were holding up after the stroke, like a head just se-
vered by the axe of the headsman ; for Oh ! on this

form the wounds, from which the three-edged dagger
had been drawn, are all fallen firmly together, and the
blood is flowing from them in secret into the choking
heart. O Thiennette, go away from the sick-bed, and
hide that face which is saying to us : " Now do I know
that I shall not have any happiness on Earth ; now do
I give over hoping—would this life were but soon
done."

You will not comprehend my sympathy, if you know
not what, some hours ago, the too loud lamenting mother told me. Thiennette, who of old had always trem-
bled for his thirty-second year, had encountered this
superstition with a nobler one : she had purposely stood
farther back at the marriage-altar, and in the bridal-
night fallen sooner asleep than he ; thereby—as is the
popular belief—so to order it that she might also die
sooner. Nay, she has determined if he die, to lay with
his corpse a piece of her apparel, that so she may de-
scend the sooner to keep him company in his narrow
house. Thou good, thou faithful wife, but thou unhappy one !—

CHAPTER LAST.

I HAVE left Hukelum, and my gossip his bed ; and
the one is as sound as the other. The cure was as foolish as the malady.

It first occurred to me, that as Boerhaave used to

remedy convulsions by convulsions, one fancy might in my gossip's case be remedied by another; namely, by the fancy that he was yet no man of thirty-two, but only a man of six or nine.   Deliriums are dreams not encircled by sleep; and all dreams transport us back into youth, why not deliriums too? I accordingly directed every one to leave the patient: only his mother, while the fiercest meteors were darting and hissing before his fevered soul, was to sit down by him alone, and speak to him as if he were a child of eight years. The bed-mirror also I directed her to cover. She did so; she spoke to him as if he had the small-pox fever; and when he cried: "Death is standing with two-and-thirty pointed teeth before me, to eat my heart," she said to him: "Little dear, I will give thee thy roller-hat, and thy copy-book, and thy case, and thy hussar-cloak again, and more too, if thou wilt be good." A reasonable speech he would have taken up and heeded much less than he did this foolish one.

At last she said—for to women in the depth of sorrow, dissimulation becomes easy: "Well, I will try it this once, and give thee thy playthings: but do the like again, thou rogue, and roll thyself about in the bed so, with the small-pox on thee!" And with this, from her full apron she shook out on the bed the whole stock of playthings and dressing-ware, which I had found in the press of the drowned brother.   First of all his copy-book, where Egidius in his eighth year had put down his name, which he necessarily recognised as

his own hand-writing; then the black velvet *fall-hat*
or roller-cap; then the red and white leading-strings;
his knife-case, with a little pamphlet of tin-leaves; his
green hussar-cloak, with its stiff facings; and a whole
orbis pictus or *fictus* of Nürnberg puppets. . . .

The sick man recognised in a moment these pro-
jecting peaks of a spring-world sunk in the stream of
Time,—these half shadows, this dusk of down-gone
days,—this conflagration-place and Golgotha of a heavenly time, which none of us forgets, which we love
for ever, and look back to even from the grave. . . . And
when he saw all this, he slowly turned round his head,
as if he were awakening from a long heavy dream;
and his whole heart flowed down in warm showers of
tears, and he said, fixing his full eyes on the eyes of
his mother: " But are my father and brother still
living, then ?"—" They are dead lately," said the
wounded mother; but her heart was overpowered,
and she turned away her eyes, and bitter tears fell
unseen from her down-bent head. And now at once
that evening, when he lay confined to bed by the death
of his father, and was cured by his playthings, overflowed his soul with splendour and lights, and presence
of the Past.

And so Delirium dyed for itself rosy wings in the
Aurora of life, and fanned the panting soul,—and shook
down golden butterfly-dust from its plumage on the
path, on the flowerage of the suffering man;—in the
far distance rose lovely tones, in the distance floated

lovely clouds—O his heart was like to fall in pieces, but only into fluttering flower-stamina, into soft sentient nerves; his eyes were like to melt away, but only into dew-drops for the cups of joy-blossoms, into blood-drops for loving hearts; his soul was floating, palpitating, drinking, and swimming in the warm relaxing rose-perfume of the brightest delusion. . . . .

The rapture bridled his feverish heart; and his mad pulse grew calm. Next morning, his mother, when she saw that all was prospering, would have had the church-bells rung, to make him think that the second Sunday was already here. But his wife (perhaps out of shame in my presence) was averse to the lying; and said it would be all the same if we moved the month-hand of his clock (but otherwise than Hezekiah's Dial) eight days forward; especially as he was wont rather to rise and look at his clock for the day of the month, than to turn it up in the Almanack. I for my own part simply went up to the bedside, and asked him : " If he was cracked—what in the world he meant with his mad death-dreams, when he had lain so long, and passed clean over the Cantata-Sunday, and yet, out of sheer terror, was withering to a lath ?"

A glorious reinforcement joined me; the Flesher or Quartermaster. In his anxiety, he rushed into the room, without saluting the women, and I forthwith addressed him aloud : " My gossip here is giving me trouble enough, Mr Regiments-Quartermaster : last night, he let them persuade him he was little older

than his own son : here is the child's fall-hat he was
for putting on." The Guardian deuced and devilled,
and said : " Ward, are you a parson or a fool ?—Have
not I told you twenty times, there was a maggot in
your head about this ?"—

At last he himself perceived that he was not rightly
wise, and so grew better : besides the guardian's invectives, my oaths contributed a good deal ; for I
swore I would hold him as no right gossip, and edite
no word of his Biography, unless he rose directly and
got better.....

—In short, he showed so much politeness to me
that he rose and got better.—He was still sickly, it is
true, on Saturday ; and on Sunday could not preach a
sermon (something of the sort the Schoolmaster read,
instead) ; but yet he took Confessions on Saturday,
and at the altar next day he dispensed the Sacrament.
Service ended, the feast of his recovery was celebrated,
my farewell-feast included ; for I was to go in the afternoon.

This last afternoon I will chalk out with all possible
breadth, and then, with the pantagraph of free garru-
lity, fill up the outline and draw on the great scale.

During the Thanksgiving-repast, there arrived considerable personal tribute from his catechumens, and
fairings by way of bonfire for his recovery; proving
how much the people loved him, and how well he deserved it : for one is oftener hated without reason by
the many, than without reason loved by them. But

Fixlein was friendly to every child; was none of those clergy, who never pardon their enemies except in— God's stead ; and he praised at once the whole world, his wife, and himself.

I then attended at his afternoon's catechising ; and looked down (as he did in the first Letter-Box) from the choir, under the wing of the wooden cherub. Behind this angel, I drew out my note-book, and shifted a little under the cover of the Black Board, with its white Psalm-cyphers,* and wrote down what I was there—thinking. I was well aware, that when I to-day, on the twenty-fifth of May, retired from this *Salernic*† spinning-school, where one is taught to spin out the thread of life, in fairer wise, and without wetting it by foreign mixtures,—I was well aware, I say, that I should carry off with me far more elementary principles of the Science of Happiness, than the whole Chamberlain piquet ever muster all their days. I noted down my first impression, in the following Rules of Life for myself and the press :

" Little joys refresh us constantly like house-bread, and never bring disgust; and great ones, like sugar-bread, briefly, and then bring it.—Trifles we should let, not plague us only, but also gratify us ; we should

---

* Indicating to the congregation what Psalm is to be sung.—ED.

† Salerno was once famous for its medical science ; but here, as in many other cases, we could desire the aid of Herr Reinhold with his *Lexicon-Commentary.*—ED.

seize not their poison-bags only, but their honey-bags
also : and if flies often buz about our room, we should,
like Domitian, amuse ourselves with flies, or, like a
certain still living Elector,* feed them.—For *civic* life
and its micrologies, for which the Parson has a natural taste, we must acquire an artificial one ; must learn
to love without esteeming it ; learn, far as it ranks beneath *human* life, to enjoy it like another twig of this
human life, as poetically as we do the pictures of it in
romances.   The loftiest mortal loves and seeks the
same sort of things with the meanest ; only from higher
grounds and by higher paths.   Be every minute, Man,
a full life to thee !—Despise anxiety and wishing, the
Future and the Past !—If the *Second-pointer* can be no
road-pointer into an Eden for thy soul, the *Month-
pointer* will still less be so, for thou livest not from
month to month, but from second to second ! Enjoy thy
Existence more than thy Manner of Existence, and let
the dearest object of thy Consciousness be this Consciousness itself !—Make not the Present a means of
thy Future ; for this Future is nothing but a coming
Present ; and the Present, which thou despisest, was
once a Future which thou desiredst !—Stake in no lot-
teries,—keep at home,—give and accept no pompous
entertainments,—travel not abroad every year !—Conceal not from thyself, by long plans, thy household

---

* This hospitable Potentate is as unknown to me as to any of
my readers.—ED.

goods, thy chamber, thy acquaintance !—Despise Life,
that thou mayst enjoy it !—Inspect the neighbourhood
of thy life ; every shelf, every nook of thy abode ; and
nestling in, quarter thyself in the farthest and most
domestic winding of thy snail-house !—Look upon a
capital but as a collection of villages, a village as some
blind-alley of a capital ; fame as the talk of neigh-
bours at the street-door ; a library as a learned conversation, joy as a second, sorrow as a minute, life as
a day ; and three things as all in all : God, Creation,
Virtue !"— —

And if I would follow myself and these rules, it will
behove me not to make so much of this Biography ;
but once for all, like a moderate man, to let it sound
out.

After the Catechising, I stept down to my wide-
gowned and black-gowned gossip. The congregation
gone, we clambered up to all high places, perused the
plates on the pews—I took a lesson on the altar on its
inscription incrusted with the *sediment of Time* (I speak
not metaphorically) ; I organed, my gossip managing
the bellows ; I mounted the pulpit, and was happy
enough there to alight on one other rose-shoot, which,
in the farewell minute, I could still plant in the rose-
garden of my Fixlein. For I descried aloft, on the
back of a wooden Apostle, the name *Lavater*, which
the Zurich Physiognomist had been pleased to leave
on this sacred Torso in the course of his wayfaring.
Fixlein did not know the hand, but I did, for I had

seen it frequently in Flachsenfingen, not only on the tapestry of a Court Lady there, but also in his *Hand-Library ;** and met with it besides in many country churches, forming, as it were, the Directory and Address-Calendar of this wandering name, for Lavater likes to inscribe in pulpits, as a shepherd does in trees, the name of his beloved.   I could now advise my gossip prudently to cut away the name, with the chip of wood containing it, from the back of the Apostle, and to preserve it carefully among his *curiosa.*

On returning to the parsonage, I made for my hat and stick ; but the design, as it were the projection and contour of a supper in the acacia-grove, had already been sketched by Thiennette. I declared that I would stay till evening, in case the young mother went out with us to the proposed meal . . . . and truly the Biographer at length got his way, all doctors' regulations notwithstanding.

I then constrained the Parson to put on his Kräutermütze,† or Herb-cap, which he had stitched together out of simples for the strengthening of his memory ;

---

    * A little work printed in manuscript types ; and seldom given by him to any but Princes. This piece of print-writing he intentionally passes off to the great as a piece of hand-writing ; these persons being both more habituated and inclined to the reading of manuscript than of print.

    † Thus defined by Adelung in his Lexicon : " *Kräutermütze,* in Medicine, a cap with various dried herbs sewed into it, and which is worn for all manner of troubles in the head."—ED.

" Would to Heaven," said I, " that Princes instead of
their Princely Hats, Doctors and Cardinals instead of
theirs, and Saints instead of martyr-crowns, would clap
such memory-bonnets on their heads!"—Thereupon,
till the roasting and cooking within doors were over,
we marched out alone over the parsonage meadows,
and talked of learned matters, we packed ourselves
into the ruined Robber-Castle, on which my gossip, as
already mentioned, has a literary work in hand.   I
deeply approved, the rather as this Kidnapper-tower
had once belonged to an Aufhammer, his intention of
dedicating the description to the Rittmeister : that nobleman, I think, will sooner give his name to the Book
than to the Shock.   For the rest, I exhorted my fellow-
craftsman to pluck up literary heart, and said to him :
" A fearless pen, good gossip ! Let Subrector Hans
von Füchslein be, if he like, the Dragon of the Apoca-
lypse, lying in wait for the delivery of the fugitive Woman, to swallow the offspring ; I am there too, and have
my friend the Editor of the *Litteraturzeitung* at my
side, who will gladly permit me to give an *anticritique*,
on paying the insertion-dues !"—I especially excited
him to new fillings and return-freights of his Letter-
Boxes.   I have not taken oath that into this biographical chest-of-drawers, I will not in the course of time
introduce another Box. " Neither to my godson, worthy gossip, will it do any harm that he is presented,
poor child, even now to the reading public, when he

does not count more months than, as Horace will have
it, a literary child should count years, namely, *nine*."

In walking homewards, I praised his wife. " If
marriage," said I to him, " is the madder, which in
maids, as in cotton, makes the colours visible, then I
contend, that Thiennette, when a maid, could scarcely
be so good as she is now when a wife. By Heaven!
in such a marriage, I should write Books of quite another sort, divine ones; in a marriage, I mean, where
beside the writing-table (as beside the great voting-table
at the Regensburg Diets, there are little tables of con-
fectionary); where in like manner, I say, a little jar of
marmalade were standing by me, namely, a sweetened,
dainty, lovely face, and out of measure fond of the Let-
ter-Box-writer, gossip! Your marriage will resemble the
Acacia-grove we are now going to, the leaves of which
grow thicker with the heat of summer, while other
shrubs are yielding only shrunk and porous shade."

As we entered through the upper garden-door into
this same bower, the supper and the good mistress were
already there. Nothing is more pure and tender than
the respect with which a wife treats the benefactor or
comrade of her husband: and happily the Biographer
himself was this comrade, and the object of this respect.
Our talk was cheerful, but my spirit was oppressed.
The fetters, which bind the mere reader to my heroes,
were in my case of triple force; as I was at once their
guest and their portrait-painter. I told the Parson that

he would live to a greater age than I, for that his temperate temperament was balanced as if by a doctor so equally between the nervousness of refinement, and the hot thick-bloodedness of the rustic. Fixlein said that if he lived but as long as he had done, namely, two-and-thirty years, it would amount, exclusive of the leap-year-days, to 280,320 seconds, which in itself was something considerable ; and that he often reckoned up with satisfaction the many thousand persons of his own age that would have a life equally long.

At last I tried to get in motion ; for the red lights of the falling sun were mounting up over the grove, and dipping us still deeper in the shadows of night : the young mother had grown chill in the evening dew. In confused mood, I invited the Parson to visit me soon in the city, where I would show him not only all the chambers of the Palace, but the Prince himself. Gladder there was nothing this day on our old world than the face to which I said so ; and than the other one which was the mild reflexion of the former.—For the Biographer it would have been too hard, if now in that minute, when his fancy, like mirror-telescopes, was representing every object in a *tremulous* form, he had been obliged to cut and run ; if, I will say, it had not occurred to him that to the young mother it could do little harm (but much good) were she to take a short walk, and assist in escorting the Author and architect of the present Letter-Box out of the garden to his road.

In short, I took this couple one in each hand, instead of under each arm, and moved with them through
the garden to the Flachsenfingen highway. I often
abruptly turned round my head between them, as if I
had heard some one coming after us ; but in reality I
only meant once more, though mournfully, to look
back into the happy hamlet, whose houses were all
dwellings of contented still Sabbath-joy, and which
is happy enough, though over its wide-parted pave-
ment-stones there passes every week but one barber,
every holiday but one dresser of hair, and every year
but one hawker of parasols. Then truly I had again to
turn round my head, and look at the happy pair beside
me. My otherwise affectionate gossip could not rightly
suit himself to these tokens of sorrow : but in thy
heart, thou good, so oft afflicted sex, every mourning-
bell soon finds its unison ; and Thiennette, ennobled
with the thin trembling *resonance* of a reverberating
soul, gave me back all my tones with the beauties of
an echo. — — At last we reached the boundary, over
which Thiennette could not be allowed to walk; and
now must I part from my gossip, with whom I had
talked so gaily every morning (each of us from his
bed), and from the still circuit of modest hope where
he dwelt, and return once more to the rioting, fermenting Court-sphere, where men in bull-beggar tone demand from Fate a root of Life-Licorice, thick as the
arm, like the botanical one on the Wolga, not so much
that they may chew the sweet beam themselves, as fell
others to earth with it.

As I thought to myself that I would say, Farewell! to them, all the coming plagues, all the corpses, and all the marred wishes of this good pair, arose before my heart; and I remembered that little save the falling asleep of joy-flowers would mark the current of their Life-day, as it does of mine and of every one's.—And yet is it fairer, if they measure their years not by the *Water-clock* of falling tears, but by the *Flower-clock* * of asleep-going flowers, whose bells in our short-lived garden are sinking together before us from hour to hour.—

I would even now—for I still recollect how I hung with streaming eyes over these two loved ones, as over their corpses—address myself, and say : Far too soft, *Jean Paul,* whose chalk still sketches the models of Nature on a ground of Melancholy; harden thy heart like thy frame, and waste not thyself and others by such thoughts.   Yet why should I do it, why should I not confess directly what, in the softest emotion, I said to these two beings ?   " May all go right with you, ye mild beings," I said, for I no longer thought of courtesies, " may the arm of Providence bear gently your lacerated hearts, and the good Father, above all these suns which are now looking down on us, keep you

---

* Linné formed in Upsal a flower-clock, the flowers of which, by their different times of falling asleep, indicated the hours of the day.

ever united, and exalt you still undivided to his bosom
and his lips !"—" Be you too right happy and glad !"
said Thiennette.—" And to you, Thiennette," continued I, " Ah! to your pale cheeks, to your oppressed
heart, to your long cold maltreated youth, I can never,
never wish enough.   No !   But all that can soothe a
wounded soul, that can please a pure one, that can still
the hidden sigh—O all that you deserve—may this be
given you ; and when you see me again, then say to
me, ' I am now much happier !' "

We were all of us too deeply moved.   We at last
tore ourselves asunder from repeated embraces ; my
friend retired with the soul whom he loves—I remained alone behind him with the Night.

And I walked without aim through woods, through
valleys, and over brooks, and through sleeping villages,
to enjoy the great Night like a Day.   I walked, and
still looked like the magnet, to the region of midnight,
to strengthen my heart at the gleaming twilight, at
this upstretching Aurora of a morning beneath our feet.
White night-butterflies flitted, white blossoms flutter-
ed, white stars fell, and the white snow-powder hung
silvery in the high Shadow of the Earth, which reaches
beyond the Moon, and which is our Night.   Then began the Eolian Harp of the Creation to tremble and
to sound, blown on from above, and my immortal soul
was a string in this Harp.—The heart of a brother
everlasting Man swelled under the everlasting Heaven,
as the seas swell under the Sun and under the Moon.

—The distant village-clocks struck midnight, mingling, as it were, with the ever-pealing tone of ancient Eternity.—The limbs of my buried ones touched cold on my soul, and drove away its blots, as dead hands heal eruptions of the skin.—I walked silently through little hamlets, and close by their outer churchyards, where crumbled upcast coffin-boards were glimmering, while the once bright eyes that had lain in them were mouldered into grey ashes.—Cold thought! clutch not like a cold spectre at my heart; I look up to the starry sky, and an everlasting chain stretches thither, and over and below; and all is Life, and Warmth, and Light, and all is godlike or God.....

Towards morning I descried thy late lights, little city of my dwelling, which I belong to on this side the grave; I returned to the Earth; and in thy steeples, behind the by-advanced great Midnight, it struck half past two; about this hour, in 1794, Mars went down in the west, and the Moon rose in the east; and my soul desired, in grief for the noble warlike blood which is still streaming on the blossoms of Spring: " Ah retire, bloody War, like red Mars; and thou, still Peace, come forth like the mild divided Moon!"—

END OF VOLUME THIRD.

EDINBURGH:
PRINTED BY JAMES BALLANTYNE & CO.